psychoanalysis never lets go

psychoanalysis never lets go

by FRANÇOIS ROUSTANG
translated by Ned Lukacher

THE JOHNS HOPKINS UNIVERSITY PRESS
Baltimore and London

Originally published in 1980 by Les Editions de Minuit,
Paris, as . . . *Elle ne le lâche plus*
Copyright © 1980 by Les Editions de Minuit

English translation and author's preface copyright © 1983
by The Johns Hopkins University Press
All rights reserved
Printed in the United States of America

The Johns Hopkins University Press, Baltimore,
Maryland 21218
The Johns Hopkins Press Ltd., London

Library of Congress Cataloging in Publication Data

Roustang, François.
    Psychoanalysis never lets go.

    Translation of: —elle ne le lâche plus.
    Includes bibliographical references.
    1. Psychoanalysis—Philosophy. 2. Transference (Psychology) 3. Hypnotism—Therapeutic use.
4. Freud, Sigmund, 1856-1939. I. Title.
[DNLM: 1. Psychoanalysis. WM 460 R868e (P)]
BF 173. R713 1983   150. 19′5   82-10042
ISBN 0-8018-2674-8

contents

author's preface to the English-language edition   vii
one   Freud's style   *1*
two   quite often   *26*
three   suggestion over the long term   *43*
four   transference: the dream   *66*
five   the game of the other   *93*
six   the effects of analysis   *117*
seven   the patient: a novelist?   *134*
notes   *151*

author's preface to the English-language edition

I did not feel the need to write a preface to the French edition, because prefaces in the French style tend to be regarded as magic tricks. Prefaces want to pretend that the book about to be opened deals, in a new way and for the first time, with questions that no intelligent reader will fail to find fascinating. But one must refrain from being too precise and above all from revealing the book's content, which would make reading the book superfluous. On the other hand one must learnedly expatiate on the necessity of following the author step by step, on the impossibility of disregarding his train of thought. Hegel of course made this question one of the keystones of his philosophy: the only introduction is to have read the work. Kierkegaard, in counterpoint, would have preferred to write only prefaces or postscripts. And Derrida, to bring us up to date, has worked very hard to put an end to this debate.

So here I am writing a preface in the French style (it is a national vice), showing you my lucidity (saying, in effect, that whether or not I write a preface, I really know what I am doing), my culture (that like the cream of the Parisian intelligentsia, I know my classics), and occasionally my style, at the same time well-documented and entertaining. All of that, however, is quite useless in the eyes of American readers, who prefer to my pirouettes those of Christian Dior's models or Roland Petit's ballets.

This is why I crossed the Atlantic: in order to take refuge from the grins of my French friends and to tell you as directly as possible what I wanted to do in this book; the criticism that I can formulate now that it has been published, now that I have distanced myself from it; and finally, the way in which it can be read most effectively.

Over the years that I have spent with psychoanalysts and people who have been psychoanalyzed, I have uneasily and repeatedly wondered why a therapeutic method whose explicit aim is the liberation of forces with a view toward being capable "of enjoyment and efficiency" (Freud's description of the cure) so often ends in alienation either on the analyst's part, because the treatment turns out to be interminable, or in regard to the patient, who adopts the manner of speech and thought, the theses as well as the prejudices, of psychoanalysis.

You will say that this question interests only analysts or those who have been analyzed. In that case I will not have many readers, simply because those who analyze or are analyzed are so taken up by what we call analytic discourse that they cannot distance themselves enough to question it. Or else they have adopted as established fact hypotheses that cannot be proved, and they above all do not wish to call into question the certainties that henceforth form the basis of their existence. In other words, they become believers. How can you expect them radically to criticize their faith? The proof of it is that some of my acquaintances, upon learning of my book, said to me: "But you are sawing off the branch that you are sitting on." Less generous members of the same profession added that "your book should not only not be read, it should not even be touched," suggesting that they would get too involved if they began considering the problems that I raise. The paradox is that I am not at all opposed to psychoanalysis—if I were, how could I practice it? I wish only to retain the opportunity to ask the most radical questions of it, even those that I cannot answer, because I want to know something about what I am doing as a psychoanalyst while you are questioning psychoanalysis in this way?" I answer, "In order to be a psychoanalyst must one be an idiot or blind to what one is doing? Does not psychoanalysis, by its be an idiot or blind to what one is doing? Does not psychoanalysis, by its very definition, give us the opportunity to question the very foundations of our practice and our theory?"

Why do analysts or those who have been analyzed have so little inclination to ask themselves what they are doing and what is at work in the treatment? To put it as plainly as I can, it is because *psychoanalysis, through its intermediary the transference, has not really disengaged itself from hypnosis and suggestion.* The result of this is that the treatment, without even being noticed, risks leading to a more or less latent form of blindness. This is the context of the title of this book in French, . . . *It never lets go,* which is taken from Ludwig Binswanger's remark, "He whom psychoanalysis has once seized, it never lets go." The fundamental connection between transference and hypnosis is the subject of chapters 3, 4, and 5, which form the heart of the book.

It seems to me that these questions should interest a larger public than the one directly involved in analysis, since this analytic audience only reveals in a magnifying glass what is at work in every relationship. In the seduction necessary to love, in the inherent human need for imitation, and in the fascination that seizes the crowd, there is more than a mere resemblance to the mechanisms of hypnosis or suggestion.

In chapter 3 I show that Freud on the one hand had always been very interested in telepathy and thought-transference and on the other took considerable efforts to prevent these phenomena from invading psychoanalysis, because he more or less consciously knew how close it was to them.

In order to prepare chapter 4 I reread all of Freud's texts on the transference and hypnosis to discover whether he had been duped, or taken in by the game of believing to the point of tranquil certitude that his method had taken a definitive distance from treatment through hypnosis, which he had seen practiced by Bernheim at Nancy. But this is not at all the case: if one looks into the complexity of the texts, one notices that on numerous occasions Freud thinks he has found the solution—of the problem of distinguishing the transference from hypnosis—only to admit failure the next moment. He finally recognizes that the transference is an indirect suggestion.

Psychoanalysts since Freud are less scrupulous and often disdainfully reject all questions on this subject. In chapter 5 I analyze, as an example, some pages of Jacques Lacan, and I show not only that his demonstration of the separation between transference and hypnosis does not stand up but that it tends to prove the contrary, to what might be a horrible extreme. In this chapter, taking my distance from Freud and relying on clinical practice, I try on the one hand to propose a radical definition of the transference as an ahistorical non-relation and on the other to suggest that if one wishes to escape from alienation, which should be the result of the analysis, one must experience this aberrant fact of the transference.

I should say that chapter 5 is the most original part of the book and goes furthest toward understanding the very principle of all communication. But these pages, perhaps precisely because they are original, might appear disconcerting. I am not making fun of you by proposing that every relation is based on its own negation, that is, that it is *at the same time impossible either to distinguish oneself from the other or to tolerate his existence.* Language never abolishes the primordial need to absorb the other and the primitive necessity to reject him. I must acknowledge, however, that these developments are not sufficient to deal with the relations between language and the transference. I suggest that two antagonistic forces are involved here, the first tending to form a distinct and specific individual, the second always trying to suppress the differences. The play of these forces is, however, very complex: language may be prevented from fulfilling its role and may function entirely in favor of a loss of distinctness and a prohibition against individuation. It then only helps to fabricate the identical under the appearances of the most specific differentiation. This problem requires much more development than I have provided here.

Without wanting to play at divination, I feel certain that something essential to our civilization is at stake in these problems. Recently I read an article by an American professor of physics and the history of science stating that every kind of interaction of forces (gravitational, electromagnetic, the strong and the weak nuclear forces) can be thought of as resulting "from processes resembling an *emission* or an *absorption* of particles between two objects in the interaction, the *emitted* or *absorbed* particle being characteristic of every interaction."[1] The words *absorption* and *emission* are fundamental to the psychoanalytic experience. Freud uses them (*Ausstossung* and *Einbeziehung*) in his famous text "Negation" (1925) to describe the first moments of the birth of thought in very early childhood, or, one may say, the contrary movements to which the human psyche submits as the condition for its emergence. What we are able to learn from psychoanalysis, however, is precisely that this emergence is never complete and that when these two movements do not combine or combine poorly, a whole series of pathological forms appears, ranging from schizophrenic separation (pure expulsion) to depressiuon or melancholy confusion (absorbing indistinctness). These pathological forms, which are much more characteristic of our era than hysteria, obsessional neurosis, or paranoia, alert each of us to the dangers that confront us and on whose axes our efforts to exist as individuals inevitably depend. If we consider these ideas in relation to Gerald Holton's remarks, we might conclude that scientific and technological investigation, taken collectively in their infinite variety, is motivated by the need to coordinate contrary movements that risk tearing apart or annihilating the individual. In other words, all scientific effort could be considered as a treatment on a planetary scale to bring an end to madness, or what amounts to the same thing, to resolve, through the manipulation of matter, the insoluble problem of communication: to maintain a relationship without losing individuality, to give and receive without annihilating.

Putting these considerations aside in order to return to the object of the preface, there still remain four chapters to be accounted for. It has been suggested to me that chapter 1 might be transferred to the end of the book so as not to discourage the reader by beginning with a detailed study of Freud's style. That is possible indeed, because the reading of this chapter is not indispensable to an understanding of those that follow. On the other hand, if you are interested in literary criticism,[2] and in Freud's manner of composition, in effect, his unconscious manner, chapter 1 will not leave you indifferent. To any questions about the utility of the first chapter, I can only answer that my investigation began to develop along this path. If I had not studied Freud's style, I could never have written the rest of the book. I had to discover how Freud's thinking operated, what the principle of the seductive power of its discourse was and where it derives its force and therefore its weakness. I had to dismantle this machine in order no longer to be overtaken by it; I had to ask questions of psychoanalysis that Freud himself sought to hide at the same time that he unveiled them.

I applied this method of literary analysis to an article on Freud's "Constructions in Analysis," which appears here as chapter 2. I show that Freud very often recognized that the interpretation imposed by the analyst leads the patient to the limits of hallucination, while the analyst himself is led to the limits of delirium. I then examine Freud's notion of "historical truth" and propose a solution that I develop more fully in chapter 7: in order to bring the patient out of alienation, the analyst must in one way or another be placed in a state of ignorance. In other words, what occurs in an analysis is that after a more or less extensive period the analyst no longer understands his patient (in the two senses of the word: *intelligere*, "to comprehend," and *capere* "to seize, to captivate"), and the patient gets free of the hold of this figure to whom he has given an excessive importance. But this applies to all relationships: although understanding is desirable, it may become the weapon of absolute tyranny.

If you are interested in literature, or more exactly, in the problem of literary or artistic creation, the last chapter may hold some attraction for you. I now realize that by proposing the use of novelistic creation in psychoanalysis as a means of not succumbing to alienation, I become part of a currently widespread preoccupation. If I understand Christopher Lasch, our culture is the producer of many little Narcissuses. In this context artistic creation would be the most developed, the most respectable, form but also the most effective in forming a Narcissus capable of enduring solitude and of making a contribution to his culture, perhaps a way of communicating. Unfortunately, one cannot decide to be a creative artist, and as I emphasize in chapter 7, the inevitable proximity of madness for those who dare to go beyond the well-beaten paths would alone discourage any prospective candidates.

We come now to chapter 6, the last chapter to be written. It is the easiest to read, although I consider it poorly composed. It juxtaposes what are in effect two diametrically opposed interests: one tries to place psychoanalysis in the social field by disposing of psychoanalysts who claim to revolutionize society; the other leads us to imagine under which conditions the treatment of limit-cases becomes possible. Some will find this chapter superficial and to some extent they will be right. It seems to me, however, that if something still remains to be written about psychoanalysis, it will involve these two interests. In France and also, but differently, in the United States, psychoanalysis has become a very large cultural phenomenon; and it would be interesting to study in detail the reciprocal influences between psychoanalysis and the social field. By contrast, the limit-cases, whom I call the "borderline cases," require, if they are to be understood in a treatment, something completely different from the well-known Oedipal scenarios; they will indeed be able to inform us about the fields of force that define our culture.

To sum up, Chapter 1 concerns the techniques of persuasion that characterize Freud's style. (You can read this chapter first or last.) Chapter 2 concerns the dangers that the patient can run into as a result of the analyst's interpretations. Chapter 3 deals with the proximity between the transference and thought-transference, or telepathy, and chapter 4 deals with the proximity between the transference and hypnosis. Chapter 5 discusses the transference as defining all relationships, as well as the means of resolving the transference. Chapter 6 deals with the social effects expected from analytic treatment as well as with the regressions necessary in the treatment of limit-cases. Finally, chapter 7 discusses the connections between the success of the treatment and literary creation.

FRANÇOIS ROUSTANG

psychoanalysis never lets go

one

Freud's style

French readers know Walter Muschg's article "Freud as Writer" through the well-annotated translation by J. Schotte.[1] Nothing better or more penetrating has been written on the style of the inventor of psychoanalysis. Muschg's remarks on the link between Freud's way of writing and the objectivce of Freud's research are particularly interesting. Here, for example, is what seems to be a description of an analytic session:

> He often enters the field of inquiry from any point whatsoever, without any apparent importance; he discovers an insight here, another there, as he finds them, examines them and turns to a third. He soon has a multitude in each hand, rejects something in order to exchange it for something that came before, strikes some more blows with his spade, uncovers new insights and suddenly finds that he has turned up all the ground around him and is buried waist-deep, and digs until he reaches the bottom. It is always a renewed pleasure to experience this with him.[2]

Although Muschg has truly grasped the specificity of Freud's style in relation to analysis and although Schotte, his commentator, accentuates this aspect, it is nonetheless true that what motivates his work is a writer's desire to pay homage to Freud the writer. The relation of psychoanalysis to style rarely comes to the forefront.

In comparison, Walter Schönau's book,[3] the only one devoted solely to Freud's prose, is deceiving indeed. It explicitly bypasses the question that interests us: "The aim of this study is not to trace an exhaustive image of Freud's individual style. It is the work preliminary to that. It seeks to furnish a founding hypothesis and an interpretation of particular literary elements and aspects in their interrelation in order to answer the question of the characteristic trait and quality of Freud's prose."[4] The author is concerned with proving a thesis: that Freud's prose is a scientific prose that aims, as does rhetoric, to teach, persuade, and move; his second thesis is that Freud's style conforms to Lessing's model. From this study, as well-documented as a doctoral dissertation, there is unfortunately nothing to be drawn.[5]

We find ourselves before a question that has been outlined by some German critics but never addressed by psychoanalysts. But does not the difficulty of the question become insurmountable if one tries to make non-German-speaking readers guess the specific characteristics of Freud's style? Unquestionably, all the literary nuances, everything that deals with the language itself, all that makes up the author's manner, which is inseparable from the genius of his language—all these things are lost in translation, regardless of its quality. Moreover, Freud, like every writer, has several styles; he writes differently in his letters than he does in his theoretical works. We must limit ourselves to an aspect of his style, the most striking one, which will remain perceptible through the transposition from one language to another. Or better still, to restrict the global interrogation of Freud's style to the following question: are we able to transfer Freud's style from German to another language?

Anxious or desperate to take these difficulties into account and to respond to this question in the best way I could, I undertook an analysis of several paragraphs chosen at random from Freud's theoretical work. I then established that he repeatedly used a certain number of procedures. I then tried, unsuccessfully, to find these same stylistic procedures, on the one hand, in the works of psychiatrists and psychoanalysts of the period[6] and, on the other hand, in philosophical texts.[7] I thought that I had discovered in the latter a certain number of traits characteristic of Freud's writing.

It is impossible to present to the reader the multiplicity of these attempts, which were never more than probes into a field of immense complexity. What was important to me about these comparisons was that they enabled me to verify a difference; I was now anxious only to make the reader aware of the difference in a limited number of pages and in a form in which the reading was not overly fastidious. I then wanted to analyze the famous chapter 7 in *The Interpretation of Dreams.* I discovered there, in effect, everything I had found elsewhere, but it was even more impossible to make it clear. The available French and English translations would never enable the reader to find the connections, the relationships, the repetitions that I wanted to suggest, for the simple reason that they cannot be grasped, they cannot be found, in translation.

I then decided to retranslate, for the purposes of my argument, the conclusion of the first section of chapter 7, which forms in itself a small unit.[8] I did not retranslate with the pretense that every translation should be of this type, because it is probably unreadable, but with care to conform to the German, to change the word order as little as possible, to avoid changing the construction of sentences or cutting them into several fragments, to utilize as much as possible the same English words for the same German words.[9]

3 / Freud's Style

In the translation that follows each paragraph can be read in its entirety. I have marked each sentence as a paragraph in order to make the progress of the argument more visible. I have italicized words that correspond to others within the paragraph or to words in the other paragraphs—at least the most important ones. I have numbered the paragraphs from 1 to 10 in order that we may return to them more easily.

1

There is another set of *objections* to our *method* of dream-interpretation with which we must now concern ourselves.

We proceed in such a way that we *abandon* all the *representations of a dominant aim* that usually govern our *reflection*; we direct our attention to a *particular element of the dream* and then we note whatever involuntary thoughts occur to us in connection with it.

Then we seize the next trait of the dream-content and repeat the same work with it, and *without concerning* ourselves with the direction in which the thoughts are driving, we let ourselves be led by them where, as we tend to say, we *fall* from hundreds to thousands.

There we cherish the confident belief of *falling* at the end, without any intervention on our part, onto the *dream-thoughts* from which the dream originated.

2

Against this the critic will now have *to object* nearly as follows: that the fact that a *particular element of the dream* leads somewhere or other [*irgendwohin*] is nothing wonderful.

To each representation something lets itself be joined associatively; it is curious indeed that one should *fall* through this *aimless and arbitrary stream of thoughts* precisely onto the *dream-thoughts*.

Probably we are deceiving ourselves; one follows the chain of associations from one element until, for one reason or another [*irgendeinem*], one notices that it is broken; if we then take a second element, it is indeed natural that the original nonlimitation of the association now undergoes a narrowing.

One still has the earlier *chain of thoughts* in memory and is therefore likely to hit upon, during the analysis of the second dream-representation, the ideas that also have something or other [*irgend etwas*] in common with ideas from the first chain.

Then one imagines oneself to have found a thought that manifests a nodal point between two dream-elements.

Since we permit ourselves elsewhere every liberty of *thought-connection* and exclude precisely only the transitions from one representation to another that operate in normal thinking, it is not finally difficult, from a series of "intermediate thoughts," to concoct something that we name the *dream-thoughts*, and without any *guarantee*, since they are not known through other means, we allege them to be the psychical substitute of the dream.

But that is completely *arbitrary* and a utilization of chance connections which appear *witty* [*witzig*], and whoever takes this useless trouble can, from any dream whatsoever [*beliebigen*], through this path, work out any interpretation whatsoever [*beliebige*].

3

If such *objections* were really advanced to us, we could appeal in our defense to the impression of our dream-interpretations, to the surprising connections with other dream-elements that emerge during the pursuit of particular representations, and to the improbability that something which covers and explains the dream so exhaustively as our interpretations could be acquired otherwise than by following the psychical connections already in place.

We could also advance for our justification that the method used during the dream-interpretation is identical with that used in the resolution of hysterical symptoms, where the rectitude of the *method* is *guaranteed* by the emergence and the disappearance of the symptoms from their place, where the exegesis of the text thus finds support in the interpolated illustrations.

But we have no reason to put aside the problem of how one can reach, through the pursuit of a *chain of thoughts* spun yet further in an *arbitrary and aimless way*, a preexistent end, since we cannot resolve this problem but are able to put it completely aside.

4

It is demonstrably untrue that we give ourselves up to an aimless stream of representations when we, as in the work of dream-interpretation, *abandon reflection* and permit involuntary representations to emerge.

It can be shown that we can never be rid of *representations of aims* that are known to us and that with their cessation, immediately the unknown— or as we imprecisely say, unconscious—*representations of aims*, which determine the stream of involuntary representations, come into force.

A thought without *representations of aims* cannot be produced by our own influence on our psychical life; but it is also unknown to me in which states of psychical confusion it is produced.

Psychiatrists have here too soon renounced the solidity of psychical structures.

I know that an unregulated *stream of thoughts*, without *representations of aims*, occurs in the context of hysteria and paranoia as little as in the formations and the resolution of dreams.

5 / Freud's Style

Perhaps it does not occur at all in the endogenous psychical disorders; even the deliria of confusional states are, according to Leuret's brilliant conjecture, full of meaning and are only incomprehensible to us through their omissions.

I have formed the same conviction where the occasion to observe it was given to me.

The deliria are the work of a *censorship* which no longer takes the trouble to conceal its operation, which instead of lending its cooperation to a modification that is no longer objectionable ruthlessly deletes whatever is in *opposition*, so that what remains becomes *disconnected*.

This censorship acts exactly like the Russian censorship of newspapers at the frontier, which allows only foreign journals with passages blackened out to fall into the hands of protected readers.

5

The free *play* of representations according to whatever [*beliebig*] linkage of associations appears perhaps in destructive organic cerebral processes; what is regarded as such in the psychoneuroses can be explained each time through the intervention of the *censorship* upon a series of thoughts that is pushed into the forefront by still concealed representations of aims.

As an unfailing sign of the free association of the representations of aims, one observes that the representations (or images) that emerge appear *joined* by the link of so-called *superficial associations*, that is, through assonance, double meaning of words, temporal coincidence without internal relation of meaning, through all the associations that we allow in *wit* and in *wordplay*.

This characteristic is present in *thought-connections* which lead us from the elements of the dream-content to the *intermediate thoughts* and from these to the dream-thoughts proper; we have in numerous dream analyses found examples of it that must awake our astonishment.

No connection was too loose, no *wit* [*Witz*, "joke"] too reprehensible, that it could not form the bridge from one thought to another.

But the exact comprehension of such indulgence is not far off.

Each time a psychical element is linked with another through an objectionable and *superficial association*, there also exists between the two a correct and deeper *junction* which submits to the resistance of the censorship.

6

Pressure from the censorship, not the abandonment of the representations of aims, is the exact reason for the prevalence of *superficial associations*.

The *superficial associations* replace the presentation of the depths if the censorship makes impracticable the paths of *normal* connections.

It is as if a general interruption of circulation, for example, a flood, makes impassable in the mountains the large and major routes; the circulation will then be maintained over the inconvenient and steep footpaths that otherwise only the hunter has used.

7

Here one can distinguish two cases that are essentially one.

Either the *censorship* is directed only against the *connection* between two thoughts which when separated from one another elude *opposition*.

Then the two thoughts, one after the other, enter into consciousness; their *connection* remains concealed, but in its place comes a *superficial junction* between the two, of which we have not thought until now and which is generally attached to a point of the complex of representations other than that from which proceeds the suppressed but *essential link*.

Or instead, the two thoughts subject themselves to the *censorship* on account of their content; then they do not appear under their exact form but modified and substituted, and the two substitute thoughts are chosen in such a way that through a superficial association they render the *essential link*, in which the two that have been replaced are related.

Under the pressure of the *censorship* has occurred in the two cases a displacement from a *normal*, serious *association* to a *superficial* one which appears absurd.

8

Since we are aware of these displacements, we also rely, during the dream-interpretation, upon *superficial associations* without any reservation.

9

Of the following two propositions—that with the abandonment of conscious representation of aims the mastery over the stream of representations passes to the concealed representations of aims, and that the superficial associations are only a substitute by displacement for the more profound, suppressed associations—the *psychoanalysis* of the neuroses makes the greatest use; it elevates the two propositions as the founding pillars of its *technique*.

If I ask a patient to abandon all reflection and to tell me all that comes to his mind, I am then relying on the presumption that he cannot abandon the *representation of aim* in the treatment, and I feel justified in inferring that what appears most harmless and most *arbitrary* in what he tells me has a connection with his illness.

Another *representation of aim*, of which the patient suspects nothing, is that of myself.

The full appreciation as the detailed proof of these two formulations thus appears in the presentation of *psychoanalytic technique* as therapeutic method.

We have here one of the points of correspondence in which we deliberately abandon the theme of the dream-interpretation.

10

One thing is exact and remains of these *objections*, namely, that we have no need to transpose all ideas of the work of interpretation into the nocturnal dream-work.

We make, during the waking interpretation, a path that leads back from the dream-elements to the dream-thoughts.

The dream-work has followed the opposite path, and it is not probable that these paths are passable in the opposite direction.

It appears rather that during the day, over new dream-connections, we drive shafts that reach the intermediate thoughts and the dream-thoughts now at one place, now at another.

We can see how the fresh thought-material of the day inserts itself in the series of interpretations, and also, the increase of the resistance, which has set in during the night, probably makes necessary new and more involved detours.

But the number or the nature of the collateral lines that we spin during the day is psychologically totally without importance so long as they open to us the paths toward the sought-after dream-thoughts.

All of section A in chapter 7 is in response to criticisms of Freud's dream-interpretation. After having overturned the principle of determinism by founding it henceforth on doubt, particularity, forgetfulness, and error[10] and having given some advice and details to the reader who would like to interpret his own dreams,[11] the text—which is the passage translated above—returns to the objections to the method used during the interpretation. Paragraph 1 briefly recapitulates this method; paragraph 2 states the objections;[12] paragraphs 3, 4, and 5 answer them, which allows paragraphs 6, 7, and 8 to address the problem of censorship; then paragraph 9 deals with the analytic treatment; and paragraph 10 concludes on the problem of epistemology.

We must now undertake a detailed analysis of these paragraphs regarding their own constitution and their links to one another.

Paragraph 1 emphasizes the unexpected, bizarre, and finally scandalous character of the method of interpretation. This method is characterized by three phases: (1) the active break in relation to usual intellectual functions and its displacement; (2) the abandonment of reflection on behalf of attention to the involuntary (second sentence); and (3) the drift; following the stream of thoughts (third sentence), the passive expectation of the dream's latent content (fourth sentence). The words and the rhythm of the third sentence evoke, above all, the dangerous and somewhat dramatic aspect of the process. They impress upon the reader the image of a swimmer seized by the current; he has abandoned the solid ground of reflection and of his notes to seize, to catch (*aufgreifen*), in passing, a rope, by which he lets himself be pulled while jumping from one obstacle to another.

Through this succession of abandonment, drifting, and expectation, Freud stages an event—an advent or an accident—that he has instigated and that he will have to account for later on. On the basis of these few sentences, though it appears that the new interpretation of the dream is to be carried out according to a method that claims a certain scientific rigor, this method is nonetheless marked by an adventurous tone that will provoke the objections of the scientists. This underlines the opposition of the words *concern ourselves — without concerning ourselves,* since if it is a question of being concerned to respond to criticism, this can only be done through the nonconcern of this scientific research.

Through its vocabulary, this first paragraph is throughout turned toward what is to follow. The word *method* (first sentence) reappears in the middle of paragraph 3. *Abandon, reflection, representations of aims, involuntary* (second sentence) reappear in the beginning of paragraph 4. *Particular element of the dream* (second sentence) and *falling . . . onto the dream-thoughts* (fourth sentence) reappear in the beginning of paragraph 2. There is no word in the third sentence (except for *geraten*, which I have translated as *to fall* in order to use the same word that appears in the next sentence), which precisely sets the tone of this paragraph, that is not taken up again later.

In order to object to the method, paragraph 2 adopts the ironic tone of the prosecutor. In effect, it is punctuated with stock phrases: *nothing wonderful; it is curious indeed; one imagines oneself to have found;* it is not *. . . difficult . . . to concoct something.* Moreover, the paragraph is structured through the repetition, in inverted order, of certain words. Reading the beginning and the end of the paragraph, one can see the following succession:

> *aimless and arbitrary (ziellos und willkürlich)*
> *dream-thoughts*
> *dream-thoughts*
> *arbitrary and witty (willkür und witzig)*

This succession, which is a figure of style known as inclusion, which comprises chiasmus, is important here because in itself it gives meaning to the paragraph; the dream-thoughts, to which the work of interpretation leads, arise arbitrarily, aimlessly, like a joke.

Paragraph 2 is linked to paragraph 1 by the words *to object, particular element*, and *dream-thoughts*, which appear at the beginning. Freud constantly uses this classical procedure of concatenation, in which the words of the preceding paragraph are repeated at the beginning of the following one.

The two adjectives *aimless and arbitrary*, which appear here at the beginning, appear again at the end of paragraph 3, but in reverse order: *arbitrary and aimless* (*willkürlich und ziellos*), enclosing the objection of paragraph 2 and the response of paragraph 3 with an inclusion-chiasmus. The expression *chain of thoughts* (*Gedankenkette*), here in the center, will reappear at the end of the next paragraph. Inversely, the expression *stream of thoughts* (*Gedankenablauf*), here in the first part of the paragraph, will reappear at the center of paragraph 4. The two other expressions formed with the word *thought—thought-consciousness* (*Gedankenverbindung*) and *intermediate thoughts* (*Zwischengedanken*), which are here in the second half of the paragraph—will reappear at the center of paragraph 5.

The reader who has taken the trouble to get this far will wonder whether these multiple connections are the result of chance. I can affirm that whenever the interrelationships appeared insignificant to me it was because I had not pursued the analysis far enough. For example, at the beginning of paragraph 5 Freud could have reused the word *chain* (*Kette*) to describe the chain of associations; yet he avoids the word and uses *linkage* (*Verkettung*), as if to maintain the tension in the thread that links together the words composed with *thoughts* (*Gedanken*), since it is precisely the point of this passage of chapter 7 to show that what at first appears as a simple stream can be organized as a chain and that the nature of the connections can be determined.

Another example: what is the effect of the word *witzig* at the end of paragraph 2? Here is the sentence in German: *Es ist aber alles Willkür und witzig erscheinende Ausnützung des Zufalls.* Word for word: "But that is a completely arbitrary and witty-appearing utilization of chance." The juxtaposition of the substantive *Willkür* and the adjective-adverb *witzig* responds in paragraph 2, as we have seen, to the juxtaposition of *ziellos* and *willkürlich*, thus forming an inclusion. The link between *ziellos* and *witzig* is worth noting, since *ziellos* will reappear at the beginning of paragraph 4 in order to present the objection that will have to be answered, and *witzig* will reappear twice in the substantive form of *Witz* in the middle of paragraph 5, where it will be central to the argument.

Here, more clearly, are the links between paragraphs 2, 3, and 4:

> —paragraph 2: *ziellos und willkürlich* → paragraph 3: *willkürlich und ziellos*;
> —end of paragraph 3: *ziellos* → beginning of paragraph 4: *ziellos*;

—paragraph 2: *ziellos und willkürlich* → beginning of paragraph 4: *ziellos*;
— paragraph 2: *Willkür und witzig* → center of paragraph 5: *Witz*;
—first part of paragraph 2: *Gedankenablauf* → center of paragraph 4;
—center of paragraph 2: *Gedankenkette* → end of paragraph 3;
—second part of paragraph 2: *Gedankenverbindung* → center of paragraph 5.

From here on we are in the presence of the principle figures of style used by Freud: *concatenation,* repetition at the beginning of a paragraph of words from the end of the preceding one; *chiasmus,* often known by the evocative name of *usteron-proteron* (in Greek, "second-first"), repetition of a series of words in reverse order; and *inclusion,* repetition of the same words at the beginning and the end of a paragraph. These three figures are well known to students of literary texts in ancient languages, for example, Hebrew and Greek. Freud's text brings to light another figure which to my knowledge has never been analyzed and which consists in the repetition in the middle of a paragraph of one or several words which appeared on the periphery of a preceding paragraph. I will name it *pericenter* in order to indicate that what is circling around moves to the center.

Freud was not unaware that his writing was produced by the imperatives through which he made his discoveries. But was he conscious of the utilization of these procedures? The question cannot be answered. What is certain, as we will see later, is that these procedures arise from infantile and archaic sources whose force Freud wanted to make known. But we must now follow through with our close analysis of these paragraphs.

After having heard the singular admission of the researcher (paragraph 1) and the raillery of the prosecutor (paragraph 2), we see in paragraph 3 the amplification of the characteristic voice of the lawyer. For example, the repetitions in the first sentence—*to appeal to . . . , to . . . , and to . . .* —and those that conclude the second sentence—*where the . . . , where thus . . .* —before the problem is expelled with a sleight of hand.

The links of the vocabulary to the preceding paragraphs have already been cited, except for one word, *guarantee,* which appears at the end of the preceding paragraph. So one finds in the second sentence of paragraph 3 the word *method* (*Verfahren*), which appeared in the beginning of paragraph 1, and *guaranteed* (*gewährleistet*), while *guarantee* (*Gewähr*) appeared near the end of paragraph 2. The first two paragraphs are thus reassembled in the middle of paragraph 3 through these words, as though through a retroactive inclusion around the central question, How can the method be guaranteed? These same words likewise form a pericenter, because what is on the periphery of paragraphs 1 and 2 appears at the center of paragraph 3.

These figures, however, suggest something else, since the content of the second sentence of paragraph 3 indicates what the evidence is, not only for this retranslated passage, but for section A and even the whole of chapter 7: the guarantee for the work of the dream-interpretation is to be sought in the discoveries Freud made during the treatment of the psychoneuroses, especially hysteria. What he proposed for the dream is only an application to another domain of the results of "my previous work on the psychology of the neuroses."[13] That is why this paragraph is constructed in such a way that it includes a sentence on symptoms, the second, between two sentences on dreams, the first and the third. This yields the following sequence: dream, hysterical symptoms, dream. Taken together, the following paragraphs, 4 and 5, will reveal the same sequence.

Concerning paragraph 3, one could say, as one could concerning many passages in Freud, that he proceeds with an astonishing slowness (as astonishing as what we encounter in an analytic session), repeatedly returning to the same words, swelling the sentence without the least bit of haste while repeating what went before in order to introduce a new element (which is visible in the first two sentences), or again turning his sentence upon itself (as in the third) until it rediscovers its point of departure. Translators are unable to refrain from compressing these tentative procedures in order to get straight to the principal idea. Freud, however, cannot be summarized or shortened; one cannot economize upon his careful reexaminations and siftings. He cannot prove himself, and he no longer wants to, because the object he is treating—to which I will return later—does not permit it; his only possible demonstration is the implementation of a pathway into which all the elements he uses must be integrated without missing any stage, so that wave after wave, the obstacle will be eroded because the sea cannot use what remains solid ground.

The first half of paragraph 4 returns to the basic objection about the existence of aimless representations and tries to dispose of it in three sentences: the first in a negative form, the second positive, and the third, doubling back again, concluding in a generalization first negative, then positive. All the principal propositions of these sentences have a neuter subject:

> *Es ist*
> *Es lässt sich*
> *Ein Denken lässt sich nicht*
> *Es ist mir*

Neuter subjects because Freud assumes the distance necessary to produce a scientific thesis, which one finds in the *demonstrable* (*nachweisbar*), or that which can be *shown* (*zeigen*). In reality, however, nothing is demonstrated or shown. When all is said and done, nothing will have been demonstrated. Although it is something that always worries Freud, it is also something he always avoids, something he cannot let go, because it is what urges him on, the urge to link what is demonstrable in the dream to other things that arise from his personal opinion. This divided attitude toward the first-person singular is initiated in the second part of the third sentence: *it is also unknown to me*. That is to say, the second half of the paragraph will be punctuated by the alternation from *I* to *it* in the principal propositions: *I know . . . , it does not occur . . . , I have formed the same conviction . . . , The deliria . . . .*

Under the heading of the representation of aims, hysteria, paranoia, confusional states, and deliria are linked to dreams; and all that is in order to introduce a decisive word: *censorship*. This forced introduction would have no significance here were it not to prepare for the role it will be given in the following paragraphs. Freud does not deduce a certain number of consequences from a well-established concept; he surreptitiously introduces a word, here sustained by a comparison that leads to a multiplicity of meanings, and he then plays with it in his own way, more through the way he positions it in the text than by his explanations. It is the art of progressive induction through the play of successive introductions.

This paragraph does not use words that explain very much. The reason for this is obvious: the paragraph is preparing for what follows. Paragraph 3 presented the same sequence: dream, hysterical symptoms, dream. Now we have:

— paragraph 4: dream
    hysteria, paranoia, confusional states, deliria
— paragraph 5: destructive cerebral processes, psychoneuroses
    dream

Paragraphs 4 and 5 inflate paragraph 3 only in order to link the processes of all mental disorders to the dream processes and to introduce censorship as an explanation of thoughts that appear to be involuntary. The answer to the objection of paragraph 2 will be given at the end of paragraph 5. We can clearly see something here about Freud's style: he does not respond directly to objections; he makes a detour and displaces the facts by drawing the reader's attention to another problem. It is not gratuitously that the word *detour* appears in paragraph 6, and the word *displacement* in paragraph 7. Freud's style carries out precisely what he reveals as the characteristic processes of the dream.

Two remarks emphasize that paragraphs 4 and 5, though clearly distinct, are inseparable. Paragraph 4 ends with a comparison, though comparisons are regularly found in the middle of Freud's paragraphs;[14] it is as if the end of this paragraph were presented as though it were the middle. Paragraph 4 likewise opens with the only concession to the thesis about aimless representations; it is as though it were caught in the center of the disclaimers that preceded it in paragraph 4 and that follow it in paragraph 5.

Paragraph 5 is constructed according to the order of the *usteron-proteron:*

> *censorship*
> *superficial associations*
> *wit*
> > *thought-connections, intermediate thoughts*
> *wit*
> *superficial associations*
> *censorship*

These words and their respective positions indicate, in themselves alone, the possible meaning or meanings of the paragraph, that is, working from them and linking them in various ways, one can display their meaning. But there are obviously other connections in the vocabulary, be it between this paragraph and the preceding ones or within the paragraph itself: the adjective *ziellos,* "aimless," used at the beginning of paragraph 2, reappears at the beginning of paragraph 5; the adjective *beliebig,* "whatever," used at the end of paragraph 2, reappears at the beginning of paragraph 5 in order to sum up the objection that must be answered. There is a still more subtle interconnection: the word *play* appears at the beginning of paragraph 5 and will reappear in the middle in the expression *wordplay*; the participle *joined* appears earlier in the same sentence, and at the end of the paragraph we find the substantive *junction.* This yields the following sequence:

> *play*
> *joined, wordplay*
> *junction*

This is indeed a way to resume the fundamental theme of the paragraph, which is at the heart of the demonstration: the junction as play.

All this is obviously a bit too precious, perhaps even annoyingly so for the purposes of discovery and explication. But in the face of so many subtle relations, how can we doubt, not whether they are intentional, but whether they were imposed upon the writer, whether they manifest an internal imperative, whether they are the marks of a style of writing, as well as a way of thinking and understanding? We cannot attribute it to chance. For example, Freud uses the participle of the verb *verknüpfen,* "to join." Why does he wait until the end of the paragraph to use the substantive form, *Verknüpfung*, "junction," when he already had it at his disposal in the interval where he preferred a synonym, *Anknüpfung*, "connection"? Ask a musician if he knows why he places a particular note or sequence of notes in one place in his composition rather than in another. He will be unable to answer you; he knows only that it is necessary. It is up the critic to imagine the reasons, and, of course, he must first show the necessity for a particular sequence.

For the moment, let us leave aside paragraph 6, a paragraph that will be understood at the end of this section. Let us say that it makes a unit only in conjunction with the following paragraph, since the words *pressure of the censorship, superficial, association,* and *normal* will reapper to form an inclusion at the end of paragraph 7.

Paragraph 7 is structured by the dichotomy *either... or instead,* or more precisely, by *either..., then..., or instead..., then....* This fits the content of the paragraph perfectly, since its concern is to describe how the censorship disrupts two thoughts. The words *link* and *opposition* are introduced in the first half of the paragraph along with the word *censorship* from the end of paragraph 4. The second half resumes the words *exact, substitute,* and *superficial association* from the beginning of paragraph 6, thus preparing the inclusion that will appear in the last sentence.

Through a unique and brief sentence in paragraph 8, Freud returns to his own experience and thereby prepares for the next paragraph, the meaning of which is not in the context. One must relate everything that is said to the psychoanalytic technique. After a first sentence which resumes the affirmations of paragraph 7, the figure of the *usteron-proteron* appears to underlie the description of the patient-analyst relationship:

> *psychoanalysis... technique*
> *representation of aim*
> *arbitrary*
> *representation of aim*
> *psychoanalytic technique*

The appearance twice of the word *Zielvorstellung*, "representation of aim," is obviously forced, for it is no longer used in the same sense as before; here it is the result of the treatment sought by the patient and even of his interest in the therapist or of the latter's objective. The word *arbitrary, willkürlich*, which appeared at the beginning and at the end of paragraph 2 in order to find itself here at the center, is by contrast the true link between this paragraph and the preceding one, because the associations in the dream-interpretation can appear aimless in the same sense that the patient's discourse can. Later we will see the decisive importance of this paragraph, when we will establish, through style, the relation between theory and practice.

15 / *Freud's Style*

Paragraph 10, the final one in this section, has several functions. First, it settles the epistemological question, Does the work of dream-interpretation reproduce in reverse order the work of dream-elaboration? Then it introduces a theme that will be resumed in the next section and that will be fundamental: the relation between progression and regression. More obviously still, it closes this section by referring back to the end of the introduction of chapter 7, where the theme of the path was introduced and where Freud's objective and manner are clearly expressed.

This final paragraph of the introduction, which is a veritable discourse on method, is a model of the *usteron-proteron* construction already encountered. Before reproducing it, let us note that the word *Unvollständigkeit*, "incompleteness, imperfection," which is plainly in the middle of the paragraph, appeared in the last sentence of the preceding paragraph: "After the removal of interpretation, we can notice how incomplete [*unvollständig*] our psychology of dreams stands."[15] Here is another example of pericenter:

> But before adapting our thoughts to this new path, we must *pause* [*haltmachen*] [5] and look back to see whether in the course of our journey we have been inattentive to anything important. For it must be clear to us that the easy and agreeable part of our journey lies behind us. Hitherto, all the paths we have traveled, unless I am greatly mistaken, have led us toward the light, toward elucidation and fuller understanding; from the moment we want to penetrate more deeply into the mental *processes* [4] of dreams, all the senses fall into darkness. We can regard it as impossible to elucidate the dream as a psychical *process* [4], since to explain means to trace it back to something known, and there is at present no psychological knowledge under which we could subsume what the psychological examination of dreams enables us to infer as a *foundation* [3] for explanation. We shall be obliged, on the contrary, to propose a series of new hypotheses that mark, with the aid of conjectures, the *structure of the psychical apparatus* [2] and the play of forces operating on it, and regarding which we should be careful not to spin our too far beyond the first logical articulations, for otherwise their value is lost in the indeterminable. Even if we make no faults in our conclusions and *account* [1] for all the possibilities that logically follow, we are threatened with the probable *incompleteness* [*Unvollständigkeit*] [0] in the assessment of elements and with the total failure of our *reckoning* [1]. An explanation of the *construction* and mode of work of the *psychical instrument* [2] cannot be reached or at least given a *foundation* [3] by even the most attentive investigation of dreams or of another isolated function; to reach this objective, one must gather, from a comparative study, a whole series of psychical functions whose correlation is constantly necessary. Thus the psychological hypotheses that we derive from the analysis of the dream *processes* [4] must likewise wait at a *halting place* [*Haltestelle*] [5], until they have been related to the results of other research which desires to penetrate to the kernel of the same problem from another point of attack.[16]

The metaphor of the path[17] is like a thread that runs through this section; this is not astonishing, since it is a preparation for the construction of the psychical apparatus whose only model, according to Freud, is the "reflex apparatus."[18] In the pages retranslated earlier, this metaphor appeared at the end of paragraph 2, which contains the objections, between two *whatsoevers* [*beliebig*], because the objections thus mark the way to a solution; the metaphor returns at the end of paragraph 3, which contains the response, and from there the obstacle arises that bars the path to this solution and, in so doing, requires paragraph 6, after the further response of paragraphs 4 and 5, to take a detour because the direct route is impassable. This is repeated in paragraph 10; if one could return by the same route, the diurnal interpretation could account for what happened in the nocturnal elaboration; the interpretation would reproduce the elaboration, which is to say that the work of analysis would reveal the psychical synthesis to us; the reconstitution would be complete. But it is not to be, and we must make new and longer detours.

The more discreet metaphor of threading is linked to that of the path. The word *spinnen* appears three times: in the last paragraph of the introduction retranslated above, *ausspinnen,* "to spin out," but it also means "to imagine, to devise, to plot"; at the end of paragraph 3, *weiterspinnen,* "to spin further" but also "to follow through, to plot"; and at the end of paragraph 10, *anspinnen,* "to spin together" but also "to knot, to devise." Even in their succession these words alone indicate one of the characteristic movements of the style of chapter 7: to lengthen the thread, to spin further, to spin together. Once again Freud does not prove anything, not that he denies it to himself or that he is not interested in doing so but simply because in his domain it is not possible to prove, to demonstrate, to deduce. "To explain means to trace it back to something known, and there is at present no psychological knowledge under which we could subsume what the psychological examination of dreams enables us to infer as a foundation for explanation." He can never do more than induce, relate, or join in order finally to establish connections (*Anschluss*) of meaning in the sense that this word carries in German when it is used to signify that one has to go some place to change trains en route to one's destination, that is, to make a connection. One could also say that Freud changes threads in order better to take up the preceding ones and weave them together.

This creates a combination of delay and acceleration, of continuity and rupture. The constant repetition of all three prior processes creates the impression of returning to the beginning; but the sudden introduction of new elements gives the reverse impression of a profoundly transformed perspective. On that basis the form of many paragraphs seems at first to develop linearly, reaching a difficulty, seizing upon an hypothesis or conjecture and then turning back to what had been posed at the start, all of which leaves the pathways overloaded by the time they are complete.

Linearity imposes circularity upon itself, because one can only retrace one's steps through detours.

I have already emphasized several times how Freud's style is adapted, in every detail, to the content of what he expresses (the dramatic tone, the prosecutor's tone, the lawyer's tone), which, after all, is commonplace for a style. What is less commonplace is that here the style creates its object, which is to say that the container and the contained are no longer separable, that they are even interchangeable. The psychical apparatus that Freud constructs in the course of chapter 7 is chapter 7 itself. We begin to see it at a distance, in the simplicity of some of its elements; and as we get closer, we see its diversification to the point that we must use a microscope in order to see the intricate multiplication of its elements, of its assembled machinery, of its infinite circuits. Each time a new piece is introduced into the system, the whole system is transformed and must be explained again. It is this work of exposition, however, that is truly the construction of the system, that is the system itself. *The psychical apparatus is the discourse that renders an account of itself.* This statement deserves some explanation.

The figures of style revealed in Freud's text—concatenation, inclusion, chiasmus or *usteron-proteron,* pericenter—indicate that the Freudian syntax is subtended and sustained by paratactic forms. Parataxis is defined as the place given to the words in a sentence, or in a series of sentences, independent of the liasons furnished by the prepositions, conjunctions, declensions, and conjugations necessary to syntax.[19] This is why Freud's writing loses all its vigor and even all its meaning in the majority of French translations and even in the English translation of the *Standard Edition,* because translators are only interested in rendering the overall meaning of a sentence defined by its syntax without concerning themselves with word placement and repetition. If parataxis is to be respected in Freud's text, it is because his writing is itself the machine that he puts together; in other words, this machine is his discourse, and one cannot displace its parts without disrupting its function. One ought not to fear affirming that a translation that follows the German while it abuses the French or the English, even to the point of unreadability, is finally less unreadable, less unintelligible, than a translation in good French or English that puts each sentence in the syntactic forms of the respective language. When one moves from one syntax to another, it is parataxis that disappears.

Freud's use of parataxis is not fortuitous. If his style is marked by it, it is because he must bring to the forefront what is characteristic of infantilism, the archaic, and the psychoneuroses. Freud gives us a genuine definition of parataxis in a passage from his *New Introductory Lectures* dealing with dreams: "All the linguistic means by which the finer relations of thoughts are expressed, the conjunctions and prepositions, the changes of declension and conjugation, escape, because there are no means of expression for it; as in a primitive language without grammar, only the raw material of thought is expressed, the abstract returns to the concrete on which it is based."[20] Freud perhaps ignored that in writing on the dream whose energy derives from infantile sources, in showing the link between the dream and the psychoneuroses, in trying to discover there "some primaeval relic of humanity,"[21] his style underwent, through all the subtleties of syntax[22] and through their omission, a paratactic regression.

Parataxis, however, is not to be considered only at the level of words; it also appears at the level of sentences and paragraphs. We have seen an example of this in paragraph 3 and in paragraphs 4 and 5, where the sentences concerning the dream preceded others dealing with different symptoms or followed them. The relative position of the sentences, as much as the syntactical links between them, determines the meaning, even when their succession is suspended. We must go even further: very often the syntax does not indicate where the parataxis is. Here, for example, what Freud wants to show but cannot explicitly tell us is that all psychical processes arise from the same processes. Similarly, it often happens that a question posed at the beginning of one or several of the paragraphs appears to be abandoned in the following sentences because its solution is to be found only at the end of this or that paragraph. This is also the case for the question of censorship in paragraphs 4 and 5 and in the last paragraph of the introduction cited above: the important thing, mentioned in the first sentence, to which one might have been inattentive, is the recourse in the final sentences to other psychical processes in order to explain the processes of the dream; the unity of the whole paragraph, along with its objective, is to be found through this inclusion of paratactic order.[23]

To parataxis as a characteristic of Freud's style we must add what I will call *diataxis* (to order by separating), which cuts the order of the sentence by introducing a new element and organizing it differently. Diataxis gives parataxis its dynamism, puts it in motion, makes the difference by ensuring that the psychical apparatus does not arise from a purely taxonomic description. The most obvious example of diataxis appears in the figure of pericenter: *incompleteness* at the center of the last paragraph of the introduction, *arbitrariness* at the center of paragraph 9, and then *censorship* at the center of paragraphs 4 and 5 considered as a unit.

Diataxis has a decisive role in the work of theorization. We must emphasize that Freud cannot make proofs, that he cannot deduce, because he cannot trace the processes of the dream to the already known of a general psychology that does not exist. He can only establish correspondences between dream-processes and other psychical functions. Through a series of paratactic procedures, he can weave the threads of his discoveries and make them appear as a fabric. If, however, he wants to show that all psychical functions arise from a single apparatus, as he clearly explains in the last paragraph of the introduction and throughout chapter 7, he is compelled to introduce hypotheses and conjectures progressively, according to the procedure of diataxis.

From this perspective, diataxis is at once the dynamic principle of Freud's style and his theory. Through diataxis analytic theory achieves its peculiar status; for analytic theory is nothing other than a style. An hypothesis appears whenever the writing comes upon an insurmountable difficulty, which is to say, whenever the psychical apparatus can no longer function. In order to put it in motion, which is the motion of the text itself, he must resort to conjectures (*Vermutungen*), which are no different from suppositions or presumptions. Freud never allows us to believe in the objective reality of his constructions for long, and even less long in the truth of his theory.

Before describing the psychical apparatus in section B of chapter 7, he clearly sees what is at stake: "I think that we should give free rein to our conjectures [*Vermutungen*] as long as we retain our cool judgment and do not mistake the scaffolding for the building. Since we need nothing other than the aid of representations for a first approach to something unknown, we will prefer the crudest and most readily seized hypotheses to all the others."[24] And when in section E he returns to the description of the total apparatus that he has, little by little, put into place in the course of the chapter, he recalls the successive hypotheses that he has introduced by carefully opening the discussion as follows: "We were buried in the fiction of a primitive psychical apparatus whose work is regulated by the effort to avoid an accumulation of excitation and to maintain itself so far as possible without excitation."[25] He corroborates this on the following page by admitting that "the mechanism of these processes is totally unknown to me"; he asserts this a little later by speaking of "a theoretical fiction."[26]

Meyerson's French translation, which is faithfully reproduced by Denise Berger, modestly reads: "We have adopted the fiction of a psychical apparatus."[27] In the always dignified *Standard Edition,* we find: "We have already explored the fiction of a primitive psychical apparatus,"[28] while Freud writes: *"Wir hatten uns in die Fiktion eines primitiven psychischen Apparats vertieft,"* which unquestionably means, above all because *vertiefen* is followed by *in* and the accusative, that we have buried ourselves, absorbed ourselves in, as one might in reveries. This is an important nuance. Freud has plunged into the fiction he spins, as one spins a dream; he is absorbed by it, and now and then he will get out of it, remake the argument, anticipate the reader, because the fiction will soon risk taking on all the traits of reality. One would end up believing in it, or more precisely, one would end up no longer dreaming that one believes in it; one would know it, one would prove it. This would be madness, for what distinguishes madness from theory is precisely that theory is recognized as fiction.

But it is not so simple. Freud doubtless stops, at decisive moments on his path, to wonder what he is doing so that he can maintain a good distance and avoid being absorbed or engulfed. On the other hand, however, it is up to him to make this apparatus work, to give it the consistency of reality. The general hypotheses that permit him to advance can take a few pages, but he needs one hundred, not to make a proof, but in order for it to hold, in order for it to give the impression, the illusion, that everything has been taken into account[29] and that the entire psyche is caught in the net, or that the psyche is itself the net. To this end, the extreme care and patience of the style. The reader who follows the net from knot to knot, the weaving from point to point, is no longer on guard, and so intricate and firm is the texture that he is absorbed into it. And he thinks that everything is as it should be.

The purpose of a style is to impose its discourse. And when Freud again insists on the fictive character of his theory,[30] when he recalls that it is only hypothesis and conjecture, one no longer hears him, one no longer pauses there. Of course, but it hangs together so well. Quite simply, one starts to think as Freud does; one no longer questions whether this is verifiable, verified, and finally true. Slippage is always possible there, and perhaps it is even necessary in order for the work to continue. Freud is not the last to let himself be caught up. He says, for example, "It is highly doubtful to me that a wish that has not been fulfilled during the day suffices, in an adult, to produce a dream." A few lines further on, in one of these turnabouts that we see in many paragraphs, he writes, "But in general, I believe, the wish that has remained unfulfilled during the day will not be sufficient to produce a dream."[31] The formulation remains reasonable, since it is a question, not of defining a universal law, but of remaining at the general level of opinion. On the next page, however, these nuances will disappear, and a universal law will be formulated: "The wish that is presented in the dream must [*muss*] be an infantile one." What appeared doubtful when considered negatively is now endowed with the traits of a generally received opinion, and can be stated as a law.[32] If the writing takes such long detours, it is perhaps to get used to an explanation. With time and repetition one turns a question into a certainty; the idea becomes an integral part of the discourse, and indispensable to its consistency. A law is universal because those who speak or write about it consider it as such. In other words, what is universal for a style is its constitutive law or one of its laws. This is not a tautology, because inversely, the law that Freud enacts concerning the role of infantile desire in the formation of a dream would be without force were it not integrally sustained by his style: here, for example, the relation between parataxis and the infantile.

The theoretical fiction can exist only if it tends to assert itself as a reality; if not, it is only a passing fancy, an interesting novel or film. The psychiatrists who want us to believe that it is easy to distinguish between theory and delirium, because they know and have seen and understood what delirium is, would be well advised to consider these unsettling questions. Freud's genius in having forged a style that conforms to the fiction he wanted to develop and impose is what makes fiction pass into reality. The difference between the theoretician and the madman would no longer consist in the fact that the first recognizes that his theory is fiction, but in the fact that it can be written and given a style, that he does not command knowledge and truth, but only puts into operation an investigative and inventive form of writing.

The difficulty doubles if one ventures into the realm of practice.[33] At the beginning of section E, Freud makes a comment about methodology:

> When I attempt to penetrate more deeply into the psychology of dream-processes, I have undertaken a difficult task, to which my art of presentation scarcely extends. To render such a complex simultaneity through a succession in the description, while in every arrangement appearing without presupposition—this will be too arduous for my forces. It brings home to me the fact that I cannot follow in the presentation of the dream-psychology the historical development of my insights. The perspectives for the understanding of the dream were provided to me by my earlier work in the psychology of the neuroses, to which I should [*soll*] not refer and to which, however, I must [*muss*] always refer when I must go into the opposite direction and, with dreams as the connection [*Anschluss*], reach the psychology of the neuroses. I know of no means of avoiding them.[34]

One can read this paragraph in a theoretical perspective and understand that it underlines the difficulty in presenting the simultaneity of unconscious processes in succession. But one can also see there a question about clinical practice: How can one, through the thread of analytic sessions, disentangle the skein of the unconscious in such a way that one can still utter words in successive order? To do so, Freud had to create a style of discourse,[35] characterized essentially by permitting the play of associations. Now, this style, as Freud often emphasizes, here particularly in paragraph 4, regarding its relation to delirium, is clearly marked by the prevalence of parataxis. The analyst who really listens is not interested in syntax, in the way the words are linked together in order to produce meaning, but in the words themselves, in their respective positions—the proximity, the distance, the intervals which constitute the fundamental relations that syntax most often veils.

One could go so far as to say that syntax is a secondary process, while parataxis is a primary process. The importance of the effect of parataxis on Freud's style is that it perfectly fits it to its object and that it enables clinical practice to speak in the style of the theory. The temporalization of unconscious simultaneity can be accomplished only through parataxis. Parataxis therefore appears not as the form of a meaningless or unfinished discourse; it depends no more on meaning than on non-meaning. It is characterized by a reserve of meaning, reserve in the sense of withholding, like a reservoir.

The analysand's discourse also combines parataxis and syntax. In a sequence of associations, the unexpected or sudden word or sentence at once divides and halts the sequence and leads it to disorder and reorganization. From many aspects Freud's style is that of the analysand, when the spoken (written) formulation immediately provokes a turnabout or when the repetition of a sentence that appeared at the beginning of the session (paragraph) automatically marks its end. Did not Freud write to Fliess, probably regarding the *Traumdeutung* on which he was working, "[My work] was all written by the unconscious following the well-known principle of Itzig, the Sunday horseman: 'Itzig, where are you going? —Don't ask me, ask the horse.' At the beginning of none of the paragraphs did I know where I would land. It is obviously not written for the reader; the concern for style was abandoned after the first two pages."[36]

Diataxis is more precisely the figure of the style of interpretation. It is entrusted with the task of shifting the discourse, of turning it in every sense of the word, or more simply, of making it go forward by placing itself at the heart of the paratactic sentence. Like the style of Freud's theory, the analyst's intervention, at moments when the analysand's discourse hits an obstacle that blocks his way (*Weg*), tries to open a detour (*Umweg*) in the form of an hypothesis. That is to say, the intervention does not present itself as the truth. It is not an explanation derived from something known in advance, or a translation in a more profound or more authentic language; it is a conjecture (*Vermutung*) that can always be invalidated, whose status inheres in its capacity to be invalidated, and whose only function is to allow the analysand's discourse to continue constructing or undoing itself.

The style of interpretation can be described by Freud's words in section E: "In every arrangement [that is, analytic session] appearing without presupposition." Putting this style to work is not easy, however, because the psychoanalyst is encumbered by his so-called knowledge and his so-called experience. He would rewrite Freud in this way: "I acquired the point of view that enables me to understand the analysand's discourse from my earlier work, to which I should not refer and to which I cannot, however, stop myself from referrring, whereas I should go in the opposite direction and, through the analysand's discourse, arrive at and change the results of my former labors."

The paradox of the intervention-hypothesis is that its introduction into the analysand's discourse should be disruptive, but in a way consistent with that discourse so that its insertion should be expected and yet inevitably have an appearance of suddenness; it can penetrate only by breaking into the place that was presented to it. The diatactic style of the intervention-hypothesis, which is essential to associative parataxis, resembles Freud's written style to the point of becoming indistinguishable from it. Freud's writing also moves forward by inserting an element that at first seems surprising, like the sight of wreckage on the open sea, but at a second glance becomes absorbed into the advancing liquid mass. The particular style that constitutes analytic practice is precisely the one that makes the writing theoretical.

It now becomes quite understandable why Freud, before concluding the first section of chapter 7 with paragraph 10, introduced a paragraph on psychoanalytic practice and the relation between patient and analyst, even though the expression *Zielvorstellung* no longer has the same meaning there that it had in the preceding pages. The point is precisely that the distance between the arbitrariness of discourse and the objectives pursued appears greatest from the perspective of analytic technique. Through the cure the practice of analysis is constantly generating theory; it is constantly taking into account the associative data, which appear under a dissociated form, and then accounting for them through the intervention-hypothesis. Analytic practice is theorization because it is constituted by a particular style, without which it would cease to be analytic.

It is neither a particular form of practice nor a particular theoretical thesis but rather style which determines what analysis is. At the end of the introduction to chapter 7, Freud writes that "we should be careful not to draw out the thread [of hypotheses] too far beyond the first logical articulations, for otherwise their value is lost in the interminable." To study analytic theory in order to deduce the theory from it is absolutely impossible unless it is understood that in this way one departs from the field of analysis only in order to do academic philosophy or, more likely, to produce an ideology. Freud well knows that he is limited to induction, that is, to testing an always problematic generalization by constantly returning to what the "unconscious dictates" to him. In other texts, each time he draws the thread past the first logical articulation in order to propose applications of psychoanalysis, he leaves the field of analytic theory and practice.

If chapter 7 seems to us obscure or even confused, it is because we have failed to follow the way it unfolds. It does not give us results but reveals the road that has been followed. It gives us a detailed description of its experiments and its mistakes. Writing what the unconscious dictates has nothing to do with a rough draft or automatic writing. In a rough draft one puts on paper ideas that come surreptitiously, but without taking them seriously, because one suspects they are fanciful. When Freud writes, even if it is for himself, he does not make things easy for himself: he tests what he has written; he criticizes himself, in deferred action and all along the way. He lets come what may, as in automatic writing, but always in order to question immediately afterwards what it could signify, and whether he is on the right track, before he continues. Something like this happens in analysis when the possibility of letting anything whatsoever emerge becomes mixed up with astonishment and interrogative reexamination. As Freud said in paragraph 1, when he described his method, it is a question of joining the involuntary, free associations and the work of intervention and notation. I believe that this process could be compared to some extent to the work of a mathematician. His writing must be as precise and rigorous as possible, but at the same time he cannot know where it will lead. He is attentive to and confident in his findings, but he also lets himself be guided by the writing itself and by the formulations that emerge from it. He can run into a dead end or a contradiction, in which case he returns to his point of departure or waits for it to reappear and then resumes his rigorous inquiry.[37] Freud's writing is at once endlessly drifting (what happens is involuntary) and endlessly put to the test, drawing the thread out as far as it can go.

The difficulty of reading chapter 7 arises when we fail to take into account the way words are used, their repetition and their respective position, when, in other words, we are not attentive to parataxis. Difficulties emerge when we are unaware of the ruptures that diataxis provokes in the text. Diataxis is a way of describing everything that is the result of an upheaval of difference, a difference of energy, of cathexis, of excitation, that is to say, every difference that is introduced through sexuality. Every hypothesis and conjecture that makes Freud's text move forward is of this order. The logos of parataxis, of that which expresses the infantile, the archaic, and the psychoneurotic, is therefore divided, undone, and reorganized by the sexuality of diataxis. This is not done all at once, but step by step, leap by leap, thread by thread. One could say, by comparison, that if the discourse heard in a session is not yet analytic, at once theory and practice, it is because syntax is still an obstacle and because, as a consequence, diataxis has not yet been able to emerge.

The progressive constitution of the psychical apparatus, as it appears in chapter 7, is nothing other than an analysand's discourse from which only the complexity has been eliminated or which has been simplified for the sake of brevity. The consequence of this is that the hypothetical and conjectural character of the apparatus is an integral part of the discourse. In practice, the style of the analysis produces analysis, even if the practice, like the theory (if there is still a reason to distinguish these two terms), must also be recognized as a fiction, as a construction of style that finally has no content. Analytic practice has this peculiarity: in order for the process to be carried out, it must be constantly undone so that it can be redone, like Penelope's tapestry. It is maintained only by being undone. One is led to a generalized fiction that is sustained only by a style.

"He whom psychoanalysis has once seized, it never lets go."[38] As analysts or analysands, we doubtless adopt Freud's style. A style cannot be imitated, however, without becoming meaningless and laughable. Read a page of Flaubert or Nietzsche, Hegel or Diderot, however little you know these authors, and you will recognize them after reading a line. There is something that belongs uniquely to each of them, and you will be able to reproduce it only as a caricature. Freud himself also has this sort of recognizable and inimitable style, which gives him a place in German literature. But he also created a style of analysis: a procedure that abandons syntax for parataxis and that opens the way to diataxis. A path, a detour, a way without an end. Exactly the sort of style that everyone must put to work from his own particular perspective, and precisely not the sort of writing that is indissociable from a thought that could alienate one individuality, which is what happens if one believes in the consistency of analytic theory. Perhaps it will be necessary to pursue this question still further: Freud's style, such as I construe it, supposes a certain relation to the unconscious that is marked by its own cultural moment (and this is still how we enter into analysis today); it is not at all certain whether this relation can be changed or has already been changed.

two

quite often

In 1937, in a brief text entitled "Constructions in Analysis,"[1] Freud returns to the technical notion that he introduced much earlier, particularly in the account of his analysis of the Ratman,[2] in "The Psychogenesis of a Case of Homosexuality in a Woman," and at the beginning of chapter 3 of *Beyond the Pleasure Principle*.[3] Through these apparently unobtrusive observations that simply discuss the handling of the treatment, the very foundations of analytic method come under interrogation.

Construction is a key notion in psychoanalytic technique. It is distinguished by its amplitude from interpretation (*Deutung*). While interpretation applies to "a single element of the material, to an idea [*Einfall*], a parapraxis,"[4] construction means that the analyst proposes to the patient something that he supposes or guesses (*erraten*)[5] about the patient's prehistory. Freud gives an example in this text: "'Up to your nth year you regarded yourself as the sole and unlimited possessor of your mother, then came a second baby and with him severe disillusionment. Your mother left you for some time and afterwards she was no longer devoted to you exclusively. Your feelings toward your mother became ambivalent, your father gained a new importance for you.'"[6] It is easy to see from this example how construction can be a technical notion that joins theory and practice, because analysis uses theory—in this case the Oedipus complex—in order to apply or to remodel it to the particular case in question.

Freud's reliance upon construction is obviously inseparable from his total conception of analysis. He is going to develop here, using the same words, what he described more briefly almost twenty years earlier in "Psychogenesis of a Case of Homosexuality in a Woman":

> In a great number of cases, the analysis falls into two clearly distinguishable phases: in the first phase, the physician acquires the necessary information from the patient, familiarizes him with the presuppositions and the postulates of the analysis, and develops before him the *construction* of the genesis of his disorder to which he feels authorized on the basis of the material brought up in the analysis. In the second phase the patient himself gets hold of the material put before him; he works on it, *recollects* what he can recall of the apparently repressed

memories, and as for the rest, he tries to repeat it as if he were reliving it. In this way he can confirm, complete, and correct the physician's inferences. It is only during this work that he experiences, by overcoming resistances, the internal change that is the objective, and that he acquires the *convictions* that make him independent of the physician's authority.[7]

This passage shows how Freud tries to submit analysis to the model of the hypothetical-deductive sciences. The construction is deduced from a general theory with a view toward the verification of a particular case, a particular case that can, in its turn, lead the psychoanalyst to enlarge or modify his construction and, through it, the general theory itself.

"Constructions in Analysis" begins with a paragraph that develops an objection made about psychoanalytic technique, namely, that whether the patient approves or opposes an interpretation, the analyst is always right. In the first case, there is no problem; in the second, the opposition is attributed to resistance. This paragraph uses the terms of the legal trial. It is enclosed by the words *justice/unjust* at the beginning and *justification* at the end. In the middle, we are in the presence of the victim, who is no longer called, as he is before and after, the *patient*, but the *poor helpless person*. At the end of the two halves of the paragraph we find the terms of a dispute: *to agree, to oppose* and *agreement, opposition*. The debate will obviously be displaced, and everything will be centered on what happens between analyst and patient.

The question of their agreement and disagreement will not, however, be developed immediately. Freud takes his time and wishes to underline slowly what is at stake. A paragraph is devoted to recalling that the objective of analytic work is to make the patient remember what he has forgotten of his most remote past, and to make these memories appear through dreams, associations and repetitions. The next paragraph, concerning the patient who must exercise his memory, directs the analyst whose task is "to make out what has been forgotten from the traces which it has left behind, or, more correctly to construct it." Then, two paragraphs complete the first part of the text by developing the resemblances and differences between the archeologist's work of reconstruction and that of the analyst. This allows him to mention, in passing, the advantages and disadvantages of the conditions of their respective work.

This comparison could have been the occasion to consider the part played by subjectivity in the reconstitutive work of the archeologist and the analyst. Freud has posed this question on other occasions. He saw how other psychoanalysts work and decided to move in another direction: "It is now no longer a question of the patient's fantasies but of the analyst's fantasies, who imposes them upon the patient on account of his own personal complexes."[8] He believes himself free of this type of misconduct. A lengthy justification follows this passage from his analysis of the Wolfman: the slowness and the details of the process of reconstruction would be sufficient proof that the analyst's fantasies had been eliminated. Freud is somewhat quick to claim objectivity, since it is obvious that slowness and detail can only be the means necessary to consolidate a subtle rationalization. When one knows, for example, that the text Freud published on the Ratman transcribes nothing about this patient's relationship to his mother—which one can see by comparing it with the notes Freud took during the treatment[9]—one may suspect that this omission served the analyst. Similar suspicions arise when the patient in the case of feminine homosexuality responds to Freud's remarks on his theory as though she were being taken through a museum.[10] One could easily deduce from this that Freud had reconstructed her story in an optic that appeared to the young woman literally out of another age, old-fashioned to her, like the words of the dead.

Freud, however, retains an unshakable confidence in his method, even though in the course of thirty years (from the Ratman case to "Constructions") he experienced failures and recognized them as such (Dora fled prematurely; the Wolfman's illness got worse; the Ratman was cured too early; the so-called female homosexual quickly vanished; and so on). Why this faithfulness to his method? There are several fundamental reasons. The first—the others will appear later—dominates the entire second part of our text: Freud believes he can apply the experimental method to psychoanalysis through the process of construction. He does not believe in the experimental method as a dogma, but as a universal rule that cannot be called into question, and which he never dreams of questioning, since without it there would no longer be science nor, consequently, rationality, nor any possibility for research.

Of course, he is not going to imitate the sciences to which he feels closest, here, for example, archeology. While "reconstruction is the aim and the end" of the archeologist's endeavours,[11] it is only preliminary work for the psychoanalyst. Not only is construction done piece by piece, but it must be submitted to the patient, who will judge its accuracy or its imprecision. Therein lies the proof of the experiment. The adaptation of the experimental method, however, is submitted to still other imperatives. Not only is the patient not a pillar of stone, a fossil, or a footprint, but he is alive, for he is a psychical object who reacts when he hears the analyst's construction. He is "incomparably more complicated than the excavator's material . . . and its finer structure still conceals so many mysteries."[12] More precisely, the possible but not immediately verifiable effects of resistance make the patient's no and yes ambiguous or, at best, always plurivocal.

But Freud accepts these difficulties, which do not appear insurmountable to him. The analyst does not avoid risking the error of "offering to the patient a wrong construction as the probable historical truth,"[13] because in this case the patient reacts to it with neither a yes nor a no. The hypothesis is invalidated, and another must be found.

"Construction" and "historical truth" are two decisive constituents of the science that Freud dreams of founding. On the one hand, we have construction and hypothesis, which are the tools, and on the other hand, the object, which must be both constituted and discovered; that is, historical truth. If psychoanalysis is at once similar to and different from archeology, it is because for both of them the object is buried (*verschüttet*), but the object of psychoanalysis can be reconstituted. The psychoanalyst is an archeologist who succeeds, piece by piece, in making reappear not only the ruins but the whole city. For the archeologist, Mycenae will always remain the site of important ruins; for the psychoanalyst, the city itself will rise again, and not even Agamemnon and Clytemnestra will be missing, because the patient who will appear there is indeed living.

We see here the second reason why Freud is so committed to the technique of construction in analysis: he believes—and this is something to which we will return in detail—in historical truth as in a force that is always at work, and that the road to it is barred only by resistance. Agreement or opposition will appear later in the text like two subtle weapons that the patient uses either to bring this truth to light or to suppress it. Sometimes the patient's agreement with the construction that has been proposed to him will enable him "to conceal the undiscovered truth"[14]: "you are right," he says to the analyst, "it is useless to go further"; at other times the patient's no will signify that the construction does not account for "the whole truth."[15] That indeed is Freud's objective in the experiment whose conditions he sets up: to make the whole truth appear, all of Mycenae in one patient, all of Knossos in another.

Such is the resistance against the appearance of this historical truth "that from the direct utterances of the patient after the transmission of the construction, one can only acquire little evidence from which to know whether we have been right or wrong."[16] The text goes on to the need to resort to indirect evidence from associations or from direct oppositions that betray themselves in a parapraxis. That is to say, the historical truth that sustains the construction can appear only without the patient's knowledge. This conforms to analytic experience, because resistances can never be broken directly, and thus they pose some problems to the method. At the end of the second part of his text, in the face of complexities, contradictions, and the always possible reversals of agreement and opposition, Freud reduces the level of his pretensions:

> These reactions of the patient are, at the least, multivocal [*vieldeutig*] and do not permit a final decision. Only the further course of the analysis can

bear a decision on the correct or useless character of our construction. We do not regard particular construction as anything but a conjecture [*Vermutung*] which awaits examination, confirmation or rejection. We claim no authority for it; we require no direct agreement from the patient; we do not discuss it with him if he at first opposes it. In short, we conduct ourselves after the model of the well-known figure in one of Nestroy's farces, that of the servant who has prepared one answer to all questions and objections: everything will become clear in the course of events.[17]

In this late text, Freud seems less assured than he was when he treated the same subject in earlier works. Three terms that define the stages of analytic method appear throughout: *Konstruktion, Erinnerung, Überzeugung*.[18] The analyst's transmission of his *construction* should induce *memory* (or failing that, repetition), with which the patient works in order to lead to the *conviction* through which he verifies that the construction-hypothesis-conjecture (*Vermutung*) was grafted upon the historical truth. As a note to the analysis of the Ratman emphasizes, the fullness of the patient's conviction is the totalization of the sources of this truth: "The patient acquires conviction only after having himself reworked the material (through memory). As long as conviction is wavering, the material must be considered unexhausted."[19]

At the beginning of the third part of our text, the three terms reappear, as though they were expected, since the first part is devoted to defining the place of construction and the second to describing the complex play of reactions to construction. In the first sentence of this third part, conviction poses no problems for Freud, because it has been placed in line with earlier texts: "How this occurs in the process of the analysis, through which ways our conjecture is transformed into the patient's conviction, it is hardly worth describing; through daily experience all of that is known to every analyst and presents no difficulties to understanding."[20] If these lines did not refer to what Freud has believed for several decades—which gives them their tone of authority—one would not understand why they precede a major exception that calls the entire method into question: the analyst's construction leads to the patient's conviction without the (up to this point) necessary detour of recollection. The text just cited continues:

> Only one point requires investigation and examination. The path that starts from the analyst's construction should end in the patient's recollection: it does not always lead so far. *Quite often* we do not succeed in leading the patient to recollect the repressed. Instead of that, one obtains in him, through a correct handling of the analysis, an assured conviction of the truth of the construction which achieves therapeutically the same thing as a recaptured memory. In which circumstances this happens and how it is possible that an apparently incomplete substitute [that is to say, construction] nevertheless produces the full effect, all of this remains a matter for a later inquiry.

The tone of these observations, as though they were made in passing, poorly conceals the abyss that Freud has opened beneath his feet. Without recollection or its complement, repetition, without the work that the patient should perform on the material transmitted to him, what is left of the analytic method? Nothing more than an effort to cure through suggestion, of which Freud does not here seem suspicious—we will see why —because from here on, as the following paragraphs will show, Freud will open an even larger abyss.

He had alerted us to it a few pages earlier, by suggesting that the patient's yes could be "'hypocritical'"[21] and could signify the desire to hide the truth and to maintain the resistance. All the more reason for the yes of the cure to put an end to all this pain and effort. But the way this cure is obtained leaves no doubts: the analyst holds the truth of the patient; he imposes it upon him in such a way that the patient begins to act according to this truth and that those acts of the patient that necessitated the symptoms no longer have a basis, and therefore the symptoms disappear.

At the beginning of the second part, Freud had dismissed this objection:

> The danger of our leading a patient astray by suggestion, by persuading him to accept things which we ourselves believe, but which he should not accept, has certainly been greatly exaggerated. The analyst would have behaved very incorrectly if such a misfortune happened to him; above all, he would have to blame himself for not allowing the patient to have his say. I can assert without boasting that such an abuse of suggestion has never occurred in my practice.[22]

One could hardly be less affirmative. Does he not speak elsewhere, in a similar context, of "inducing the patient to abandon his resistances through human influence (here, the role of suggestion operating as 'transference')"?[23] And if the time of remembering is suppressed in order to obtain conviction immediately, is this a way to prevent "the patient [from having] his say"? Besides, this is not an exceptional fact, since Freud recognizes that there is "not always" recollection, that "quite often" there is none at all.

He seems here to have little regard for the patient's discourse, under the pretext of no longer needing it, since the therapeutic effect has been fully obtained. This is obviously not an argument, since on the preceding page he explains that in the case of "a negative therapeutic reaction," that is, a negative transference, the patient reacts to a correct construction or one close to the truth with "an unmistakable aggravation of his symptoms and of his general condition";[24] if the anti-cure cuts off the discourse and annuls the time of recollection, the disappearance of the symptoms would not justify these events. Moreover, Freud repeated that this disappearance prevents the possibility of research.[25] What therapy gains becomes a loss as much for the patient, who can no longer be "independent of the physician's authority," as for the analyst, who is prevented from developing his science.

If Freud dispenses with recollection, if he accepts the cancellation of the patient's discourse, it is because he is fascinated by the truth and its efficacy (*Wahrheit, Wirkung*). That the analyst has formulated this truth seems secondary to Freud; it only matters to him that the patient (as well as himself) submits to it and sacrifices his symptoms (whether they disappear or get worse) and his discourse (there is no need to work on the material). Everything happens as if Freud were alarmed by the seriousness of his own assertions and felt constrained, on the one hand, to multiply his formulations about the cure—the passage from the analyst's conjecture to the patient's conviction, "it is hardly useful to present it," "his understanding presents no difficulty"; and on the other hand, to disconnect as completely as possible his assertions from the consequences he is going to have to draw from them. This is why the paragraph in which he jumps from construction to conviction by passing over recollection ends with the words "all of this remains a matter for a later inquiry" and the following paragraph begins, "I shall conclude this brief communication with some remarks which open up a wider perspective."[26] In other words: beware, everything I am going to say now has only a very vague link with what went before. Such a heavy negation should persuade us to listen closely.

The premises having been defined above, we must be ready to read the deductions of an implacable logic. To the question, What happens to the patient when he allows himself to be convinced of the truth of the analyst's construction? Freud will answer, "He does not remember the event that was the content of the construction," but the related details under an "'ultra-clear [*überdeutlich*],'" an "'ultra-sharp [*überscharf*],'" a hypermnesic form. Why?

The truth of the construction is, in a sense, the patient's, and he recognizes himself in it, since he supplied its elements. But its peculiarity is that it has been created through another, according to his way of thinking and interpreting. The patient's memories, associations, and actions are returned to him like things that have been first stolen from him, like jewels that have been removed and then reset differently, at once recognizable and unrecognizable. Because they are recognizable, he accepts them as true; because they are unrecognizable, he can only accept with an encompassing, absolute, and faultless conviction and therefore by halting the process of association and the work of his own discourse. The "truth of the construction," which leads the patient to "assured conviction," forces everything that construction could not use to fall to the level of hallucination. If the patient adheres, through conviction, to the analyst's reconstitutive discourse, it can be only by abandoning himself and by casting outside discourse, into an hallucinatory hypermnesia, the fragmented memories, the "details" that were closely related to the event whose actor has been expropriated. What returns is no longer attributable to anyone, and it falls into pieces in the margins of his discourse.

In the second paragraph of the third part of this text appears the first consequence of the suppression of the time of recollection between construction and conviction: the appearance of related memories. A rapid reading of the following paragraphs would make us believe—and that, indeed, is Freud's apparent intention—that he uses the link between hypermnesia and related memories to present a mini-theory of hallucination, then delirium, in their relation to historical truth so that he can reintroduce them into his general conception of the neuroses and, particularly, of hysteria. It is certainly permissable to read these pages like this, but then one does not see clearly, in fact, one does not see at all, why Freud makes it the conclusion to an article devoted to "Constructions in Analysis."

In my opinion, he presents phenomena in which conviction does away with remembering and its substitutes—repetitions, actions within and outside the analytic situation[27]—in order to base them directly on historical truth. For example, the link is explicitly made at the beginning of the third paragraph of the third part between hyper-clearness (hypermnesia), which he has just treated as a consequence of communication and construction, and hallucination, which he describes here:

> These recollections [that is, the related details] could be called hallucinations if to their distinctiveness [*Deutlichkeit*, an allusion to *überdeutlich* in the preceding paragraph] were added a belief in their actuality. But the analogy gains importance when I am attentive to the occasional occurrence of true hallucinations in other, non-psychotic, cases.[28]

One is therefore right to conclude that the hallucinations that can appear during an analysis are to be equated with construction-conviction. The text continues: "Perhaps this is a general characteristic of hallucination to which insufficient value has been given, that, in it, something experienced in early childhood and then forgotten returns, something that the child saw and heard when he was still hardly able to speak, and that now forces its way into consciousness, probably distorted and displaced owing to the operation of forces opposed to such a return." Now, this is also the case of the patient who has been rendered speechless and unable to remember his repressed experience by the truth that the analyst has transmitted. He sees, he hears, pieces of his life, "details" without a context, in an untransmissable form, both because it is no longer possible for him to make his interlocutor understand them and because he wants to prevent the analyst from interpreting them, that is, from taking them away from him. Hallucination thus includes a conviction which the person who hallucinates keeps for himself alone and which will allow him to escape from the conviction that is imposed by the analyst's discourse.

Freud says nothing about truth in relation to hallucination, because the latter is not of the order of discourse but is a reaction to a discourse of truth held by another who does not leave it to the disposition of the one who hallucinates. The madman is in a very different situation: he is the only master of his discourse, and that of the others matters to him only when he can use it to pursue his own. Regarding madness, Freud writes: "A fragment of historical truth is contained in it, and we are close to admitting that the compulsive belief met with in madness derives its force from such an infantile source." One would do better, not to try to persuade madmen of their delirium or of their opposition to reality, "but rather to find, in the recognition of its kernel of truth, a common ground on which the therapeutic work can be developed."[29]

One has no hesitation on a first reading. Freud takes advantage of the occasion to return with some new perspectives to his conception of the psychoneuroses; as he often does, he posits some new interrelations in these pages. The third paragraph of this third part establishes links between hallucination and madness; the fourth paragraph links madness and neurosis; the fifth, madness and hysteria; and the sixth and final one enlarges the perspective by moving from the individual to humanity as a whole.

But why does he insert in the fifth paragraph a comparison between madness and construction in analysis? Through all these developments he never loses sight of the subject of his article. He cannot, however, directly enter into this new relationship. It must be done as though in passing, but without appearing as such, without appearing as such to Freud himself, because that would involve him in it too much:

> I know that it is of small service to treat in passing, as I have done here, such an important theme. I am, however, carried forward by the attraction of an analogy. The delusions of patients appear to me to be the equivalent of the constructions that we build in analytic treatment, attempts at explanation and cure, which, under the conditions of psychosis, can do no more than replace a fragment of reality that one disavows in the present with another fragment that one had disavowed in the remote past. To discover the intimate connections between the disavowed material of the present and that of the former repression is the task of each individual investigation. Just as our construction is effective only because it recovers a fragment of individual experience that has been lost, so also madness owes its convincing force to the element of historical truth that it inserts in the place of the rejected reality.[30]

From here on, we can conjecture a very different mode of composition than the one that appeared earlier. The fourth paragraph, with its comparison of madness to construction, is an answer to the second, in which the consequences for analysis of the suppression of the time for recollection are discussed. If one pushes to the extreme the hypermnesia that characterizes the second paragraph, one ends up with hallucination in the third paragraph; if one goes beyond the equivalence between madness and construction in the fifth paragraph, one falls into the pure madness discussed in paragraph four:

$$\left.\begin{array}{l}\text{2 hypermnesia}\\ \text{3 hallucination}\end{array}\right\} \text{the patient}$$
$$\left.\begin{array}{l}\text{4 madness}\\ \text{5 construction}\end{array}\right\} \text{the analyst}$$

Madness and hallucination meet at the center here only in order to emphasize that no link is made between the analyst's constructions and their effects on the patient. By pursuing this type of reading, we are forced to consider that if the relation between analyst and patient risks becoming that of a madman and someone who hallucinates, the reason is to be sought in the fact that the construction is based on historical truth and that the analyst who adheres to it with an unshakable faith (*zwanghafte Glaube*) forces it on the patient in order to make him respond with conviction. Each time one is involved with construction and conviction, one puts truth in the place of memory and risks producing effects that are close to psychosis. Through this operation the psychoanalyst comes nearer to being a madman, and his theoretical construction to being madness.

In this text, Freud oscillates between two positions: either what he proposes as an analyst is pure supposition, simple conjecture that claims no authority, but only awaits, as a result of this limitation, the continuation of the analysis through the play of associations, and very carefully tries to remain in the realm of the plurivocal and the undecidable; or he maniacally seeks verification, wants to know, through every means, direct or indirect, whether his ideas are right or wrong, and he then embarks upon a process of justification in which the patient is only a machine to corroborate his theories.

Paradoxically, when the theory places itself on the side of truth, the threat of psychosis arises. On a first reading, the patient's historical truth is all that interests Freud; at this point there is no forcing, no expropriation of the patient's discourse for the benefit of the analyst's discourse. But from the moment the analyst is seized by the illusion that he can bring forth the whole truth, or by the frantic desire to use up all the material, as though it were quantitatively defined, he imposes a closure on the patient's discourse to which he, the analyst, alone has the key. He instantaneously makes the patient's discourse pass under the rod of his own, which he claims to be the measure of totality and truth.

On the other hand, if he admits, for the constructions, interpretations, and interventions, which are always based on an already formulated theory (whether or not one recognizes it), and which is also true for the patient's discourse, that the only possible course is that of conjecture and fiction, then it is no longer a question of truth or falsehood, but of the hypothetical, where the only objective is to ensure that the discourse goes on. There is nothing to confirm or invalidate; he can only set in motion the discourse in which he is engulfed. He does not aim at an end and knows there will never be an end, but only awakens as best he can what is asleep.

Construction (which is always a part of the theory) is in an unstable position and can readily turn into madness if one takes it too seriously, if one forgets that, like an hysteric, it suffers from memories, that is, it cannot be separated from the particular discourse of a particular analyst. Construction can just as soon turn into fiction, into a fleeting game, into an imaginary realm that has been patched up with a little coherence but still leaks no matter how slightly one puts pressure on it. As for memory, it can fall to the side of truth as well as it can serve as the basis for an hallucination where discourse has been abandoned and conviction has been replaced by a belief in the reality of what has definitively marked the individual, or it can wander in the direction of dreams and fantasies, which in themselves are neither true nor false but are satisfied with making the psychical apparatus function. If to dream or to fantasize is still to remember,[31] then remembering does not risk being used in an analysis whose task would be to verify the constructions that the analyst has already created or that he is presently working out. It is true that one can dream in the direction wished by the analyst, for the patient's need to sacrifice himself to the analyst-theorist does not stop, and the dream and the fantasy are finally plurivocal enough that now that the analyst has made deductions from his construction, there remains a sufficiently rich and rebellious basis to permit the patient to escape from his dependence on "the authority of the physician."

This equivalence between madness and construction on the one hand and attempts at explanation and cure on the other is enough to puzzle us. Freud says that he was "carried forward by the attraction [*Verlockung*] of an analogy." One thinks of a child who could not resist violently juxtaposed colors or a young architect who plays with models he will never actually build. He tries to be casual when he proposes things that could overturn his discovery; he would like to skip over the difficulty, but he does not succeed at all because he allows himself to be carried away by his blindness—so much the better—when it concerns historical truth. Just like everybody else, he believes in God or something omnipotent. With historical truth, the prehistory of childhood, the forgotten years, he wanted to shelter psychoanalysis from the *Schwärmereien*,[32] on the side of science. But he was obliged to recognize, a few years before his death, that things had not gone as well as he has wished. In the last paragraph of "Constructions in Analysis" (1937) he has to have the last word:

> If we consider mankind as a whole and substitute it for the single human individual, we find that it has developed delusions which are inaccessible to logical criticism and which contradict reality. If, in spite of that, they can exert an extraordinary power over men, investigation leads us to the same conclusion as for the single individual. They owe their force to the content of historical truth that they have brought up from the repression of forgotten origins.[33]

Now we understand why *quite often* the patient cannot remember this historical truth: because his truth, like that of mankind as a whole, is mythical. This truth is certainly endowed with an irresistible force, because it is identified with what we would today call the combinatory power of the signifier, which makes us speak, love, and die, or perhaps more precisely, the way according to which we speak, love, and die, provided that we stress culture as the cause or the form. Historical truth exists no more than do the origins of revolutions or of the Indo-European languages. What exist are delusions founded upon the supposition of its existence. These delusions, for those who want to believe in them, are as solid as rock: Mithra or Varuna, the goddess Reason, or the Oedipus complex.

Historical truth, forgotten origins, and repression are the signs of a culture, and Freud knew how to find the words that defined it. But although culture can now recognize itself in those words, this recognition may have come a little late to be of much use. Because they gave an account of a cultural situation, these mythic words, as always, possessed an extraordinary, one might say magical, power. Freud emphasizes this in the relation between truth and power. The link between these two terms cannot be undone without ignoring that truth has always had a strength which comes from the fact that it has none, that is, that it draws all its force from its nonexistence and that this nonexistence is precisely what provokes, through a horror of the void, the feverish and indefinite production of cultural substitutes. The nonexistence of truth is its power and not, as is often said, belief. Belief only veils the absence of truth a little more completely, by identifying the latter with cultural productions.

To return to Freud's three terms—construction, recollection, conviction—we could say that when recollection disappears in order to make way for truth, what the patient adheres to, since truth does not exist, is the fiction produced by the analyst, which the patient simply takes for the truth. This fiction is nothing other than a return to the patient's situation in such a way that it becomes pertinent and eventually coherent.

This situation is impenetrable in the patient's eyes; it appears to him in scattered, meaningless fragments. The analyst tries to insert it into a discourse that can account for it at least partially, since it is known that this discourse leaves many elements unaccounted for. If the patient recognizes himself in it, he makes this discourse his own, and this gives him a certain coherence. But to suggest that this discourse is the patient's truth is to make a qualitative leap: it is "to confuse the scaffolding with the building"[34]; to attribute to the statements of the analyst and, if the occasion presents itself, to those of the patient the value of an enunciation; to identify these statements that are never more than "distortions and displacements" of an absence of truth with this absence itself, in other words, to make this absence present. The force of this truth, which has only the limitless power of its nonexistence, finds itself improperly transferred to positive statements.

Through this operation, psychoanalysis ceases, paradoxically, to be scientific and becomes one cultural formation among others. If psychoanalysis were a science, it would not leave the terrain of fiction, of a temporary fiction that could be invalidated. Freud does this when he lets the patient speak, that is, when he gives him the chance to agree, to expand, to confirm or reject the psychoanalytic discourse that has been made for him alone. In reality, however, the opposite happens: if the patient continues to speak, it is finally in order to approve the truth of the analyst's construction, to bring analyst and patient into agreement. And this agreement, it must be recognized, is nothing but joint submission to the analytic discourse such as they have been able to constitute or reconstitute it. In so doing, they bring about the culmination of an analysis; this is particularly true in what is called didactic psychoanalysis when analyst and patient end up speaking the same language, in which there are differences only in order to avoid the appearance of impropriety. One could say that analyst and patient finally enter into the same cultural mini-universe, or to return to Freud's terms, they situate origins in just about the same place and they describe them in the same way; that is, their delusions, which are based on the same supposed historical truth, have become similar enough to allow them to communicate and to found a mini-society.

They then become, in Octave Mannoni's words, "cured psychotics,"[35] people who are alienated from the analytic discourse which is their truth and which they will say belongs to no one, since it is the manifest truth which absorbs them all. An analyst said to me, "I always thought that the end or objective of my analysis was to be in agreement with my analyst. Now he treats me as if I were shit. I can no longer say I." One might call it caricature or simply a coarse expression of something widespread. Cured because they escape isolation and can speak a language that some people, a small number, pretend to understand (and, as Hegel said, what is well understood does not differ from the most misunderstood), but psychotics nonetheless because they can exist as bearers of this discourse only by sacrificing their individuality and the possibility of speaking in their own name and of tranquilly saying, even if some think it foolish, "I." We are reminded of, among others, the figure of the Wolfman, whom Freud and then generations of psychoanalysts have carefully studied. He did not succeed in finding his way into the successive discourses, however intelligent, that were proposed to him, and finished his days, rather poorly, in the Vienna where his fame began. He was prohibited by conventional psychoanalysts from making public what a journalist had permitted him to say about his own life after so many accounts of it had been so amply presented to him.[36]

It must be acknowledged that not all psychoanalysts are stifled by epistemological concerns and that not all of them fanatically interrogate the premises and objectives of their practice. Their moderation in this domain would be understandable if psychoanalysis, like the other delusional human activities of which Freud speaks, needed to protect itself from, to shun, "logical criticism" and "the objections of reality."

According to some—and this would be the cause of the difficulties raised here, but brilliantly overcome since then—Freud's conception of analysis remains dominated by the dual relationship between analyst and patient, that is, by an imaginary relationship. It is a difficult question to settle, and there are several ways in which it can be considered.

In "Constructions in Analysis," Freud constantly stumbles upon the difficulty in psychoanalysis, as compared with the experimental sciences, of verifying an hypothesis through experience.[37] If construction is possible for the analyst only through the application to a particular case of a simple generalization acquired from the results of earlier experiences, then one is still within the rules common to all hermeneutics. Freud, however, pretends to have founded his theory—more precisely, his metapsychology—in universal terms that make it independent of experience. Analysts and patients are therefore both subjected to the laws of this third party who prohibits them from being content with each other's reflection.

Has Freud succeeded in his effort? Since the conditions for theory are identical to those of practice, we can legitimately pose this question in the context of the analytic situation. Either the theory, particularly the metapsychology, is independent of experience and therefore unverifiable (for example, in the case of psychical energy), or the theory is taken from experience and is therefore only the description or the more or less structured account of it through a new and more appropriate terminology. One is in the presence either of fictions that develop in the margins of the analytic situation (for example, the constitution of the psychical apparatus) or of a process of theorization in which experience is always doubly inadequate.

Analytic theory may never emerge from this circle. Because of the reason that constitutes both the force and the specificity of analysis—namely, that it is the movement through which the subject resumes accounting for his own life and the belief that analysis could contain, as do the experimental sciences, a universal logic that is independent of it but capable of regulating it and verifying the authenticity of its direction—analytic theory would set this condition, as do the sciences: that the subject be placed in parentheses, that is, excluded.

Does not the effort that brought about the creation of the mathemes[38] also fall within the compass of this dilemma? Have they been derived from analytic experience in order to codify it? Were that the case, the conditions of their appearance would be attributable to the same factors and the same hazards as analytic experience itself and could be no more than a generalization; on one hand, one could deduce nothing from them that could not be known through other means, even if one pretended to ignore those means; on the other hand, the mathemes take on a multitude of meanings according to the ways they are interpreted and applied. Perhaps they arose from the logic of language, but then they would account for analytic experience only inasmuch as it resembles ordinary language, and thus this explanation would not address the specificity of analysis. The mathemes, or any logic inscribed in the analytic field, can take on an appearance of validity that is distinct from practice; but in reality the mathemes can only be a translation or a figuration of practice.

There still remains the possibility of an escape from the imaginary through access to the symbolic.[39] It seems to me that the problem is not solved in this way, but only deferred. In effect, one finds another dilemma there. From one point of view, the symbolic represents the laws, legends, rituals, and beliefs that permit a society to function. In this case, it is not that the imaginary is flexible in every direction according to the individual's needs and desires but rather that the subject is confronted with a world that has been constituted in advance. But then the relation between analyst and patient amounts, through the analyst's intervention, to an effort at education or reformation. The subject no doubt encounters there what is called symbolic castration. One is nonetheless led to the same problem. In other words, the psychoanalyst again becomes the one who must present a construction (that is, who must conform to the symbolic) and demand from the patient a faultless conviction or lead him to it. Nothing is changed if the analyst is silent, for he then becomes the representative, in person, of this symbolic order to which the patient must submit.

From another point of view, the symbolic presents the Other as the locus of the wealth of the signifier, as the site of the enunciation or the condition for the possibility of every utterance, and one is then led toward a transcendental deduction, in the Kantian sense, that is not without interest for the psychoanalyst but whose a priori status is, by definition, detached from experience.

By combining these two fundamentally different points of view in the same word, one creates the illusion, on the one hand, of escaping the closure of particular social laws thanks to the universality of the great Other and, on the other hand, of conjuring up the transcendental abstraction through a reference to the concrete form of these laws. Analytic theory is doubtless right not to choose prematurely from the possible meanings of the symbolic, because it does not even know its own limits very well and because the confusion of meanings could have uncontrollable consequences for analytic practice.

These difficult questions obviously deserve further discussion. The preceding remarks are simply an effort to prevent the specific difficulties of analysis from being swept away by a sleight of hand and to ensure that the circle in which analysis is enclosed by its very objective is also taken into consideration.

The question remains, Is it possible for the patient not to be absorbed by the analytic discourse such as it is now, such as it is presented or represented by the analyst, even if he were the most silent analyst? The most simple solution, but one that obviously resolves nothing, is for the patient to break away. Freud and others have experienced it. The patient leaves because he refuses to be apprchended, both in the sense of being spied upon and in the sense of being seized. He does not want to be locked up in a museum, transformed into a statue through repeated conceptual pressures which are not really related to him, or turned into a mummy wrapped in the bandages of someone else's preconceptions. But this breaking away, which appears like a resurgence of the patient's vitality, only allows him to leave in just about the same condition he was in when he came. For the analyst, the rupture can provide the occasion to perceive when and how his own discourse, or his effectively particularized silence, has cut off the patient's discourse. But it will then be a question, as Freud demonstrated when he did this, of making repairs and changes that will render analytic discourse more subtle, more complex, more flexible, and thus more effective through its refinement and extension; that is, it will be even more difficult not to let oneself be caught and assimilated by it.

Must we then hope that psychoanalytic discourse will not develop and transform itself, that it will not try to become more intelligible? That is obviously absurd, even though the analyst's stupidity does have a temporary but indispensable function in the cure. It is useless to aim at noncomprehension, since it already exists in abundance, whether or not the analyst wishes it. A considerable part of the patient's discourse is not generalizable, because, on the one hand, the theory is incapable of explaining it and, on the other, because of its own particularity and that of the way in which it is said. During an analysis a truly private discourse is constituted, if one knows how to let it happen—Freud called it a dialect, but that misses the point, since a dialect is used for communication within a limited group—a properly impenetrable discourse that is made not for communication but to provide an echo for the most isolated individuality. This discourse uses words and even the syntax of ordinary language; it can thus receive information from the outside, but on the whole it is without a transmissible meaning, and the patient cannot understand it any more than the analyst can; he lets it speak. It is not, however, a discourse spun or woven by chance; it gradually acquires its own consistency, and this allows the patient, if not to rediscover, then to find his own consistency. We could call this particular discourse the *monopheme*, the expression of one alone.

It is obvious that certain elements of this discourse are translatable, interpretable, theorizable, whether in an already acquired conceptual organization or in those that are invented for the case at hand. If the psychoanalyst were to lose sight of the task of understanding, if he were not even there, the patient would be unable to make the monopheme the support or the starting point for the Interlocutor of the totality of his discourse. The mistake would be to confuse this monophemic discourse with what the analyst can lay hold of or with what the theory enables him to grasp, because what remains would only be a lost discourse, not only for the analyst but for the patient as well. One or the other—either the patient would reject into the margins, in a psychotic mode, as Freud describes it, all that remains to be said or his discourse would be extinguished.

We can schematize the situation. From the totality of the monopheme (M), the psychoanalyst makes a deduction (d) that enables M to develop, because the patient, during the transference, makes the psychoanalyst (p) the interlocutor (I) of the same dimension that we designate as M. The motive force of the discourse is the double difference $M\text{-}d$ and $I\text{-}p$, a double difference that is recognized, admitted, and sustained by the analyst, who should expect during the treatment to see d and p moving toward zero, in order that the patient can be released. Freud's mistake could be summarized as the wish to make M equal to d during construction, and I equal to p during conviction.

three

suggestion over the long term

Among the examples Freud cited as material for the study, discussion, and interpretation of telepathic or occult phenomena, the only one in which he is personally involved as an analyst appears in *The New Introductory Lectures on Psychoanalysis* (1932).[1] In the autumn of 1919, Dr. Forsyth went to see Freud, who could not receive him immediately. A few minutes later Mr. P., a patient of long standing, arrives and tells Freud that the young woman whom he has often mentioned used to call him (Mr. P.) Mr. *Vorsicht,* which means Mr. *Foresight.*[2] Had thought-transference taken place between the analyst, who is very interested in the visit of his respected English colleague, Dr. Forsyth, and the patient, who at this precise moment comes up with the very word that corresponds to Forsyth in his own language?

Freud refrains from rushing into this question. He presents all the mediating elements between Forsyth and Vorsicht in order to dissipate the immediately uncanny relation between the two words. By seeking to invalidate the impression of thought-transference, he will eventually be able to reinforce it.

To begin with, P. acquainted Freud with the works of Galsworthy, which are centered around the Forsyte family: "The name 'Forsyte,' and everything typical that the author has sought to embody in it, had also played a part in my conversations with P.; it had become part of the secret language [*Geheimsprache*] which so easily grows up between two people who see a lot of each other."

Freud then offers two other associations brought up during the same session, which also seem to indicate the presence of thought-transference but which should explain analytically why P. produced them. First, the patient asks, "Is the Freud-Ottorego who teaches English at the People's University [*Volksuniversität*] perhaps your daughter?" But instead of "Freud" he says "Freund." The week before, after having waited in vain for Mr. P. to arrive for his appointment, Freud had gone to visit Dr. von Freund, who lives in the same building as P. Second, at the end of the same session, P. says that he had a nightmare; he forgets the English word and says "mare's nest" instead. P. had recognized another English doctor, Ernest Jones, in Freud's waiting room; and Jones had published a monograph on the nightmare.

Freud explains all these associations through P.'s jealousy. Whenever he saw the arrival of foreign patients, P. anticipated there would no longer be time to receive him. It was as if he had said, "After all, I'm a Forsyth too, though it's true I'm only a Herr von *Vorsicht.*" The other two associations, whose link with the first is through the use of English, are also expressions of jealousy. They say, in effect, "It's not me you wanted to see in my building, but a certain von Freund" and "Of course, you would prefer this other Englishman, Jones, who has written on the nightmare."

Freud thus relates the patient's statements to the jealousy that provoked them. But between the arrival of Dr. Forsyth and the *Vorsicht* that appears on the same day, between the visit to von Freund and the confusion of Mrs. Freud-Ottorego and Mrs. Freud-Ottorego, between the forgotten nightmare and Ernest Jones, the possibility of thought-transference remains an unanswered question. Regarding the third one, Freud says that his patient, who was unaware of analytic literature, had the opportunity to see the cover and thus the title of Jones's book. For the second, Freud might have told P. that he had visited von Freund in his building. Freud is more perplexed, however, about the first, since he does not remember having pronounced the name Forsyth, but without totally excluding the possibility, he feels that "the scales weigh in favor of thought-transference." Here Freud obviously is unable to invalidate the hypothesis of telepathy. He cannot find the probable connections permitting him to establish an associative and discursive continuity between Forsyth and Vorsicht.

Freud then resumes his narrative. There are still, however, several features in these few pages that can provide us with another path to the solution of this problem, more by way of the analyst than by way of the patient. It is worth noticing that in order to interpret P.'s statements, Freud attributes a whole series of associations to him, while in fact they are Freud's invention and reveal much more about him than about his patient.

When Freud recalls his visit to von Freund in connection with the second lapsus, he is talking about himself and about the grief he felt at the death of this friend. Why does he introduce at this point the deaths of Anton von Freund (1920) and Karl Abraham (1926) as "the gravest misfortunes which have befallen the development of psychoanalysis" if not because, in speaking of telepathy, he remembers Abraham's reservations and recalls the dangers of putting psychoanalysis on the wrong path.

Freud is the one who associates the word *nightmare* with Jones in the third lapsus. We know that Jones had implored Freud not to write on telepathy and the occult, in order not to jeopardize the chances for the acceptance of psychoanalysis in England. Since Freud disregarded that, it is normal that the reproachful figure of Jones appears before him; and for Jones this story of telepathy is indeed a ghost story, a nightmare—and Freud knows it. We could even go so far as to suggest a meaning to this lapsus, with which Freud certainly does not bother. Is he not the analyst who prevents the patient from remembering his nightmare by immediately evoking the critical presence of Jones? Is not Freud the one who provokes a displacement onto the mare's nest and thus unleashes the return of the repressed and gives the patient's aggressiveness free rein? It is as if the patient says "the analysis from which you are going to eject me is a mare's nest, an illusion," or as Freud says, "a cock-and-bull story." Since P. has just learned that because of Dr. Forsyth's arrival, Freud will not be able to see him for some time, and that he will soon be gotten rid of, why not have a go at the first scientific interpreter of dreams: "You, who say you take nightmares seriously, should know it is only illusion and nonsense." Not a very sophisticated reaction, but understandable.

In contrast, we see much more clearly why Freud privileges the link between Forsyth and Vorsicht. In 1919, with the war over, Freud is especially preoccupied with the expansion of the psychoanalytic movement, and Dr. Forsyth appears to him as "the first dove after the Deluge," who announces a new era, who is able to foresee (*voraussehen*) a happy future. That is why Freud translates the English *foresight* not only by *Vorsicht* ("foresight, precaution") but also by *Voraussicht* ("prescience, foresight"). In asking P. to relinquish his appointment to the recently arrived foreigners, Freud makes him prescient, he forces him into becoming Mr. Foresight, to which the latter reacts with his story and by quickly transforming himself into Mr. Precaution. Freud, however, again outdoes P. by making him become *Vorsicht*; that is, from today on, Forsyth will take his place.

If Freud publishes the account of this session in 1932, it is obviously because he sees it as an occasion to examine thought-transference, but it is also because he can use it to express his preoccupations and anxieties concerning "the development of psychoanalysis" and its encounter with occultism. More than ever, Freud needs to produce as his double a Mr. Foresight, Mr. Prescience, or Mr. Precaution. It is no longer a question of knowing whether thought-transference, that is, the passing to another of a word secretly held by someone, has occured, but one of knowing whether the many parameters that constitute the network of relations between two people do not make it probable that certain signifiers will emerge from both of them at the same time. Does not "the secret language which so easily grows up between two people who see a lot of each other" imply the formation of similar or identical associative chains that can be activated at the same time in both of them by an external event, whether through words exchanged between them, gestures, or simple movements imperceptible to anyone else? These questions must be left open for the moment, until the discussion is widened beyond this one example, which may have impressed Freud the most.

Although Jones has collected the evidence against Freud, who in his eyes was guilty of encouraging, through his superstitious side, the fullfledged return of the old Celtic depths, replete with phantoms and haunted houses,[3] and although this question has recently been studied in detail by Charles Moreau,[4] it is necessary, for the reader who has not had the chance to look into these books, to retrace briefly the domain of telepathy and occultism. Moreover, this will allow us to emphasize certain aspects that more directly concern the relation of psychoanalysis to these phenomena.

From 1899, Freud believed that a dream could predict an event that would take place the next day. In his opinion, Frau B. became certain that she had dreamed only at the moment when she encountered the foreseen event, and then reconstructed the dream from there. He concludes his analysis of Frau B. in "A Premonitory Dream Fulfilled" (1899) by saying: "The formation of the dream after the event, which makes prophetic dreams possible, is nothing other than a form of censorship which makes the dream's penetration into consciousness possible."[5] In *The Psychopathology of Everyday Life* (1901), the same example reappears with the same interpretation, but with the addition of this remark: "Belief in prophetic dreams can claim many adherents, because it can take support from the fact that a number of things do in reality turn out in the future in the way in which the wish had previously arranged them in the dream."[6] In these texts, the telepathic phenomenon is completely assimilated by psychoanalysis.

Twenty years later, the perspective has changed considerably. Freud succumbed, over several years, to the influence of questions posed by Jung and Ferenczi, and he conducted his own experiments in thoughttransference, which resulted in his taking occultism and telepathy much more seriously and in his making them the domains in relation to which psychoanalysis must be defined. In his lecture to the International Psychoanalytical Association in the Harz Mountains in August 1921, Freud tried to establish resemblances and differences between "Psychoanalysis and Telepathy"[7] (the title of his lecture) and the difficulty or danger of their relation. He discusses a first case, to which he will return later in the *New Introductory Lectures on Psychoanalysis*, in which a young man hears a fortuneteller foretell the death of his brother-in-law by poisoning. The poisoning took place, but not the death. Here is Freud's conclusion:

> Psychoanalysis teaches us that what has been communicated by this means of induction from one person to another is not merely a chance piece of indifferent knowledge, but an extraordinary wish of one person that was in a particular relation to his consciousness, and that could, with the aid of another person, find conscious expression in a slightly veiled form, exactly as the invisible end of the spectrum reveals itself on a light-sensitive plate as a colored extension.[8]

Freud's observation merits close attention: he wants to be true to the facts, but he wants to refrain from justifying the existence of thought-transference. For that reason, he does not say that the fortuneteller has perceived and expressed the client's secret wish, but only that the wish reached conscious expression "with the aid of another person"; in reading this sentence, we do not know whether the conscious expression is the client's or the fortuneteller's. This ambiguity tends to reduce the prophecy to nothing more than the realization of a desire.

We state without hesitation that what is at stake here is the similarity between the fortuneteller and the psychoanalyst. Freud wants, at any cost, to prevent us from perceiving this relationship. This is why the second case he presents does not go as far, and why he explains it by reconstituting the conversation with the fortuneteller according to the same principle of intelligibility as that of the prophetic dream. Above all, that is why he forgot to tell his most trusted disciples in the Harz mountains about the Forsyth case, because the question of thought-transference in analysis would have been posed directly.

Despite Freud's precautions and visible hesitations, the opposition of Eitingon and Jones was so determined that this lecture was neither published nor even communicated to a larger public during Freud's lifetime. It is not astonishing that the article written at the end of the same year, "Dreams and Telepathy" (1921),[9] is still more restrained and defensive. He is concerned with maintaining that even "if the existence of telepathic dreams were to be established there would be no need to alter our conception of dreams in any way";[10] that the telepathic dream is nonetheless "a dream like any other,"[11] that is, it must be understood as the realization of an Oedipal desire; or, again, that "telepathic messages—if we are justified in admitting their existence—can thus change nothing about the essential nature of dreams."[12] The reason is therefore clear: if one is protected by two principles—that dreams are produced by unconscious desire and that the reconstitution of the event after the fact creates the object of prediction—then one is assured that telepathy poses no questions for the theory of the dream or for psychoanalysis in general.

Several years go by, and in 1925 Freud seems to have changed his mind: he decides to advocate the existence of thought-transference,[13] to which a sequel to *The Interpretation of Dreams* bears witness.[14] For example, he no longer says, as he had regarding a similar case in 1921, that the wish reached conscious expression "with the aid of another person" but asserts that

> there was no better explanation of the whole, so univocally determined, than through the hypothesis that a strong desire on the part of the questioner—in reality, the strongest unconscious wish of her emotional life and the motive force of her impending neurosis—was made known to the fortuneteller through an immediate transference while her [the questioner's] attention was distracted by diversions.
>
> I have long had the impression, through the repeated actions of my intimate circle, that the transferences of strongly emotionally accentuated memories succeeded without difficulty. If one risks submitting to an analytic examination the thoughts of the person to whom the thoughts are to be transferred, correspondences often appear, which would otherwise have remained undiscovered. On the basis of many experiences, I am inclined to draw the conclusion that such thought-transferences succeed particularly well at the moment at which a representation emerges from the unconscious; in theoretical terms, as it passes from the "primary process" to the "secondary process."[15]

A considerable step is taken here, but even though Freud uses the word *transference* (*Übertragung*), he does not connect it to the transference in analysis. It is nonetheless a modification of his use of the term, since he is no longer using the compound substantive *Gedankenübertragung*, which means "thought-transference." Freud's objective in this paragraph remains limited, however, to the attempt to explain telepathic phenomena that can be better understood through the aid of psychoanalysis, which he believes is really something quite different.

In the *New Introductory Lectures* (1932) Freud returns to the same themes and maintains the same distrust of telepathy: psychoanalysis and its interpretation of dreams are capable of making sense of dreams called telepathic: "the fortuneteller had merely brought to expression the thoughts, and more particularly the secret wishes, of the person who questioned him."[16] One might believe that Freud, who now acknowledges thought-transference, will be surprised at the fact that the fortuneteller can know something about his client's secret wishes. Not at all; the sentence just cited continues: "We were therefore justified in analyzing such prophecies as though they were subjective productions, fantasies or dreams of the person concerned." Through significant and inevitable gesture, Freud returns to his former position, that is, to the study of psychical processes in an individual considered in isolation, and not in light of the phenomena of transmission and communication. He believes he has explained everything, while he has only led the facts onto his own terrain, and he has done so in good conscience and with an honesty that warrants as little suspicion as does the belief he evinces in those who believe in thought-transference. Freud's repeated blindness here is interesting, and we must try to explain it.

He then discusses two other cases, the conclusion to which is still the same. In the first, "the fortuneteller simply expressed the patient's own expectation";[17] in the second, when the graphologist "promised that the writer of the specimen presented to him would commit suicide in the next few days, he had once again only brought to light a powerful secret wish of the person who questioned him."[18] It becomes clear that Freud treats the words of the fortuneteller, the graphologist, and the astrologer as the text of a dream, or more precisely, as a dream-text elaborated in such a way that he can already see through to the latent content. To return to Freud's metaphor, these people are sensitive photographic plates on which the client's colored desires are projected. By virtue of his reduction of all these phenomena to earlier discoveries on the dream, Freud thinks he has given occultism scientific status. This is why he concludes his presentation of these examples by reaffirming: "Ladies and Gentlemen, you have now heard what dream-interpretation and psychoanalysis in general have done for occultism. You have seen from examples that by their application occult facts become clear which would otherwise have remained incomprehensible."[19]

Freud does not stop there, however. He indeed senses that psychoanalysis is related to thought-transference, not only in the passage of thoughts from the client to the fortuneteller, the astrologer, or graphologist and therefore to the analyst but also in the inverse passage from analyst to patient. This is why he will present the Forsyth case, the notes about which he had left in Vienna before going to Gastein in the Harz Mountains in 1921, while he had remembered it as "the one which has left the strongest impression on me."[20] He cannot, however, stop himself in the introduction from repeating his subtle formulations, which are also honest but which prevent him from confronting the question directly. This explains his reference to "observations which at least have a relation to psychoanalysis, because they have been made during analytic treatment and have perhaps been rendered possible by its influence." That is, they still do not touch upon the very essence of analysis. Further on: "It is an example in which the facts came clearly to light and did not need to be developed by psychoanalysis. In discussing it, however, we will not be able to do without the aid of psychoanalysis." That is, the example is not of the order of psychoanalysis, even though we need psychoanalysis to deal with it. Finally: "I will tell you in advance that even this example of thought-transference does not eliminate all doubts and does not permit us to take an unconditional position in support of the reality of occult phenomena." In other words, you must not take what I say too seriously, since it finally proves nothing.

Freud himself says, "My personal attitude on this matter remains unenthusiastic and ambivalent."[21] But this ambivalence must have a function, which we have already seen in outline, and it is time to make it clear.

We must observe first of all that Freud repeatedly reduces occultism to telepathy, and telepathy to thought-transference.

> You see that all my material treats only the single point of thought-transference; of all the other miracles claimed by occultism I have nothing to say. My own life, as I have already openly acknowledged, has been particularly poor from the perspective of the occult. Perhaps the problem of thought-transference appears to you very restricted in comparison to the great magical world of the occult.[22]

Between telepathy proper and thought-transference as Freud speaks of it there is also a considerable difference. On several occasions, he specifically defines telepathy as communication "between people spatially distant" or "without employing words and signs."[23] Without foreseeing it, he constantly moves from cases in which the transmission is from a distance to other cases in which the individuals are present to one another. This is a major distinction for followers of the occult, but Freud takes no account of it, because it is thought-transmission itself which interests him, which gives him the strongest experience of the occult, and which he must protect himself against. Let us make the hypothesis that everything Freud wrote on this subject was in order to exorcise the reality of thought-transference in his life and in his invention, psychoanalysis.

Freud's experiments with his daughter Anna and Ferenczi, which the biographers have noted; the sinister creakings through the library walls after the manner of Jung; the superstitions that Freud at one time or another felt the need to display—all this is obviously insignificant in comparison with the threat of thought-transference. A threat because it is inseparable from the uncanny. In his essay on this feeling, Freud indeed identifies telepathy as the experience of the double:

> These themes are all concerned with the phenomenon of the "double," which appears in every shape and in every degree of development, that is, the production of characters who, because of their similarity in appearance, must be considered identical. This relation is intensified by psychical processes leaping from one of these characters to the other—through what we call telepathy—in such a way that one possesses the knowledge, feelings, and experience of the other; the subject's identification with the other is such that he is in doubt about his own ego or the foreign ego is put in the place of his own, that is, a doubling of the ego, a division, a substitution, of the ego—and finally the constant recurrence

of the same, the repetition of the same features of appearance, character, destiny, criminal acts, or even the same names across several successive generations.[24]

Thought-transference appears here as a constitutive element of the "double." The exchange of thoughts or psychical processes between one person and another increases, so that progressively, like a pattern that appears when the lines and traces are sufficiently numerous, one becomes the replica of the other, and it is no longer known who is who.[25]

This description accounts for an important aspect of Freud's intellectual life, which is especially prominent in his relationship to his disciples. Among others, there is the uncanny impression made upon Freud by Tausk, who could "elaborate Freud's concepts with his own clinical material, without making the distinction between what was his and what was Freud's."[26] Lou Andreas-Salomé describes Freud's uneasiness after a lecture by Tausk: "He was restless (on account of the closeness of the ideas to his own), questioned me during the lecture, passing a note to me: 'Does he know all about it already?' I wrote back: 'Of course not, nothing at all!' referring to Freud's remarks to me."[27] It is as though, in his creative work Freud constantly felt threatened by a "doubling of the ego" due to this shared possession of knowledge. As Andreas-Salomé notes after a discussion between Freud and Tausk, Freud's best defense was forgetfulness: "Freud referred favorably to this clarifying observation— having immediately forgotten who had made it. He then smilingly apologized for his error."[28] The fear or accusations of plagiarism, the concern about priority in making discoveries, and the originality of ideas, all of which so preoccupied Freud, are to be viewed from this same perspective as disturbing phenomena in which his subjectivity is dangerously entangled. If he reduced occultism to thought-transference, it is because he experienced thought-transference and because it led him to the edge of depersonalization. It is not surprising that he cultivated the sacred egotism of the creator or that he avoided reading authors who would give him the impression of having been preceded or influenced and who would expropriate his own thoughts. He wants to preserve his identity at any cost, and so he must exclude thought-transference from the field of psychoanalysis by reducing it to the experience and study of individual psychical processes based on noncommunication.

Through the invention of the transference, Freud was able to maintain telepathy and occultism theoretically and to protect himself from the risk of dissolution that could result from the constant possibility, within himself, of passing to "the knowledge, feelings, and experience of the other." With the transference, one is on the side of scientific objectivity and not in an unstable, obscure, or confused relation. By discovering one day that the amorous outbursts of one of his patients were not addressed to him but to another, a third person (*dritte Person*)[29] whom she had fantasized, Freud personally removes himself from the field of relations in order to see a "false connection" [*falsche Verknupfung*][30] in the transference. What is demanded of the analyst is that he transform himself into a pure recording machine, so that he is "like a mirror that should show nothing but what is shown to him,"[31] or like a telephone receiver: "he must turn his unconscious like a receptive organ toward the transmitting unconscious of the patient; he must adjust himself to the patient as a telephone receiver is adjusted to the transmitting microphone."[32] If the psychoanalyst must himself undergo an analysis, it is because he should not "tolerate any resistances in himself which hold back from his consciousness what has been perceived by his unconscious."[33] In that way, he can be in a position to receive the other's message without any "selection or distortion." This, indeed, involves the passage of thoughts from one person to another, but it is not thought-transference in the sense of telepathy, not so much because the message uses language as its medium but rather because at no time does the thought of one person become the thought of another. The analyst receives words addressed to another, and he records them as the patient's, never as his own, never having any part in them, never sharing anything about them. "It is the patient's problem. I have nothing to do with it; and if I do have something to do with it, it is because I have done my work poorly." This permits Freud to separate analysis from anything resembling suggestion, whether at close range or from a long distance.

All this seems clear and decisive, but it could all be quickly reversed if one allowed oneself to consider a few other connections. A page of "Psychical Treatment" [*Psychische Behandlung*], published in 1890, offers an insight into the way mediums work:

> The affects in the strict sense are characterized by a quite special connection to somatic processes, but, strictly speaking, all mental states, even those we usually consider as "processes of thought," are to some degree "affective," and none of them is without the capacity to modify the somatic processes. Even when a person is engaged in quietly thinking in "representations," there is a constant series of excitations, corresponding to the content of these representations, which are discharged into the smooth and striated muscles, and which can be distinguished by an appropriate reinforcement and can thus explain many surprising, supposedly "supernatural" phenomena. Thus, for example, so-called "thought-reading" [*Gedankenerraten*] can be explained by small, involuntary movements of the muscles that are carried out by the "medium" when he makes someone try, without guiding him, to find a hidden object. The whole phenomenon might more suitably be called "thought betraying" [*Gedankenverraten*].[34]

What does the psychoanalyst do when he interprets, if it is not "thought-reading"? For example, Freud tells the Ratman, "I will do everything possible to guess [*erraten*] the full meaning of what he tells me."[35] Elsewhere, he says that the analyst's task is "to make out [*erraten*], or more precisely, to construct, what has been forgotten from the traces it has left behind."[36] "To make out, to guess," is therefore a technical expression for an important operation that the analyst must perform in order to speak knowledgeably, but it is also the task of the medium.

The connection between the psychoanalyst and the medium is no less striking regarding the question of content. According to Freud, the medium "does no more than bring to light the thoughts of the person questioning him, and more particularly his secret wishes." But is this not precisely the same effect that analysis produces, since it also makes latent desires become manifest? And even though in German the fortuneteller is called the *Wahrsager*, "the truth-sayer," Freud would not disdain bearing this title, for he too is haunted by the search for the patient's historic or prehistoric truth and would do anything to unearth it.

The attempts at explaining the processes of divination and thought-transference are just as applicable to the transference in psychoanalysis. It is not by chance that in German the word *Übertragung* is used for both phenomena, though in the first case it is more often used in compound form (*Gedanken-übertragung*). In 1925 Freud makes the connection very clearly. In concluding a study of telepathy, he notes: "There was no better explanation of the whole, so univocally determined, than through the hypothesis that a strong desire on the part of the questioner — in reality, the strongest unconscious wish of her emotional life and the motive force of her impending neurosis — was made known to the fortuneteller through an immediate transference while her attention was distracted by diversions."[37] The fortuneteller is here distinctly in the position of the analyst who must abandon all conscious efforts in order to bring his unconscious to maximum receptivity.[38] The same text of 1925 continues: "Such thought-transferences succeed particularly well at the moment at which a representation emerges from the unconscious; in theoretical terms, as it passes from the 'primary process' to the 'secondary process.'" In other words, the force of the patient's desire, when it passes from the unconscious to consciousness, affects the unconscious of the analyst, who, in his turn, allows this impression to come to consciousness.

In her comments on this page of Freud's, Helene Deutsch has emphasized the proximity of telepathy to the analytic situation:

> The psychoanalytic situation, with its technique of free association, is, indeed, one in which "emotionally accentuated memories" are constantly found in *statu nascendi*, that is, passing from the primary to the secondary processes. The

conditions in which the second person (on whom the transference occurs) receives the complex of affective representations emerging from the unconscious are not much discussed by Freud. What he says above leaves us to suppose that there is, in this process, a reaction in the unconscious, which betrays itself only through the free associations and which reveals its content and its correspondence with the content of the representation of the person from whom the stimulation originates, only during the work of analysis. Among the presuppositions that are not clear to us but are probably connected to the transference (in its analytic sense) is that the reactive process for the person who is the object of the transference visibly penetrates into consciousness and becomes the content of perception. Since the clear perception which usually precedes this process is missing, it now acquires an "occult" character. One can easily suppose that the condition for this transference of "emotionally accentuated memories" is a certain unconscious disposition to receive these memories, and that only the fulfillment of this condition makes it possible for the person concerned to be in a "state of receptivity." The content of emotionally invested representations emerging from the unconscious must mobilize in the other's unconscious an analogous content with the same meaning, which penetrates into consciousness like an internal perception. The identity of these contents is recognized after the fact, and at that point the internal perception acquires the character of an external perception.

The more specific studies of these processes during an analysis make us recognize that the presuppositions admitted above for the production of occult phenomena are continually present in analysis.[39]

Telepathy is different from analysis, because the latter seeks to explain how the passage of thought from one person to another takes place and because it wants to establish continuity between the various facts that are presented, while those who adhere to telepathy try to preserve the mysterious and therefore leave all the intermediate elements in the realm of incomprehensibility and strangeness. Psychoanalysis wants to be irrevocably on the side of science and therefore rejects what it cannot account for. But Freud does not really go too far in the establishment of a chain of uninterrupted facts or in filling the gaps that separate two similar or identical thoughts in two different people. This is what he proposes at the end of his lecture on "Dreams and Occultism":

> What lies between two psychical acts may well be a physical process into which the psychical one is transformed back once more into the same psychical one at the other end. The analogy with other transformations, such as speaking and hearing by telephone, would then be unmistakeable. And think, if one could seize this physical equivalent of the psychical act! By inserting the unconscious between the physical and what until now was called the "psychical," I would think that psychoanalysis has prepared us to admit processes like telepathy.[40]

On the preceding page, Freud had alluded to the article by Helene Deutsch just cited. She tried to go further in the connection between psychoanalysis and telepathy, not so much in order to gain an understanding of telepathy, which does not really interest her, but simply to understand better some of the astonishing aspects of some basic analytic situations. Freud never pursued this line of research because, as he again repeats here, telepathy is too frail ever to succeed in raising itself to the level of a science and therefore needs the assistance of psychoanalysis, which is well-established as a science. It is impossible for him to consider, as Helene Deutsch does, that thought-transference is at the very heart of analytic experience.

In my opinion, all the commentators have fallen into the trap. They are either disturbed or elated that Freud is interested in parapsychic phenomena. Like him, they earnestly ponder whether or not Freud believed in such things, whereas all such considerations are purely diversionary maneuvers. If occultism, telepathy, and thought-transference are constituted as a separate field of their own, then psychoanalysis will be free to pursue its allegedly scientific principles, that is, its scientific intentions or pretensions. Even when, at the end of this same lecture, Freud cites an article by Dorothy Burlingham, who observes phenomena of this sort in analyses of child and mother, he simply concludes that such observations "put an end to the remaining doubts on the reality of thought-transference."[41] All of this suggests to him no questions about analytic work and what goes on there. He does not fail to note, however, that this mode of communication arises from archaic or infantile sources, which are not especially unfamiliar to analysis. In other words, the connections between thought-transference and transference proper cannot help but appear in Freud's writing, but it is to prevent the question of thought-transference from penetrating like a red-hot poker into the very heart of analysis.

By this distant interest in telepathy, Freud wants to repudiate a most formidable enemy, and that enemy is suggestion, which he has long practiced with hypnosis. When he speaks of the transference, it is always in the context of patient-analyst. The counter-transference is simply that which obstructs the transference. Helene Deutsch, who discusses occult processes in analysis in the article cited above, can find in several of her master's texts support for what she says about "reactions of the analyst's unconscious to unconscious processes of the patient." But when she wants to look into "the influences of the analyst's unconscious on the patient," she is venturing alone into unmarked terrain, and this is not by accident. To admit that the analyst can have an influence on the patient or that he can will or wish something for him or in his place would ruin the entire psychoanalytic discovery, since one would be led back to a variant of suggestion. But above all, one must at any cost prevent such a question from being posed, for if it is posed, one will be forced to speak not only of the analyst's conscious wishes but of his unconscious wishes, which would put him in the position of never really being able to know what he is doing. As long as the transference is well understood and summarized by saying "That's your problem," one is sure of protecting analysis from everything that could disturb its purity.

(Some will say that analysis has made progress since Freud and that Lacan, for example, has placed the analyst's desire at the very heart of the analytic cure. But could this by chance be only a more subtle way of diverting or hiding the question? If desire is without an object or has only a random object, then there are no obstacles to the analyst's desire. Such purified desire does not arouse anything in the patient but desire itself. Speaking of the analyst's desire is therefore a very shrewd way of responding to the objection, but perhaps also a way of pretending to answer while ignoring it totally, since the response supposes that the analyst's desire has nothing to do with the personality of the analyst himself; the Lacanian response omits the fact that the patient is also confronted with the analyst's own fantasies, symptoms, and desires. Along the same lines, the refusal to take the objective of the treatment into account saves the analyst from asking himself what he is looking for in analysis, in this kind of analysis, that is, crudely, the form and the content of his desire. Quite a few years ago an experienced analyst explained to me that the analyst never has an objective; when I asked him how he could manage not to vanish entirely, he was startled for a few seconds, but fortunately for him only a few seconds. Lacan is clearer and leaves us a path to follow when he turns didactic psychoanalysis into pure psychoanalysis, that is, when he makes the aim of analysis the production of analysts, in a word, the reproduction of the same.)

Freud is interested in the transference only because it can be used in treatment and thus analyzed; in this sense, he deviates radically from the practice of suggestion. He explicitly seeks "the final independence of the patient" and thus the lifting of the transference[42] as a result of the psychical work performed by the patient. The analyst is then cut off from the "third person" onto whom the patient transferred. The real question, however, is whether this lifting of the transference, which is certain on this or that point, can be applied to all the transference connections or even to the most important ones. In the case where one calls a transference, as Freud does, only what appears through resistances and can thus be perceived and analyzed, the transference has nothing to do with suggestion. But this supposes that the problem is resolved or that only the question that can be resolved is posed.

As Freud recognizes, the peculiarity of the transference is that "it exceeds, both in amount and nature, anything that could be justified on sensible or rational grounds," because it "has precisely been set up not only by the conscious anticipatory representations but also by those that have been held back or are unconscious."[43] In every sense, the transference entails a type of relationship that exceeds the limits of analysis. Through the inspired discovery of the transference—by the refusal to believe what the patient says and to respond to his demand, which amounts, once again, to removing one's individuality from the relationship in order to become an undetermined "third person"—Freud observed that he provoked an imbalance, a deformation, an excess, and that what then came to light in speech was of the order of the primitive, the archaic, the erotic. This means that for the patient, the analyst is no longer a person like others with whom one could speak but he becomes someone who, by remaining a "third person," is able to reemerge as a concrete individual (because one still speaks to him), who from now on is marked by excess and imbalance, endowed with omniscience and omnipotence, a fantastic individual whom the patient can see, hear, and encounter, only through hallucination.

One could therefore conclude that the analyst's peculiarities cannot be accounted for, since the patient does not know what to make of them. It is really a question not of his peculiarities but of his capacity to sustain the deformations to which he must submit without buckling under the weight of the excess invested in him. In doing so, he responds, not at the level of his own personality, but at the level of his own relationship to the primitive, the infantile, and the sexual. He thereby enters the scene and goes to work, but he thereby also places himself and his patient in the realm of the uncanny.

When he tries to describe this, Freud returns to the fundamental characteristics he had developed with regard to the transference: "The double is a formation dating back to a primitive psychical stage, long since surmounted, which then doubtless wore a more friendly aspect."[44] A few pages later: "That the uncanny effect of the return of the same proceeds from infantile psychical life is a question I can only lightly touch on here."[45] Then a final explanation in which he says that the uncanny proceeds from nostalgia for the maternal body or for the pleasure that was to be found there.[46] Freud does not miss the connection to psychoanalysis: "I would not be surprised to hear that psychoanalysis, which is concerned with uncovering these hidden forces, has itself become uncanny to many people for that very reason."[47] But then all the consequences must be drawn: it is not only because it is concerned with the infantile and the sexual that psychoanalysis is disturbing: it is because by concerning itself with the infantile and the sexual, by making them emerge in spite of repression and suppression, it provokes the return of the same, the appearance of the "double," and thus a return to an immediate communication with these phenomena.

At the end of his lecture on "Dreams and Occultism," after having presented the Forsyth case, when he wants to find a rationale for the transmission of a message without the aid of words or signs, Freud again takes up the same terms: the only possible explanation is the recourse to a mode of archaic, erotic, infantile communication:

> It is a familiar fact that we do not know how the collective will comes about in the great insect communities: possibly it is done by means of a direct psychical transference of this kind. One is led to suppose that this is the original, archaic method of communication between individuals and that in the course of phylogenetic evolution it has been replaced by a better method, that of communication by signs which are picked up by the sense organs. But the earlier method could have persisted in the background and still be able to put itself in effect under certain conditions, for example, in passionately excited mobs. All this is still uncertain and full of unsolved riddles, but there is no reason to be frightened by it.
>
> If there is such a thing as telepathy as a real process, we may suppose, in spite of the difficulty of proving it, that it is quite a common phenomenon. This would correspond to our expectation if we were able to point to it precisely in the psychical life of children. One is reminded here of the frequent anxiety in children over the idea that their parents know all their thoughts without having to be told them—the exact counterpart and perhaps the source of the belief of adults in the omniscience of God. Recently, a trustworthy witness, Dorothy Burlingham, has published, in an article on child analysis and the mother, some observations which, if they could be confirmed, would put an end to the remaining doubts on the reality of thought-transference.[48]

Freud obviously remains here in the same restrictive problematic: there is thought-transference in analysis, but it is an appendage, indeed an aberrant phenomenon, in relation to psychoanalysis. However, if the relation between analyst and patient makes childhood, passion, and the connection to the mother reemerge, then does not "the direct psychical transference" constitute the cement that analysis proper could never totally lift away (*aufheben*) or dissolve (*auflösen*)? One can even wonder whether the analysis of the transference is not likely to reinforce this "direct psychical transference" while it appears to undo it.

When he speaks of the interpreter whose objective is to bring the repressed to light, Freud thinks that the analyst carries with him nothing of his own and that he thus avoids suggestion, but he seems to have forgotten what he wrote in 1890, well before he discovered the transference, regarding the factor of success in a treatment:

> Foremost among such measures is the use of words; and words are the essential tool of psychical treatment. A layman will find it very difficult to understand how pathological disorders of the body and mind can be eliminated by "mere" words. He will think that he is being asked to believe in magic. And he

will not be so very wrong, for the words of our everyday discourse are nothing other than faded magic. But we shall have to follow a long detour in order to understand how science sets about restoring to words a part of their former magical power.[49]

If there is a place where words have been restored to their magical power, above and beyond what they can attain in the doctor-patient relation, it is surely in analytic treatment. The analyst, who is so easily confused with and even risks becoming the "third person," who should, in effect, be "no one"—which is, in fact, the pure condition for the possibility of the discourse, but which is most often fantasized or hallucinated—gives his words an intensity that, like the transference, surpasses "in amount and nature, anything that could be justified on sensible or rational grounds." This is because the analyst's words have a power that everyday discourse lacks, so that they can produce analytic effects, or in Freud's words, so that they will lead to "the patient's independence." But precisely because they do have a magical power, they cannot avoid having, on the one hand, the inverse effect of linking the patient more closely to the analyst (who wanted to free him from his shackles) and, on the other hand, side effects that bring on problems in the patient which the analyst cannot master, because in receiving the analyst's words, the patient also assimilates all that those words unconsciously carried. The words become the medium of communication between unconscious minds.

In order to avoid these subversive inferences, the analyst decides to be silent, and as if he also wanted to be hidden from sight, he does not risk letting anything from his unconscious appear through gestures or simple movements of his face or hands. But perhaps this procedure is not as effective as it might appear at first: it fails to take into account that silence is a language that the patient learns quickly. There is such an abyss between the silence of death and that of life, such a difference between the silence of inattention and that of alert interest, between the silence of desire and that of impotence, between that of depression and that of continuous mania! Every silence has an intensity and a coloration that is perceptible to the patient. If punctuation gives meaning to a sentence, then surely silence alone, with all its nuances, is capable of passing to the patient all sorts of preconscious or unconscious messages, which are all the more clear because the analyst thinks he is protected from communicating them.

What analytic treatment sets up and what the analyst reinforces, whether through his speech or his silence, is an immediate relationship of an archaic, infantile, erotic sort, the aim of which is the negation of all alterity. The passion of analysis becomes the same passion that binds together a mob, or lovers, or parents and their children; it is what unites them without the need to communicate. The principle of "direct psychical transference" is never to be separated; it is to remain glued to one another in order to be one, or better still, to be one in the other. Every patient, whether he knows it or not, dreams of dissolving into or being engulfed by this silent or talkative womb which leaves him no autonomy.

Freud tried to cast this immediate transference outside the analyst's concerns by including it either in the unknowable or not-yet-known field of telepathy and occultism or in the unanalyzable field of psychosis. If he casts psychosis, which knows only the immediate transference, outside the field of psychoanalysis, it is because he is content with what we could call the "mediated or indirect transference," where the analyst is taken for another, where language is king and makes possible the discovery of fantasies, the play of signifiers, the appearance of resistances, and their dissolution.

But because he did not want to assess the force of the immediate transference, and thus the existence of thought-transference and the psychotic background of every analytic relation, Freud left the door open to the return of this repressed under the form of a transference that combines both the immediacy and the mediations and that one could call the "infinite transference"; at first it is infinite in duration, in the sense of indefinitely postponed, because analysis can only undo a small part of it and because it repeatedly reinstates it, then infinite in intensity, from which it acquires uncanny forms of veneration,[50] the culmination of belief. The infinite transference uses the mediated transference in order never to have to pose the question of direct transference, in order to conceal it but also to seal it off. If this is not the case, how can we explain Binswanger's indisputable statement, "He whom psychoanalysis has once seized, it never lets go"? No longer is our concern with a discipline to which one is passionately attached, nor even with a discourse that one has assimilated; it is with an unsurpassable experience, at the limit of the inhuman, from which not even the coming of adulthood can remove us for long. The subtle detours of theory and the mathematical sophistication that represent the epitome of the mediated transference create the pretense that analysis is infinitely removed from symbiosis; they only make us forget that symbiosis is the basis and the context of its development.

If telepathy could seduce Freud in this way, it is only because it carries a myth, that of the most total communion at the greatest distance, the myth of identity in difference. The same thought is thought at the same time by two people who do not see one another, speak to one another, or hear one another. The thought of two distinct and distant people becomes the thought of one. One cannot dream of a more beautiful realization of a symbiotic relation, without the risks of absorption and annihilation that it involves. It is symbiosis without encumbrances, pure and absolute pleasure without drawbacks. Through telepathy one returns to the one in the midst of separation. If telepathy could have been given a scientific basis, the direct transference would also have attained scientific status, and psychoanalysis would no longer be encumbered by a handicap so serious that it repeatedly risks falling into charlatanism, magic, and "cock-and-bull stories."

The question is whether the immediate or the mediated transference will have the last word. If it is the mediated transference, then the fusion of one unconscious with another will last only during the analysis itself; it will only be an artifice created by an activity that controls the conditions of the experience, and this artifice will disappear once the objective is attained. But if by chance the non-said had more force than the half-said, if the mediated transference (considered alone, as if it alone were at work), which allows something of the unconscious to be heard, were only a new illusory form of the ego—which believes in mastery, objectivity, and science—because repression had been somewhat lifted, it would then be possible indeed for analysis to swing back to the side of suggestion. No longer as in hypnotic suggestion, where one or several injunctions are transmitted to the patient but where everything in the analyst's unconscious passes to the patient under the protection of the mediated transference, which, from the analyst's perspective has no influence whatsoever over the patient's speech, fantasies, and projections. A long analysis would then be the thread-by-thread production of a symbiotic fabric in which two unconscious minds would progressively and silently communicate under the cover of an analysis through language. One would not attain the always desired and always impossible symbiosis, but one at least would achieve osmosis, the optimum equilibrium of which would mark the end of the analysis. Analyst and patient would part when each could observe in the other his best possible "double"; suggestion would then no longer apply to a particular feature, but to all possible unconscious traits.

Freud has already observed that P. had come up with the word *foresight* at just the right time in his discourse, as if in response to the Forsyth with whom Freud was then preoccupied. What prevents us from imagining that this so-called singular discourse of the patient was reconstructed entirely as a function of the desire of the analyst, himself unconsciously caught in the intricate maze of the patient's unconscious? Anyone who has been to several different analysts knows very well that the past that he discovers with each one is different, and that his glance or his poor vision, his discourse or his bad hearing, have had a different effect on each of his analysands. This banal observation should not fail to open some new perspectives on the means and end of analytic treatment. This is nowhere more plainly visible than in so-called didactic analysis. How can we explain, for example, that a patient who has become an analyst adopts—or rejects, but still adopts—the discourse of his analyst? One way or the other, he has been constituted as the analyst's "double." Is this not explicitly acknowledged when one makes the production of analysts the aim of analysis? The question of the transmission of analysis no longer has to be posed, since in its very operation it enacts the principle of repetition under the form of reproduction.

Is it possible to modify this operation and in some way to break the inevitability of this repetition? Granoff cites Nacht, who proposed that at the end of analysis the analyst "reveal a little more of his being." He continues by recalling that Freud, in order to get rid of a bashful patient and put an end to an analysis that had gone poorly, had invited him to dine at his table; Granoff's conclusion is that the psychoanalyst should take his inspiration from Homer: "I am not no one, I am Ulysses of Ithaca, son of Laertes."[51] It is a question of somehow putting an end to the transference that has removed the analyst's personality in order to turn him into the other, the "third person" who has no name and no history and who should be a pure mirror, a pure receiver. The procedure one uses is entirely beside the point. By again becoming Dr. Freud, or Ulysses, or Durand, the analyst returns to day-to-day reality, but he leaves the patient's condition unchanged. The patient then finds himself in front of someone who is cut in two, who is not only "no one" but also this new character, without any connection whatsoever between the two pieces. To say "I am no no one, I am Ulysses" is to keep under cover everything that "no one" has put into place; it is to want to say nothing—to know nothing—about what went on with him. It is therefore to reinforce permanently the immediate transference that was constituted during the analysis. The analyst can now get rid of his client, but this analyst maintains his position, his power, and fixes the clownlike mask of the analyst on his face forever. That he is no longer "no one" is certain. He becomes something much worse, the analyst with a capital *A,* although there should no longer be an analyst at the end of analysis. Invitations to dinner or to have a drink at the corner do not lead to the dissolution of "no one"; they are ways of embalming him and of building a mausoleum for him.

By revealing a little more of his being, by inviting his patient to dinner, by saying his own name, the psychoanalyst maintains the initiative and redoubles the ideal of the mediated transference, since he passes from the speech of the oracle or from the silence of the magician to the hypocrisy of sociable discourse: he remains impenetrable, he reveals nothing, he remains out of reach, untouchable. He thus maintains his grotesque power beyond the time of the analysis, indefinitely holding the patient in his power. The patient enjoys this situation; he must have an idol to satisfy his incredible need to believe. And if, like a concierge, the patient takes an interest in his analyst's private life, it is in order to give himself the appearance of not believing while in reality keeping the other intact, preserving him as the larger-than-life, all-powerful figure whom he encountered face-to-face. It is important above all to hear nothing and to know nothing about the fantasies or the symptoms that the analyst was able to induce, in other words, to preserve the absolute principle of the mediated transference as the only transference in the analysis, so that nothing is known about the effects or even the existence of immediate transference.

To get out of this impasse, the patient and the analyst must come to an agreement (and this is obvious to neither of them) in order to undo the artifice that makes analysis possible. It is decisive for the analyst to enter the analysis like someone whose mind is already made up and who wants to make up the other's mind as well, thus enabling the patient to grasp, after the fact, why the analysis took a particular direction, why this or that statement was not understood, which led to one consequence or another, why this or that fantasy or event was repeatedly interpreted in a way that locked the unconscious instead of opening it. In each case, what is uncovered is the defensive character of his speech or of his silence, the implications of his ideology or his fantasies, the need to reinforce his blindness; more generally, what is revealed is how the analyst uses the patient as a compromise-formation, that is, as a symptom, at once revealing what makes him work unconsciously, but in such a way that he cannot realize it or take it into account, since he has expelled it onto the other.

This work, if it is necessary to say it, is extremely difficult, because the analyst must renounce his most deeply held convictions. If he is blind to a particular question, it is for a good reason: it is in order to protect himself, or simply in order that he may survive by not being too vulnerable. In truth, the only tenable hypothesis is that he has made some progress in conquering his earlier deafness and that he now is ready to recognize it and to reduce its hold. If this is not the case, then he still absolutely needs the other to be his symptom, and he will continue to lock the patient into that role.

An example will elucidate the preceding argument. Groddeck writes to Freud that he has made a maternal transference onto him. Freud absolutely denies it; he believes that he can arouse only a transference of the paternal type. This is a vital point for Groddeck, because he finds himself inextricably entangled in this problem. But it is just as vital for Freud to keep denying it. Let us suppose, on the contrary, that Freud grasped the problem on which Groddeck had challenged him. He would then have to rethink his entire theory, which was based on the prevalence of the father, the prohibition against incest (which always made Groddeck laugh), and an esteem for science; he would also have to question his own relation to the theory, his use of his disciples, and so on. This is an immense, perhaps impossible, task, but nevertheless the necessary condition to stop Groddeck from repeating his untiring demand, which he will repeat to the point of becoming ill and dying for its sake. Freud could not meet this condition as long as he clung to his own beliefs, as long as he remained incapable of recognizing, after the fact, his earlier misunderstanding.

It is obviously not a question of the analyst's recounting the feelings and emotions he experienced in the course of the analysis, or of dwelling on the details of his counter-transference; it is a question of giving the patient a way to distinguish his experience from that of the analyst during the analysis, while during the immediate transference they form what appears to be a single mass. This immediate transference does not have to be analyzed in its totality, which is, in any case, impossible and contradictory; it is enough that in the course of such and such a detour, at such and such a moment, "no one" appears like someone who, for his own reasons wanted to enclose (or was unable to prevent himself from enclosing) the patient in his desire, to make the patient the site where he reproduced his own image. When "no one" recognizes that "without knowing it, I was there in order to put you there," "no one" is entirely demystified; all belief in him vanishes, or at least *could* vanish for the interlocutor who wanted it to vanish. Suggestion ends, and the desires, fantasies, or stories that were intertwined to the point of being lost in one another[52] begin to unravel and now simply intersect. From the fabric woven by analysis, each one can henceforth follow those threads that are a little more his own.

The analyst is analyzed, the remover of knots is himself untied, because the analysis turns back on him. The "pass" invented by Lacan had certainly aimed at this resumption of the analysis to the second degree for the person who has become an analyst. In an afterthought, it aimed this insight at the production of analysts in and through the analysis. But since it came to completion with the production of "passers," the pure witnesses, it really could not go back again and thus lost itself in the indefinite. The "pass" is therefore also made in order to shelter the analyst, to protect him from having to fall from his position in the mediated transference, to leave the patient in the lurch, his interpretations always left in suspense, in other words, left in a haunted state of derealization, since he is confronted only with the objectivity of pure witnesses, who make no response and who appear as an uncontrollable and unattainable jury. The patient is therefore sent back to the reality of his delusions and is definitively constituted as a symptom. Quite a way to address a question ignored by psychoanalysis and to deal with it, without resolving it and finally casting it much deeper into the abyss; this makes the "pass" the institution of the infinite transference.

We must wonder whether all the solutions proposed in order to come to the end of an analysis or to theorize about something do not rigorously and automatically have an effect opposite to the aim. The patient who wants to take down the circus tent in which the analyst has been clowning around has it fall regularly on his head. The patient is so wrapped up in the grandeur of his enterprise that he cannot even laugh at it. He sometimes loses more than he anticipated. In any case, it is difficult to see how something could be untangled by looking into problems other than the ones that formed the knot in the first place. The assumption that the analyst, taken for another during the analysis, realizes that he too has taken the patient for another, would suppose such a radical interrogation of psychoanalysis that hesitation, detours, and subterfuges could easily be understood and doubtless justified.

four

transference: the dream

To resume the questions we have thus far considered, we will use a paragraph from the postscript to Freud's case history of Dora:

> If one goes into analytic technique, it becomes obvious that the transference is an inevitable necessity. Practical experience, in any event, shows conclusively that there is no way of avoiding it, and that this latest creation of the disease must be combated like all the earlier ones. This part of the work, however, is by far the most difficult. Dream-interpretation, the extraction of unconscious thoughts and memories from the patient's associations, and similar explanatory procedures are easy to learn how to do; here, the patient himself will always provide the text. On the contrary, the transference must be detected almost independently, from only the slightest clues and at the same time while being careful to avoid being guilty of making arbitrary inferences. But the transference **cannot be evaded, since it is used for the production of all the obstacles that make the material inaccessible to treatment,** and since the sense of conviction in the validity of the constructed connections is obtained by the patient only after the resolution of the transference.[1]

In these few sentences, written in January 1900 but not published until 1905, the main outlines of analytic technique are definitively traced. Freud will say nothing new about it in the numerous articles that he will devote, over the course of more than thirty years, to the connection between resistance and the transference, to the dissolution of the transference, to the right moment for the interpretation, to construction in analysis, and finally to the conviction which the patient should reach about the truth of what has been communicated to him.

The connection, frought with vicissitudes, between memory, construction, and conviction has been developed at length in chapter 2 and elsewhere in Freud's case history of Dora. The transference was not the question at this time, for a principal reason that will be elucidated later: this term had acquired, in time, such an extensive meaning that it was difficult to deal with it and other elements of technique at the same time. This passage from the Dora case is important because the word *transference* is used in a restricted sense, and can be either singular or plural, or in the singular partitive. This plural and these singular forms have their basis in Freud's first use of the word *transference* in relation to the dream, where, in the words of Laplanche and Pontalis, "he is referring to a mode of 'displacement' in which the unconscious wish is expressed in masked form through the material furnished by the preconscious residues of the day before."[2] There it is a question of the displacement, the translation, the transfer of an affect—linked to a representation—to another representation. "If the idea of the analyst enjoys a special status this is, first, because it constitutes a type of 'day's residue' that is always available to the subject; and secondly, because this kind of transference aids resistance in that it is particularly hard to admit the repressed wish when this acknowledgement has to be made to the very person the wish concerns. It is clear too that at this period Freud considers transference to be a highly localised phenomenon. Each transference is to be treated like any other symptom."[3]

In this case, analytic technique has an impeccable rigor and appears to be perfectly mastered. The operation of its three pivots—recollection, construction, and conviction—is governed by the transference, since its resolution, by permitting the return of forgotten memories, produces the patient's conviction in the truth of the analyst's construction. To resolve a transference is simply to perform a counter-displacement, or better still, a replacement; it is to return the message to the right destination, or, to use the vocabulary of dream-interpretation, to the representation to which it belongs. The displacement had disconnected the affect from the representation by linking the affect to another representation; the replacement, which makes the representation concerning the analyst pass back to the person to whom it was originally directed, brings about a reconnection and allows repression to be lifted from the affect. Analytic technique is thus analogous to the interpretation of dreams, and the transferences in treatment are like detours that are obliged to return to their starting point. There is no possibility of total alienation between patient and analyst, since the analyst is only there to permit, on the one hand, the displacement or the greater concealment of "impulses and fantasies"[4] and, on the other hand, their replacement or unveiling because they have been revealed by the analyst. "Transference, which seems destined to become the greatest obstacle for psychoanalysis, becomes its most powerful ally, if one succeeds in detecting it and in explaining it to the patient."[5]

The analyst is therefore involved in the treatment in two very different ways: first, through the patient, who uses him or his environment to find certain "details"[6] from which to work his transferences; second, through the process of detecting, of making out or determining the patient's transferences, which is the source of the analyst's interpretations and constructions. This process of detection is the key to the technique,[7] since it is the condition for the solution of transferences. Let us leave aside the extremely complex problems it poses, since it is done, as Freud recognizes, "from only the slightest clues" and since the analyst risks "being guilty of making arbitrary inferences." It is important to emphasize here that the rigor of the technique rests on the resolution of transferences. What happens when this term goes from the plural to the singular, when it becomes *the transference,* in the sense of a relation between the patient and the analyst? Freud realizes, in his account of the Dora case, that he will have to deal not only with tender and amicable transferences but also with "all the tendencies, including the hostile ones that must be awakened."[8] The sum total of all the transferences, here represented by the two extremes hostile and affectionate, will force him to regard the transference as linking the patient's total psyche to the analyst's entire personality or to what he represents.[9] In maintaining that the cure implies the resolution of the transference, Freud afterwards will no longer be able, in his technical writings, to make the resolution the decisive factor in the delicate interplay of memory, interpretation, and conviction. The interpretation in the transference, or more precisely, *of* the transference, could sustain the impeccable rigor of the technique only as long as it has not perceived the comprehensive nature of the transference.

Such an observation overturns former certainties and requires that we again pose the question of the connection between psychoanalysis and hypnosis or suggestion. In 1903, Freud thinks he can establish a decisive distinction. Psychoanalytic method turns its back on suggestion and hypnosis, since the physician refuses to exert any influence whatsoever and is content to record "the associations of the patient, that is, the involuntary thoughts, frequently regarded as disturbing and therefore ordinarily put aside."[10] Curiously, not a word is said in this article about the transference(s); there is not even an allusion. The *Traumdeutung,* and therefore self-analysis (the analytic work done by the patient himself), is considered the best introduction to the new technique. But can the clear distinction between hypnosis and psychoanalysis really be maintained if it depends on forgetting the transference?

At the end of 1904, in a lecture given at the Vienna College of Physicians entitled "On Psychotherapy," Freud lifts this oblivion by resituating psychoanalysis in the great medical tradition; he rejects the accusation of "modern mysticism" and claims to employ scientific means. He explains, for example, that the majority of the methods of primitive and ancient medicine "must be classed under the head of psychotherapy; in order to effect a cure a condition of 'credulous expectation' was induced in sick persons, we still do the same thing today." He goes on to say that suggestion such as it was practiced by Liébeault and Bernheim in the Nancy school is to be understood in this context, since it is "a factor dependent on the psychical disposition of patients, that contributes, without any intention on our part, to the effect of every therapeutic process initiated by the physician, on most occasions in a favorable sense, but also often inhibiting."[11] There is another feature that psychoanalysis can claim: "According to a saying of the ancient physicians, these illnesses [the psychoneuroses] are not cured by the drug but by the physician, that is, by the personality of the physician, inasmuch as it exerts a psychical influence."[12]

Neither is the transference explicitly mentioned in the remainder of this article, even though the transference is indeed what this article is about, since suggestion is spontaneously defined, not from the point of view of the doctor who suggests it, but from the point of view of the patient, as a psychical disposition, be it helpful or hindering. Freud reproaches suggestion for being too powerful a factor, "uncontrollable, unmeasureable, incapable of moderation." The task of "scientific psychotherapy," that is, psychoanalysis, will be to master this factor, to direct and reinforce it.

Here Freud does not dread connecting psychoanalysis to hypnosis, since the same operations are used in both. This lecture can even be considered as a sequel to his article "Psychical Treatment," published in 1890, before the discovery of the transference.[13] In that article he discussed at length the importance of this "credulous expectation" (*gläubige Erwartung*). While anguished expectation worsens the illness, "hopeful and credulous expectation is an active force which we must rigorously take into account in all our attempts at treatment and cure." This expectation is to be related to the faith that produces miraculous cures:

> Those who are without religious belief need not renounce miraculous cures. In their case, reputation and group influence amply substitute for religious faith. There are always fashionable treatments and fashionable physicians, who play an especially dominant part in high society, where the most powerful psychical drives reveal an effort to surpass one another and to do what the best people do. Such fashionable treatments develop therapeutic effects that are outside of their actual force, and the same procedures work in the hand of the fashionable doctor, well-known as the one who saved an eminent personality, much better than they can work for other physicians. Thus there are human as well as 'divine' miracle-workers.[14]

After having presented the curative value of the patient's confidence in the physician and the methods used by magicians and oracles, he observes: "The physician's personality acquired a reputation derived directly from divine power, since in its beginnings the art of healing was in the hands of priests. So that then as now the physician's personality was one of the principle conditions in order to obtain from the patient the state of mind favorable to the cure."[15]

When in 1904 Freud pursues his reflections a little further, in "On Psychotherapy," he certainly does not forget his ideas on *credulous expectation* (words which he now writes within quotation marks); he knows that if he takes this force seriously in all the procedures of the treatment, his cathartic or psychoanalytic method will be accused of being "modern mysticism" and of appearing as the opposite of scientific medicine founded on discoveries in psychical chemistry. That is why he will try to show here that, in truth, there is the greatest possible contrast between the technique of suggestion and that of psychoanalysis. Suggestion acts, like painting, *per via di porre,* that is, "it superimposes something, a suggestion, in the expectation that it will be strong enough to prevent the pathogenic idea from coming to expression"; analytic technique, on the contrary, acts, like sculpture, *per via di levare,* since it introduces nothing new, but seeks to lift away the pathogenic idea by concerning itself with the genesis of symptoms.[16]

But is this distinction so easily made? For a suggestion to come from the physician is indeed to add something. That does not, however, prevent the technique of suggestion and that of psychoanalysis from having a form of suggestion in common: the suggestion that comes from the patient and that is indeed the strongest. Freud himself defined it, in a passage cited above, as "a factor dependent on the psychical disposition of patients that contributes, without any intention on our part, to the effect of every therapeutic process initiated by the physician." Besides, the difference between the ideas suggested by the physician and those guessed and transmitted by him appears to be slight indeed.[17] Moreover, to say that in the technique of suggestion "the resistance through which the patients cling to their illness" remains concealed is not exactly right, since resistance, as Freud already observed at the end of his article of 1890, can be removed in hypnosis, when the suggestion reaches the foundations of the personality or tries to make the patient renounce his illness, which "means a great sacrifice for him and not a small one."[18]

All of Freud's work, during several decades, is marked by an effort to establish a radical difference between psychoanalysis and suggestion, but it is also marked by the difficulty of making this difference convincing. In 1909, for example, before he presents the conclusions to his analysis of Little Hans, an objection appears: "An analysis of a child conducted by his father, who went to work instilled with my theoretical views and infected with my prejudices, is totally devoid of objective worth. A child is obviously highly susceptible to suggestion, and in regard to no one, perhaps, more than his own father. . . . In short, the whole thing is here once again simply suggestion."[19] Freud responds by saying that we can clearly distinguish the occasions where the child falsifies the facts under the pressure of a resistance, and the occasions where he agreed with his father, and those where, freed from all constraints, he speaks the intimate truth and tells things that he had kept to himself until then. Furthermore, the difficulties encountered here are no greater than in the analysis of adults. "A psychoanalysis is not an impartial scientific investigation but a therapeutic intervention; its essence is not to prove anything but merely to alter something. In psychoanalysis, the physician always gives the patient *conscious anticipatory ideas,* through which he is put in a position to recognize and to grasp the unconscious material."[20] Freud concludes from this that he cannot convince those who do not want to be convinced. This clearly indicates that it is impossible to demonstrate that there is truly no suggestion in analysis; it is at least to recognize that there is as much of it in the analysis of Little Hans as there is in any analysis.

A new attempt must be made to bring psychoanalysis back to the rigor of its technique, or more specifically, to make the transference pass back again from the singular to the plural in order to render it more manageable. The notion introduced here is that of representations of expectation (*Erwarterungsvorstellungen*), translated by Strachey in the *Standard Edition* as "anticipatory ideas." This notion establishes a connection between credulous expectation (*gläubige Erwartung*), which smells of mysticism and magic, and the representations that are the object of transferences. This expression reappears in 1910 at the beginning of an article called "The Future Prospects of Psychoanalytic Therapy": "The treatment is made up of two parts: what the physician infers and tells the patient, and the patient's elaboration of what he has heard. The mechanism of our assistance is easy to understand: we give the patient the conscious anticipatory idea, and then he discovers for himself, on the basis of its similarity to the anticipatory idea, the repressed unconscious idea." At this stage, however, the transference is explicitly distinguished from this aspect of analytic technique, and Freud regards the transference as a different and "far more powerful [mechanism]."[21]

The term "anticipatory idea" is used again in 1912 in "The Dynamics of Transference."

> It must be understood that each individual, through the combined action of his innate disposition and the influences brought to bear on him during his early years, has acquired a specific method of his own in his conduct of his erotic life, including the conditions under which he falls in love, the drives he satisfies, and the aims he sets for himself in the course of it. This produces what might be described as a stereotype (or even several), which, in the course of his life, is regularly repeated, reprinted anew, so far as the external circumstances and the nature of the love-objects accessible to him permit; which is certainly not entirely invariable in the face of recent experiences. Our observations have proven that, of these impulses determining the erotic life, only a portion has reached full psychical development; this portion is directed toward reality, and

is at the disposition of the conscious personality, and constitutes a part of it. Another portion of these libidinal impulses has been held up in its development; it has been turned away from the conscious personality and from reality, and has either been developed only in fantasy or has remained totally in the unconscious, so that it is unknown to the personality's consciousness. Someone whose need for love is not completely satisfied by reality is bound to turn toward every new person he meets with libidinal *anticipatory ideas*; and it is highly probable that the two portions of his libido, the one capable of becoming conscious and the unconscious one, have a part in forming this attitude.

It is therefore perfectly normal and understandable that the libidinal investment of the unsatisfied portion, which is held ready in expectation, is also turned toward the figure of the physician. It follows from our supposition that this investment will have recourse to models, will attach itself to one of the stereotypes that are presented by the person encountered, or, to put it another way, the investment will introduce the physician into one of the psychical series that the patient has already formed. This corresponds to the patient's real relations to the physician, when, for this insertion, the father's imago (to use Jung's apt expression) is the determining factor. But the transference is not tied to this model; it can also come about through the imago of the mother, or the brother, etc. The peculiarities of the transference to the doctor, through which it exceeds, both in amount and nature, anything that could be justified on sensible rational grounds, are intelligible through not only the *conscious anticipatory ideas,* but also through the repressed and unconscious ideas that have produced this transference.[22]

In this text, the expression "anticipatory idea" no longer indicates the content of the inference made by the analyst and transmitted by him to the patient but tries to remove it from uncertainty in order to give it a genuine status in analytic theory. At the same time, the transference is no longer considered in its entirety, since the anticipatory ideas make it appear as a preliminary mechanism for the patient, a mechanism that, because of its shortcomings, will require the analyst to fill in the corresponding ideas. One rediscovers the same conception of transferences that appeared in *Studies on Hysteria* and the Dora case history. Here it is no longer explicitly called inference or constructions transmitted by the analyst, but it is still the same thing, since the transference or the anticipatory ideas, in correspondence with the images supplied by the analyst, will become manifest through resistances that will have to be explained.

The pages that follow in "The Dynamics of Transference" specifically examine the relations between transference and resistance. But in order for this to be done, the entire transference must be considered within the field of analyzable transferences. After resistance has been explained as the regression toward infantile imagos, the idea of the transference (*Übertragungsidee*) appears as a compromise between the task of investigation and resistance: "When anything of the material of the complex (of the content of the complex) is suitable for being transferred onto the figure of the physician, the transference takes place; it produces the next idea and announces itself through the signs of a resistance, sometimes through an obstruction. We conclude that this idea of transference has penetrated into consciousness before any other possible ideas because it also satisfied the resistance."[23] In other words, the infantile imagos, which engender resistance by their attraction, are manifested in a distorted way through an idea of transference, or, to return to an earlier vocabulary, in a transference. In yet other words, an anticipatory idea tied to infantile imagos finds a corresponding idea in the physician, by means of which there can be an analysis, that is, a return to the infantile imago from which the message originated. The transference expresses the resistance, while the resistance reflects the repressed infantile imago, and "finally every conflict must [and can] be settled on the field of the transference."[24]

The demonstration is conclusive; the rigor of the technique is restored because the transference could be taken apart piece by piece and analyzed and thus done away with in the course of the treatment. It has been emptied of its power (*erledigt*, "settled, discharged") because it has been "traced back to the disposition of the libido, which has remained in possession of infantile imagos." Is Freud's task finished? Not at all. Quite to the contrary, it is as though he bypassed the question. Immediately after concluding his discussion on the relations between transference and resistance, he poses the question again: "How does it come about that the transference lends itself so remarkably to the utilization of resistance?"[25] His answer: in order that resistance is able to make use of the transference, the transference cannot be affectionate and amicable; it must be a negative transference that goes back to erotic origins. In order to hold the work of investigation at bay, resistance depends upon hostility or archaic love toward the analyst.

Without saying, Freud, through the new series of responses, abandons the domain of transferences and returns to the transference. When he justifies the existence of the erotic transference in the words: "Originally we knew only sexual objects; psychoanalysis shows us that people who are merely admired and respected in our real life may still be sexual objects for our unconscious,"[26] he is forced by the facts to leave the solid ground of plural transferences to return to the singular. And then he gets involved with difficulties that he will not succeed in overcoming. He does not for a moment assert that the coming to consciousness permits the transference to be suppressed, that is, to detach from the physician the two hostile and erotic elements in order to preserve only the affectionate and friendly transference that is "the vehicle of success in psychoanalysis, as it is in other methods of treatment" (like hypnosis, for example; but then the cure would not be properly analytic).

Thus Freud is led onto the terrain where he will lose his beautiful certainty. After several paragraphs on the negative transference, he recognizes with his usual honesty that "in all these considerations, however, we have hitherto dealt only with one side of the phenomenon of the transference."[27] Then he mentions the case of the patient who rejects his real relations to the doctor and neglects the fundamental rule of speaking spontaneously as he succumbs to an intense transference-resistance; it leads him to renounce the work of recollection in order to reproduce unconscious impulses through his actions. Analysis is then held at bay. Though it begins at a lively pace, Freud's reflection on the transference and its relations to resistance becomes more and more encumbered and finally runs into an insurmountable problem, that of memory, which renders the whole technique null and void. All that remains is for him to be consoled (in the last sentence) by the fact that the phenomenon of the transference renders the "patient's hidden and forgotten erotic impulses immediate and manifest, for no one can finally be killed *in absentia* or *in effigie.*"[28] Why killed? Perhaps we will know the answer later.

Freud goes no further, but it is easy to see what he has stumbled upon. He is too preoccupied with keeping the transference within the limits of manageability to be able to think of resistance other than as a force making use of the transference, although it is plainly also the reverse process that can explain the blockage of the patient's associative discourse. If the transference takes root in erotic sources, and if the patient is given every psychical treatment, through the inevitable and obligatory means of the transference, to return to the sexual objects that were once the totality of his reality, then one understands why he becomes silent each time his discourse leads him back again to this exact point. What kind of a treatment could tear the patient away from these delights? The fact that the transference is one illness exchanged for another, of which it is difficult to cure the patient, implies that the agonies of neurosis can be exchanged, thanks to the transference, for a state of bliss that one would never abandon. The patient is silent because he finds a thread that ties him directly to the thing for which he longingly wastes away, and of which he always dreams. In this sense, it is not so much resistance that uses the transference, or that the length of the transference is an effect of resistance (as Freud repeats in this text), as it is the transference that provokes resistance and protects itself through resistance in order to last longer.

Freud does not understand it in this way and would prefer, at any cost, that the transference were for the patient what it is in the eyes of the analyst, a means of making the unconscious come to consciousness. In other words, Freud would reduce the transference to the affectionate and friendly variety where the anticipatory ideas are conspicuous and analyzable. This is the price fo the beautiful rigor of analytic technique, which is threatened by the negative transference and by the excesses of the positive erotic transference. "The patient is thrown out of his real relations to the doctor, as soon as he falls under the dominance of an intense transference-resistance [under the dominance of archaic erotic sources]; he feels at liberty to disregard the fundamental psychoanalytic rule, according to which one must say whatever comes to one's mind without criticizing it; he forgets the resolutions with which he entered into the treatment, and he becomes indifferent to logical connections and conclusions which only a short time before had made a great impression on him."[29] In other words, all the analyst's interpretations and constructions are useless and ineffective, and one cannot see in these conditions how the transference could be resolved. That indeed disturbs Freud, for his method is once more overrun by excess and irrationality.[30]

The passion with which Freud wants to come to the end of resistance and his blindness in seeing in it the only cause of all his therapeutic worries are equaled only by his lucidity in recalling the true sources of the power and uncontrollability of the transference. But his lucidity has limits. He cannot understand the proximity of the negative transference to the positive erotic transference, although he opposes these two to the friendly and affectionate transference. To speak of the ambivalence of emotions, as he does in relation to normal individuals or neurotics, is to refer to secondary psychical processes; the more one approaches the primary processes—as in the case of psychosis—the more ambivalence disappears on behalf of identity. Freud recognizes it in his own way when he writes, "Where the capacity for transference has essentially become limited to the negative, as is the case with paranoiacs, there ceases to be any possibility of influence or cure."[31] He omits emphasizing that this negative is the positive of an excess investment of primary processes where there is no relation to the object and to alterity and where the rejection of the so-called other is his absorption. Freud implicitly recognizes on the following page that we are at the limits of madness and that this is the fruit of excessive transference. "The unconscious impulses do not want to be remembered in the way the treatment desires them to be, but endeavor to reproduce themselves in accordance with the timelessness and the capacity for hallucination of the unconscious. The patient, just as in dreams [or as in psychosis], regards the products of the awakening of his unconscious impulses as contemporaneous and real; he wants to act out his passions without taking account of the real situation."[32] In the following years, Freud will turn and return to the question of excess in this negative-positive transference of archaic erotic origins; he will repeatedly be led, by the inevitability of experience, to encounter on his way the specter of hypnosis and suggestion, which he will never completely succeed in distinguishing from one another, and he will succeed even in separating them from psychoanalysis.

It is not surprising that in the same year, 1912, in his "Recommendations to Physicians Practicing Psychoanalysis," he makes an extreme effort to redefine the analyst's position in the purity of his nonintervention and of his nonimplication, as if to exorcise, if that were possible, the disturbing tone of the last pages of "The Dynamics of Transference." The physician should not try to remember, or to take notes during his sessions, nor should he go into a scientific discussion in the course of the treatment. On the contrary, he should maintain a state of fluctuating attention and let himself be surprised by new developments; in a word, he must have a surgeon's coldness of emotion so that he can put his own emotions aside in order to provide the best possible aid to the patient. This advice is explicitly presented as the counterpart for the analyst of the fundamental rule to which the patient must submit:

> Just as the patient must relate everything . . . so too must the doctor put himself in a position to make use of everything he is told for the purposes of interpretation and of the recognition of the hidden unconscious without substituting any censorship whatever for the choice proposed by the patient; in a word, he must turn his own unconscious like a receptive organ toward the transmitting unconscious of the patient; he must adjust himself to the patient as a telephone receiver is adjusted to the transmitting microphone. Just as the receiver converts back into soundwaves the electric oscillations in the telephone line which were set up by soundwaves, so the doctor's unconscious is able, from the offshoots of the unconscious which are transmitted to him, to reconstitute the unconscious that has determined the patient's ideas.[33]

We are used to Freud's formulations—it is as if they come automatically—and we accept as evidence the conclusion that he draws from them:

> However, in order for the doctor to be able to use in this way his unconscious as an instrument in the analysis, he must fulfill one psychological condition to a high degree. He may not tolerate in himself any resistances that hold back from his consciousness what is recognized by his unconscious; otherwise he would introduce a new manner of selection and distortion that would be far more detrimental than that produced by the concentration of his conscious attention.[34]

This formulation is very seductive, but absurd and utopian as well. If the analyst were without any resistance, which is recognized as impossible on the next page ("an analysis such as this of someone who is practically healthy will naturally remain incomplete"), he would know nothing of repression, and therefore he would not have an unconscious. Furthermore, why must the patient's discourse, in order to be perceived by the analyst's consciousness, make a detour that is compelled by the latter's unconscious? Why is it that the analyst's unconscious must be affected before the inference can become possible? Because, in Freud's formulation, it is this pure and virgin unconscious of the analyst that appears as the necessary receiver transforming the patient's message into a possible reconstruction. The analyst, who must remain impenetrable and who must also economize his own affective capital for the sake of chilly indifference, is called upon to put his unconscious completely and unreservedly at the patient's disposition; that is, he totally abstracts his subjectivity in order to become a pure matrix without prejudices, but also without intentions, desires, or ideas, a wax surface offered up to objectivity.

The obviously meaningful absurdity of this utopian proposal fills a ready-made place in the theory. Of the three transferences specified by Freud (negative, positive involving unconscious erotic sources, positive involving feelings admissable to consciousness),[35] only the third was really reintegrated into the technique, because it was based on anticipatory ideas to which the analyst could correspond in detail and which he could thus identify and analyze. The attitude of pure receptivity claimed by the analyst's unconscious—and it is indeed an attitude or a posture, not a reality—will give a technical status to the two other types of transference (which some say are actually one), because they pass through neither objects nor intersubjective images. In effect, there is no possible representation of the positive transference of erotic origins. In other words, the utopian idea of the analyst's pure, virgin, nonconflicting, unconscious functions as a receptacle, an anchor, or a projection screen for the archaic libidinal forces, those that "exceed, both in amount and nature, anything that could be justified on sensible or rational grounds."[36] The positive-negative transference of erotic origins, lacking specificity and language, thus receives form and discourse through the myth of the analyst's unconscious without resistances. "Originally we knew only sexual objects; psychoanalysis shows us that people who are merely admired and respected in our real life may still be sexual objects for our unconscious"[37]—above all, one could add, if these people only had ears for what, in our discourse, bears the mark of the archaic, the infantile, the erotic, the excessive. Freud's advice and injunctions can thus take on quite a different meaning: to say that the analyst's unconscious must be receptive is to assert that he must select from what he hears precisely that which arises from erotic origins, that he must specialize in this and be able to hear and transpose everything into the language of negative erotic origins, and not linger over feelings, or prejudices, or efforts at sublimation, that is, over the social expressions of these erotic forces.

In "Recommendations to Physicians Practicing Psychoanalysis," the specter of suggestion seems to have been averted. If the physician wants "to be convincing," if he abandons his "caution and self-restraint," if he shows "his defects" to the patient, if he has an "educative ambition," he has then entered into "the psychology of consciousness," and he has left "the ground of psychoanalysis and approaches treatment by suggestion"; he should know that if he ceases being a pure mirror by mixing in a bit of suggestion, "his method is not that of true psychoanalysis."[38] Everything that arises from the secondary processes, for the patient as well as for the analyst, is to be considered under the heading of suggestion; everything that arises from the primary processes constitutes analysis proper. Nothing is easier than admitting this. But is it not to see only one side of the question? The essence of suggestion is not in what the analyst suggests but in the power of the patient's suggestibility. If the analyst's position of pure receptivity suggests, in effect, nothing particular, would it not still constitute a formidable suggestion, since it arouses what is most fundamental to the patient, since it makes him depart from the real and from the present in order to send him into excess, immoderation, and unreality? Moreover, to confuse the function with the posture, that is, to believe, as Freud does, that this attitude of pure receptivity, of having analyzed every resistance, is possible — is this not to reenter the realm of magic? Is it not simply to adopt a perverse position of all-powerfulness which fixes the patient in his own corresponding state of infantile all-powerfulness? And besides, is it so obvious that the methods of suggestion only reach the secondary processes? Once again, that is to confuse what the hypnotist has suggested with the patient's suggestibility, which can lead all the way to subjection.

It would therefore be false to assume that the psychoanalyst's attitude creates the transference. In "The Dynamics of Transference," Freud is careful to observe:

> It is not a fact that the transference appears more intense and more unrestrained during the analysis than outside it. We observe in the institutions in which neurotics are not treated analytically, the most extreme intensities and the most unworthy forms of the transference extending all the way to subjection, as well as unquestionable erotic coloring.... These characteristics of the transference are therefore to be attributed not to psychoanalysis but to the neurosis itself.[39]

This is indeed well said, but by slipping in that last line about neurosis, Freud is cheating a bit. We do not ordinarily find neurotics in institutions, but psychotics, those who in Freud's eyes do not respond to psychoanalysis, not, as he sometimes says, because they are incapable of transference, but because their negative or positive erotic transference is so violent that "there ceases to be any possibility of influence or cure."[40] But it is precisely this sort of transference that analysis unleashes and that poses a problem that Freud cannot resolve, because, as we have seen, it holds the work of recollection at bay.[41]

As a result of the analyst's position, the patient sees himself overtaken by the ascendancy of forces that he had ignored up to then, because they were repressed. The analyst's pure, impenetrable receptivity tends to reproduce in the waking state the conditions of the creation of the dream. The psychoanalyst who turns away from reality in order to attend only to the psychical reality of the negative-positive erotic transference places himself at the level of infantile passion. And precisely because he wants nothing in particular, because he eliminates from his thought-processes the ballast of the affective, of the intellectual, and of the active life, because his expectation of himself is in a state of total indetermination, he pushes the bewildered patient to react by activating his fantasies, or by reproducing his infantile unconscious in reality.

Once again, the clarity of the principle and the simplicity of the advice, which had certainly given analytic method a greater rigor and specificity, are not enough to restrain the forces that have been awakened by the situation and are insufficient to be able to make a game of these forces. After the detour of "Recommendations to Physicians," we now return to the last disturbing pages of "The Dynamics of Transference": "Just as in dreams, the patient regards the products of the awakening of his unconscious impulses as contemporaneous and real; he wants to act out his passions without taking account of the real situation."[42] This is precisely what Freud will develop in 1914 in an article entitled "Remembering, Repeating, and Working-Through."[43]

At the beginning of this article, Freud appears much more uncertain about the distinction that existed between hypnosis and psychoanalysis. He begins by abandoning not only abreaction (we will have to return to this term soon) but even the act of remembering. "We must still be grateful to the old hypnotic technique, for it brought before us in an isolated and schematic form certain psychical processes of analysis. Only through this technique could we have had the courage to create complex situations in analytic treatment and keep them clear before us."[44] Further on he writes:

> There are some cases [in the new technique] that behave like those in the hypnotic technique and only cease to do so later; other cases behave differently from the beginning. If we confine ourselves to the second case in order to characterize this difference, we might say that the patient does not remember anything of what he has forgotten and repressed, but acts it out. He reproduces it not as a memory but as an action; he repeats it, without, of course, knowing that he is repeating it.[45]

The difference expressed here relates to two modes of transference or to two stages in treatment, where the first is the hypnotic technique in which symptoms disappear; but if as a result "this transference becomes hostile and overly intense and consequently in need of repression, remembering immediately gives way to acting out. From this moment on, the resistances determine the sequence of the material that is to be repeated."[46]

This refers back to two of the three types of transferences distinguished in "The Dynamics of Transference." Freud, however, does not look into the reason for the connection and for what is in fact the assimilation of the negative and the overly intense transference or of the negation and the excess. He will no longer linger over the connection that he establishes this time, on the one hand, between the easy transference and an absence of resistances and, on the other hand, between the hostile and overpowering transference and the presence of resistances. Finally, he does not ask himself why this second form of transference leads to the replacement of acting out for the work of remembering.

His perspective on the transference is the reason why he does not pose any of these questions. As we have seen, he believes that the resistance uses the transference, but he does not mention that the transference might be able to bring on the resistance. He does, however, admit it indirectly when he explains, for example, that the patient's silence at the beginning of the treatment "is, of course, nothing other than the repetition of a homosexual attitude that comes to the fore as a resistance against remembering anything."[47] But he does not draw the consequences from it. On the contrary, it is easy to admit that the blockage of the patient's associations is the effect of the impossibility of speaking about the original erotic sources that are without any representations. The patient becomes silent because there are no words at his disposal, because he finds himself or rediscovers himself in a situation where language is suspended due to insufficiency. Nonetheless, this connection to archaic erotic sources involves a libidinal charge so strong that once awakened, it forces its way to expression and thus manifests itself in acting out. Freud again recognizes it implicitly when he discusses, on the preceding page, the impossibility of remembering "experiences of the utmost importance, which occurred in very early childhood and were not understood at the time"[48]; but even there he does not connect them to the transference and to what it produces. The patient, put back into this early state, acts, as a child does, without being able to talk about what he is doing, acting simply under necessity. Moreover, if he repeats instead of passing through the detours of ordinary behavior, it is because the tranference puts him in a state in which he never encounters the pure state of social interaction but which has left some indelible traces in him, perhaps because they too were archaic and ask only to be revived with all their former intensity.

If, on the contrary, the easy, amicable transference, like hypnosis, permits the work of remembering, in both cases it is because the transference or the hypnosis does not appear to be in this sort of relation. As active and determining forces they remain silent and secretive, they do not reveal their names and their origin, which is at the limit of language, its excess and its negation, and that is why they bring forth words for experiences that have been represented and forgotten. In the article of 1913 entitled "On Beginning the Treatment," the following sentence is the only one Freud underlines: "So long as the patient's communications and ideas run on without any obstruction, the theme of the transference should be left untouched." Let sleeping dogs lie. The same text continues, "One must wait until the transference, which is the most difficult of all procedures, has become a resistance."[49] Because the transference is the resistance. To assert that the patient's resistance is that of the analyst is to psychologize the question and to plunge into the guilt-ridden process, the infinite interrogation, of the counter-transference, unless it is understood that the analyst's resistance consists in not recognizing the nature of the transference. Transference is resistance because it is the scene of a decisive struggle where the subjectivity, and therefore the life, of each of the protagonists is threatened. Freud says as much in passing when he mentions the weapons used by the patient, which must be taken from him, or the perpetual combat in order to lead the patient's impulses onto the field of the analysis.[50] Freud thus implicitly recognizes between patient and analyst a struggle that the analyst's impassibility and impenetrability, on the one hand, and the complete freedom of the patient's speech, on the other, repeatedly try to cover up. Under the pretext that the analyst must refuse, no matter what the cause, to get into a confrontation, that he must never try to defend or justify himself, but must project the patient's speech onto another scene, one fails to recognize that on another, unexpressed level the transference relation is a violent one, one of at once the most subtle and the most murderous violence to be found in any conflict. It is a question of the very existence of the subject who places himself in a position of complete dependence upon another from whom he expects all or nothing, undetermined in any case. This applies to the analyst as well as the patient. When one individual depends upon another, as though in order to enact the myth of the origins prior to object-relations, it entails the greatest violence, the sort that is defined by the alternative either to remain dependent or die, or to live thanks to this dependence or die from this very dependence.

There is nothing extraordinary in such a description, nothing pseudo-metaphysical about it, only what every analyst has heard a hundred times unless he has not had occasion to hear it, for example, because of his difficulty in getting rid of a patient,[51] or because of the patient's excessive reaction to his absence or the patient's fear of meeting him outside the sessions. These are some of the many forms that the fear of absolute abandonment takes and that underneath the exaggerated importance given to the analyst mark his negation. Because he has no real existence, the patient's dependence upon him could just as easily be called independence and self-sufficiency. The more total the dependence, the more it turns into ignorance of the other. The violence is without a tactic, without a strategy or a game plan; it is immediately a struggle to the death, a struggle to nonexistence. This does not apply only to the patient who tries to absorb the analyst, because the patient must maintain the analyst and the analyst must maintain himself in his invulnerability. By keeping his distance, by arousing the form of an archaic erotic relation, the analyst exasperates the desire and the longing to abolish this distance, which is incompatible with this relationship. In this way, he does violence to the patient by putting him in an insolvable position where he must either take refuge behind a reintensified resistance or enact, in a thousand different ways, a process of self-destruction. Freud clearly sees that the logic of repetition leads to an "often unavoidable deterioration during the treatment,"[52] which can "invalidate the prospects of recovery,"[53] because the deepest instinctual impulses may come to be repeated. But once again the text makes no allusion to the transference and restricts itself to disclosing one of its effects. It is easy, however, to see how the two types of transference, linked to resistance and to repetition, are both conjointly at work here. The excessive erotic transference is no longer distinguished from the hostile negative transference, because the original relation indissociably comprises these two aspects: the attraction to the other is his destruction; at the moment of his paroxysm, love is hate.

Freud will not lead his research in this direction, at least not directly, since this undeveloped side of the transference will reappear in another mode. In effect, what really appears in faint outline when the repetition-compulsion is presented for the first time is the death drive;[54] moreover, this compulsion to repeat will serve as the introduction to the speculations on the death drive in *Beyond the Pleasure Principle*. But this drive will then be presented without any link to the transference; it will even be explicitly said that the death drive cannot be revealed in analytic treatment, no doubt because it must not be revealed, because it would be much too dangerous to recognize it at work in the mainspring of analysis, namely, the transference. All appearances would suggest that Freud had not ceased working on this question between 1914 and 1921, while in fact he had been able to confront it directly only once, detached from the analytic treatment where he had discovered it, because a long detour through the metapsychology enabled him to forget where this question had come from.

In order to give an account of the transference without explicitly mentioning it, Freud will pursue another detour by looking into hypnosis. But it is impossible to perceive the interest and the value of what he has to say if we do not first understand the difficulty of clearly distinguishing analytic method from hypnotic method.

In "Remembering, Repeating and Working-Through," he has already placed the easy transference on the side of hypnosis, since in both procedures remembering is possible thanks to the absence of resistances. The hostile and overpowering transference is characteristic of the new technique that takes resistances into account and sees the emergence of repetition. But we must go a bit further. This hostile transference is not only a characteristic of the new technique, it is also the appearance of the hidden side of the amicable transference; it is necessary to avoid unveiling the essence of the transference unless it is absolutely indispensable to the treatment, since if it is not indispensable, it could be disastrous. Now that the amicable transference and hypnosis have been brought together, the conclusion arises that the motive force of the analysis, hidden or manifest, is the same as that of hypnotic technique.[55] We are then less surprised to read, at the end of this article, something that might have seemed strange:

> This working-through of the resistances may be an arduous task for the patient and a test of patience for the physician. But this part of the work effects the greatest changes in the patient and distinguishes analytic treatment from any kind of treatment by suggestion. Theoretically, one may compare it with the "abreaction" of the charges of affect squeezed by repression, without which hypnotic treatment remains ineffective.[56]

If in practice working-through moves away from suggestion, it approaches it in theory, because working-through is not placed in parallel with free association, which made the difference, but with abreaction, which occurred under hypnosis. Freud's hesitation in the last sentence of this article is understandable on more grounds than one. No doubt the first cause of his hesitation is the impasse between suggestion as that which the analyst has suggested and suggestion as the patient's suggestibility. But above all there is an impasse due to repetition, which is the reproduction of symptoms, the hatching of an "artificial illness," and therefore the cause of Freud's hesitation is, more than anything else, the transference neurosis, in the strictest sense of the term. Freud knows very well that he is returning to Charcot's old conception of hypnosis as nothing other than a "neurosis, and an artificially induced hysteria."[57]

There is another, much more radical link established by Freud between transference and hypnosis: through the mediation of being in love. If one reads "Observations on Transference-Love" (1915) and chapter 8 of *Group Psychology and the Analysis of the Ego* (1921), one is obliged to conclude that what is expressed in this final text on hypnosis in order to define its specificity also applies to the transference. The "Observations" are at first reluctant to recognize in the amorous expressions of patients the characteristics of genuine love, but the argument takes another turn when one considers that "this state of being in love consists of new editions of old traits and repeats infantile reactions."[58] Besides, "the resistance did not create this love; it finds it already there, makes use of it and exaggerates its manifestations. The authenticity of the phenomenon is not weakened by the resistance." To sum up, the state of being in love that makes its appearance during the analysis can be described

> by certain features that ensure it a special position. In the first place, it is provoked by the analytic situation; secondly, it is pushed to intensity by the resistance that dominates the situation; thirdly, it is lacking to a high degree in a regard for reality; it is more unreasonable, less concerned about its consequences, more blind in its appreciation of the loved person than we would want to acknowledge for a normal state of being in love. We should not forget, however, that precisely these departures from the norm constitute the essence of being in love.[59]

Freud deduces nothing from this that could illuminate the nature of the transference. He only uses it in order to repeat the injunction that he has formulated since the beginning of the article: the physician must not draw any personal benefit from and must not respond to the patient's entreaties.

If Freud does not push his observations further but seems content to expatiate on the state of being in love, it is, once again, because he remains a prisoner of his conception of resistance and as a result cannot take advantage of the occasion to work out his conception of the transference. That love is used in analysis in order to make analysis impossible, by making the analyst leave his position, emptied of feelings and opinions, tells us that love is defined by reciprocity much more than by the realization of sexual aims. Nonreciprocity is precisely what distinguishes the transference from love; but nonreciprocity also provokes love in order to avoid the effects of nonreciprocity, which are the return to infantile dependence, the awakening of the most primitive drives, and finally subjection to the other to the point of nonexistence. Throughout this article Freud insists on the necessity of not satisfying the demand for love; but that is superficial indeed in comparison with the radical nonresponse that puts the analyst at the patient's disposal in order to hear him, in such a way, however, that the patient cannot make use of the analyst. Preferring to become a sexual object that attracts the other, the patient resists a relationship without relation, an exasperated connection to a presence that vanishes in the act of presenting itself as pure re-

85 / *Transference: The Dream*

ceptivity. The resistance is at first not resistance to the treatment but resistance to the transference and to the mortal danger that it involves, a resistance all the more intense because the patient resists the state in which he is already ineluctably seized. We are beyond the question of satisfaction here, because these processes put the individual in a situation logically anterior to object-relations; he is contending with another from whom he cannot distinguish himself and yet in whom lay his own foundations. One can say then that what he experiences is unreal, or that it turns him away from reality, because it concerns the actualization of a relation that is presupposed in every relationship. Love would then only be a substitute for a relation that was first manifested in the transference.

Freud says nothing about all that, at least in regard to the transference. But if one rereads chapter 8 of *Group Psychology and the Analysis of the Ego*, one discovers that the connection established between hypnosis and being in love is exactly the same as the one in "Observations" between transference and being in love: the transference is the state of being in love, if all sexual satisfaction, direct or indirect, is excluded. In order to unveil certain decisive aspects of the transference, it is necessary to replace *hypnosis* with *transference* in the following passage:

> From being in love to hypnosis is evidently only a short step. The respects in which the two agree are obvious. There is the same humble submission, docility, absence of criticism, toward the hypnotist as toward the loved object, the same absorption of the subject's own initiatives; no one can doubt that the hypnotist is in the place of the ego ideal.[60] It is only that all the connections in hypnosis are clearer and more intense, so that it would be more appropriate to explain being in love through hypnosis than the other way around. The hypnotist is the sole object, and no one else is considered in comparison to him. That the ego experiences as a dream whatever the hypnotist requests and asserts reminds us that we have neglected to mention among the functions of the ego ideal the business of testing reality.[61] No wonder that the ego takes a perception for real if its reality is vouched for by the psychical agency ordinarily charged with the task. The complete absence of impulses that are uninhibited in their sexual aims contributes further to the extreme purity of the phenomena. The hypnotic relation is the unlimited devotion of someone in love, but to the exclusion of sexual satisfaction; whereas in the actual case of being in love this satisfaction is only temporarily held back, and remains in the background as a possible aim at a later time.[62]

To replace the word *hypnosis* with *transference*[63] in this text may seem to be overdoing it, above all if one continues on the next page: "There are still in hypnosis a great many things that we must recognize as unexplained and mystical. It contains an element of paralysis derived from the relation of someone all-powerful and someone powerless and helpless, which perhaps forms a transition toward the hypnosis of terror that occurs in animals." Is this not a description of resistance—not the subtle and intense resistance which Freud speaks of and which makes such astute use of the transference but that inevitable effect of the all-powerful transference which constitutes the analytic relation? In 1921, thirty years after his discovery, Freud cannot name the transference at this point in the text. Having invented psychoanalysis in order to free the neurotic from his symptoms, to modify his psychical life, to release forces hitherto enchained, to allow individuality to speak and to assert itself, how could he now admit that the transference, not only in its deviations or in the risks that it makes one run (*Lebensschädigungen*) but in its very nature, is the bearer of paralysis[64] and death? He has certainly observed in analytic treatment the fabulous credulity of patients who are otherwise sensible and critical, but he would not dare to write in connection with the analyst what he added in a footnote (1910) to *Three Essays on the Theory of Sexuality* (1905), namely, that "I cannot help recalling here the credulous docility of the hypnotized subject toward the hypnotist, which leads me to suppose that the essence of hypnosis lies in an unconscious fixation of the libido on the figure of the hypnotist through the means of the masochistic elements of the sexual drive."[65]

Those who are persuaded of the decisive break established by Freud which placed psychoanalysis definitively apart from hypnosis will doubtless not be inclined to accept these connections. But psychoanalysts know very well, unless they have shut their ears to it, that they constantly encounter in their practice these borderline features (manifested in the transference) that reproduce or isolate the universal and fundamental elementary factors in the nature of a relation. Certain patients understand this very clearly. Such is the need for the attention of the one he thinks he loves that he will die if the other is interested in anyone or anything but him, that is, he reduces the other to a curious nonexistence, since he permits him only to be usurped and possessed. The sexual aims of this love can be put totally in parentheses, even if they too are called upon. What matters here is that not a fiber of the other is his own, since it prolongs the undifferentiated existence of the one who loves. The other is finally perceived "as in a dream" and loses all subjective differentiation. But this goes both ways, since the other who is malleable in every sense literally becomes the ego ideal, the perfect other. Nothing is easier for oneself than to become this other, without rough edges or borders, and to place this other in the opposite position, that of an all-powerfulness that paralyzes and destroys one's own subjectivity to its very roots, since it is still my all-powerfulness that I experience when my ego ideal leads me asymptotically toward death. This is a permanently shifting game where each one makes the other and himself now the pole of his subjection and loss of subjectivity, now that of his excessive demands.

If Freud sees in hypnosis something mysterious and unexplained, it is because he only lingers over the second phase of the alternation. "The masochistic elements of the sexual drive" can be activated only on the condition that the hypnotist has been put in a state of absolute dependence and availability, that he has otherwise become an isolated object that functions only for the hypnotized subject. The annulment of the hypnotist's independence is the condition *sine qua non* of the subject's submission.

That is just how the analyst is described in "Recommendations to Physicians." He must abandon, as we have seen, every effort of memory, every scientific objective, every emotional reaction, in order to become a pure receiver who lets his unconscious work entirely at the patient's disposition. The nonreciprocity which was used earlier to distinguish the transference from being in love, this non-response by the analyst to the demands for satisfaction, is changed into an extraordinary, unhoped for, undreamed of response to the demands of the patient, who thus realizes his unexpected and unimagined desire to find at last another whom he can at once, or rather alternately, transform into the very roots of his being, into what is most withdrawn and secret, his slave and his absolute master. The analyst is the one who holds things together, who is there for me alone during this time: his concern is only for me, and I can be whatever or however I want for myself and for him; he will wait there for me. This is the height of all-powerfulness in powerlessness, because I need the other, while I can shape him as I please. One says that the analyst does not respond to demands, but is there any archaic demand to which his non-response does not answer? His non-response is the basis of hypnosis as well as of the transference. This is narcissism, because one needs neither an image nor recognition. This is at the limits of destruction and exaltation, of death and life. For at the height of amorous passion the situation can be reversed: I adore the one with whom I can do anything, and I let myself be subjugated. Because the analyst does not have a single identity, he becomes the dreamed-of other who therefore can be anything, can know anything, and to whom one can safely submit and alienate oneself.[66]

Finally, the transference is not confused with suggestion, no more than analysis is with the hypnotic method. This is obvious, but we must still state precisely what the distinctions are. They would be located neither in the patient's position nor in the analyst's impassability nor even in the use of discourse or the effort at remembering. All these things were also present in treatments using hypnosis or suggestion. *Analysis departs from earlier methods through the progressive extension of the course of the treatment and through the addition of numerous detours.* It begins by turning away from the explanation of symptoms, which defines the cathartic treatment, in order to investigate the complexes to which the symptoms have given birth. Then it veers away from this line of inquiry in order to discover and overcome resistances. Finally, instead of treating these resistances directly, analytic method waits for them to appear as repetitions. By way of these repetitions, analysis gets through to the resistances and from there to the complexes in order to end with the dissolution of the symptoms. Freud uses this elongated path to avoid a confrontation with the patient, that is, to avoid everything that involves the physician's direct action upon the patient, which is evident in hypnosis and suggestion and involves attempts to influence and coerce the patient and everything else in which force or an educative aim is used to effect the cure. Instead of freeing the patient, the establishment of a relation involving force risks enclosing him in his systems of defense. We note in passing that Freud's success on this point is not total and that military metaphors surreptitiously reappear.[67] One cannot, however, say that analytic method is heading in this direction. But if the relation involving force is not between analyst and patient, it is perhaps between two aspects of analysis, that of the transference and that of free association.

Analysis replaces hypnosis through the fundamental rule about saying everything that comes to mind without any criticism or omissions.[68] That implied getting involved in the longest detour imaginable, since it was impossible to foresee either when or how one could come to the end. The analyst loses all mastery here, since the patient, in his own way, at his own rhythm, meanders through his story and lets his fantasies and his drives appear, all of which permanently drifts in connection with everything that could be constituted as the analyst's expectations. Through free association, the patient, to his own astonishment, reinvents or invents what could have happened to him but took another course. In "A Note on the Prehistory of the Technique of Analysis" (1920),[69] in response to a polemical essay by Havelock Ellis, Freud says that the attention given to the free or random ideas that arise (*freier Einfall*)—not the free associations—and the method to make them appear came to him first while he was reading the works of Ludwig Börne, which had been given to him as a present on his fourteenth birthday and which he still possessed fifty years later, the only vestige from that time. In his "The Art of Becoming an Original Writer in Three Days," Börne advised that one "take a sheet of paper and write down everything that comes into your head," and he predicted that one would assuredly come out of these three days astonished "at the new and unheard-of thoughts you have had." This is not the place to consider the applications and developments that Freud derived from this advice; we will return to this question in chapter 7. It matters only that we see the emphasis in this procedure upon the originality and the uniqueness of the one who writes, and now of the one who speaks. By voicing every unexpected idea that comes to mind independent of one's wishes and reflection, the speaker brings to light the repressed foundations of what makes him uniquely himself. We then find ourselves at a point diametrically opposite to suggestion and to any discourse spoken under its influence.

Analysis thus finds itself inhabited by two contradictory tendencies: on the one hand, the transference whose center and motive force resides in the subjection-all-powerfulness that results, as we have seen, in the loss of subjectivity; on the other hand, the random ideas that structure or restructure the subject's uniqueness. It is easy to understand that the analysis that operates through this contradiction and claims to overcome it possesses a fascination that has no equal in the past other than the great religions that sought to unite submission and liberty. And the fact that one can only with difficulty turn away from them after one had accepted them is not at all surprising. What other mode of practice can be imagined that permits the rediscovery of *the relations of the dream in the production of its own uniqueness?* The real question is whether psychoanalysis can keep its promises, that is, what will finally become of the patient. For Freud, there is no doubt that the transference must come to an end, that it must be resolved or dissolved, undone, decomposed, once the individual has been returned to his existence, capable of enjoying and living.[70] Freud is convinced that this imperative can be effectively realized. But this is not a proof. Between the two terms of the contradiction there is a relation involving force that Freud is the first to have considered. He has told us that as long as the transference was amicable and unexpressed, the work of association was easy and consequently so also was the work of remembering. In other words, the transference in this case plays its role as the secret motive force of the treatment; it is the illusion that permits the words to flow without obstacles and that leads to the discovery of the unheard-of, and to the constitution of subjectivity. But when the transference becomes overpowering and negative, when it appears indistinguishable from a realized dream, it has become like the song of the sirens, whose voice no one can resist. What good is my uniqueness and the gigantic effort of continuous invention if I now see within range that which I have suspected from the origin and for which I have since sought in vain; one would have to be mad not to place oneself in the madness of the transference, even if it were at the price of the most complete degradation. Numerous results are possible from this forceful relation—from the patient who after some time with the analyst is sufficiently freed of his symptoms to leave the labyrinth and return to his life, to the patient who went down the road of free association and thus into his own solitude but who, having become an analyst, cannot tolerate this risk for long and in order not to withdraw from the transference becomes interested in theory and through it becomes, as Freud says, a pupil and disciple like the others.[71]

It appears as if Freud had for more than twenty years (1892-1915) regarded the work of free association as powerful enough to bring about the end of the transference, that is, the end of suggestion, and thus to free the patient from the influence of the physician. But after "Remembering, Repetition, and Working-Through," having encountered and described the power of this transference and its substitute state of being in love, he runs into a difficulty which he cannot overcome and which makes him doubt that the emergence of random ideas has a greater force than the transferential link and can therefore undo it. In any case, after these texts, he will no longer make any revision of his technique; on the contrary, he will develop, outside the context of analytic treatment, those things that he had discovered as the intrinsic limits of the treatment: the themes of narcissism, the uncanny, the death drive, and group psychology.

In 1916, in his *Introductory Lectures on Psychoanalysis*, although on the whole he remains intrepidly optimistic, he no longer pretends to have turned his back on suggestion and to have effectively replaced hypnosis with the free expression of random ideas: "It must dawn on us that in our technique we have abandoned hypnosis only to rediscover suggestion in the form of the transference."[72] In the following pages, while resuming pell-mell the earlier themes of the treatment and its effects, while making pretensions to understand the limits of the transference and "to clear up the obscurities of the case, to fill in the gaps in the patient's memory, to discover the circumstances causing the repressions," and thus to destroy (*abtragen*) the transference,[73] he uses the word *suggestion* as such a near-equivalent to *transference* that he adds to it the adjective *indirect* to differentiate from the direct suggestion of hypnosis. All of this in order to try to respond to a radical question which is posed at the end of the preceding chapter and which is no less the sign of the author's uneasiness for having been put in the mouth of one of his auditors: "'the numerous important psychological discoveries of psychoanalysis . . . are they not the result of suggestion, of unintentional suggestion?'"[74]

There is nothing new in *The Question of Lay Analysis* (1926).[75] The principal features of preceding accounts are simply integrated into the second psychical topography. One must wait until "Analysis Finite and Infinite" (1937) to see the claims of analysis directly questioned and to see the timid introduction of the death drive into the perspective on the treatment.[76]

A note to *The Ego and the Id* (1923) prohibits the analyst from doing what was fully granted to the hypnotist, namely, taking the place of the ego ideal:

The struggle against the obstacle of an unconscious sense of guilt is not made easy for the analyst. Nothing can be done against it directly, and nothing indirectly but the slow discovery of its unconscious repressed foundations in order to change it little by little into a conscious sense of guilt. One acquires a special opportunity to exert an influence if this sense of unconscious guilt is a borrowed one, that is, the result of an identification with another person who was once the object of an erotic investment. A sense of guilt that has been adopted in this way is often the sole remaining trace of the abandoned love-relation and is recognized with difficulty. The likeness between this process and melancholy is obvious here. If one can uncover this former object-investment under the unconscious sense of guilt, the therapeutic task is often brilliantly resolved; otherwise, the result of the therapeutic effort is by no means certain. That depends in the first place on the intensity of the sense of guilt, to which therapy is often unable to oppose a contrary force of a similar order of strength. Perhaps it may also depend on whether the personality of the analyst permits himself to be put by the patient in the place of his ego ideal, and this involves the temptation for the analyst to play the part of the prophet, the savior, and the redeemer to the patient. Since the rules of the analysis are decisively opposed to the physician's use of his personality in this way, one must honestly confess that here a new limit is placed on the effectiveness of the analysis, which does not set out to make morbid reactions impossible, but to give the patient's ego the freedom to decide for itself one way or the other.[77]

If one reads this note by beginning from the end (which is often the only way to graps the real movement of Freud's thought beneath its ostensibly deductive form), one gets something like this: the psychoanalyst who seeks his patient's freedom may end up with a sense of guilt, because that would suppose that the analyst's personality takes the place of the patient's ego ideal (which would lead to alienation instead of liberation); but if he took this place all the same, he would become the counterforce equal in intensity to the sense of guilt, that is, he would be the object of erotic investment with which the patient would identify himself, as he had done formerly with someone he knew. If one could discover this person beneath the analyst's features, the success of the treatment would be assured.

What Freud says is all very well, but consider what he does not say. His omissions become evident when we recall what he has often repeated elsewhere. The principle of the transference presupposes the replacement of the object of infantile love by all or part of the analyst's personality. Likewise, psychoanalysis effects the substitution of one neurosis for the transference neurosis. And again, psychoanalysis follows the most ancient therapeutic tradition by making the personality of the analyst into the physician who can heal; psychoanalysis creates the condition of credulous expectation or responds to the anticipatory ideas as healers had done in times past. But what Freud's note on the sense of guilt says most explicitly runs counter to this line of interpretation. Not only is there is no allusion made to the transference but it is suggested that the transference, which partially includes that the analyst take the place of the ego ideal, could not be used and occur in this form.

It is easy to understand why the physician's personality cannot play this role in the present argument: it would engender an extreme dependence in the patient that the treatment could not undo. The question, however, is first to know, not if the analyst should take this place, but if, by chance, he does not take it effectively and inevitably. The context of this note entirely supports this conclusion. Is it not because the psychoanalyst has taken the place of the ego ideal that the patient takes delight in self-destructive masochism, that he "manifests what is known as negative therapeutic reaction," "deteriorates during the treatment instead of getting better," "finds satisfaction in the illness and refuses to give up the punishment of suffering?"[78]

But Freud cannot connect these observations to those he made, for example, in "Remembering, Repetition, and Working-Through," where it was indeed a question of the transference. Freud must make a caricature of the position eventually taken by the analyst by bringing in the prophet, the savior, and the redeemer; he even gives up the goal of the cure (since the treatment is not meant to make morbid reactions impossible) — all to safeguard the patient's liberty. In reality, it is because this liberty, to which analysis should lead, is compromised indeed by the sense of guilt that is described in these pages, and that the analysis brings so vividly back to life. It is because the psychoanalyst has taken the place of the ego ideal, of the other person, the former object of erotic investment with whom the patient identifies himself, that this patient "can endure neither praise nor appreciation" and that he reacts to every step of the treatment with an exacerbation of his illness.

It is impossible for Freud to recognize that "in very many cases, perhaps in all the most severe cases of neurosis"[79] (why not in all cases, even if it does not appear in all of them), the transference is the privileged occasion through which one experiences or reexperiences the masochistic willingness that alleviates the guilt of the first separation.[80] It is impossible because he knows the difficulty of coming to the end of this form of transference neurosis, linked intrinsically to the overpowering transference, because from there above all the mainspring of the transference, as we saw earlier, is identified with hypnosis, and because in spite of everything, one must try to distinguish psychoanalysis from it, even if it means turning one's back for a moment on the most obvious facts.

five

the game of the other

Between the two contradictory poles that constitute psychoanalysis—the transference and the upheaval of ideas—there remains a space to be uncovered, by trying first to situate as precisely as we can this "intense affective relation" that inheres in every therapeutic enterprise, whether or not one wishes it, and that was already the decisive dynamic factor in hypnosis. If one must make use of it in order to be free from it, we must know where it derives its ineluctable character and its force.

Every analyst has experienced the situation in which after the patient has spoken freely for a while, has taken risks and developed some disturbing fantasies, he falls back upon the analyst. He sizes up the analyst and then starts to show an interest in him or her, but he no longer wants to talk about what happened or about what he thinks happened in the analytic relation. In other words, the patient uses transference love to stop the course of the analysis. All efforts to put the patient back to the work of remembering are doomed to failure. To use Freud's terms, the transference has become too passionate or too hostile to be able to overcome the resistances. But one can pose another hypothesis.

The appearance of disturbing fantasies or of a stream of archaic images leads the patient to the edge of subjective destructuration. He then takes refuge in love for the analyst in order to avoid crossing the borders of psychosis. But this hostile love is not only a protection; it can become the index of the regressive situation into which the patient has now entered, a state of primitive fusion and confusion. The analyst who then clings to his role as the analyzer of neurosis is playing the game of the patient, who speaks of love in order not to confront the limits of existence, which are life and death.

The patient gives the appearance of enjoying the realm of sexualized existence, but that is only to avoid approaching his own loss. At this stage, two possibilities are open to him: to make the analyst abandon his reserve, so that he becomes one individual among others, or to force him to become even more impenetrable, to harden his role as the receiver and transmitter of discourse.

The patient is looking for a way not to pursue the regression within his own story, that is, within this place where the first separation has not yet been carried out and where he risks disaster. At the same time, however, the indetermination of the analytic situation soon hurls him into the whirlwind of this hostile passion that constitutes the other, while it destroys him as a distinct and independent individual. In this way, the analyst, seeing himself put in the position of an omnipresent nothingness or feeling himself on the verge of losing all his freedom of movement, does not want to see this regression go any further.

But why does the regression have to work like this? Is not the analyst right to send the patient back to the work of remembering without getting into a conflict so obscure that no one ever finds his way out of it? There is certainly no necessity to make every treatment pass through this liminal experience. If one thinks in Freud's terms, there is, of course, no need to force anything when the analysis is carried out under the auspices of an "amicable and unexpressed" transference. But if, as quite often happens in a somewhat prolonged analysis, the transference becomes "hostile and excessive," how can one avoid letting things get worse without terminating the analysis or falling into unforeseeable or repetitive actions? Moreover, if, as we suggested in the preceding chapter, the essence of the transferential relation is to be sought in the states of fusion, how can the analysis of the transference, which is decisive for the treatment, be performed without going through this regression? Finally, there are a great number of cases where the analysis more or less explicitly comes up against the vital need for a primitive unity which nevertheless turns out to be deadly.

How can we manage to get a better look at this state from which, by definition, the archaic escapes from representation and from the readability of the historical event? How can we describe this relationship which is really not a relationship at all if not through the models in connection to which it becomes identifiable further down the line but which also fall outside of its range, since they assume the realization of a distinction that never took place? Is this not how Freud tries to dispell some of the mystery of hypnosis (and thus of the transference)? He sees in the hypnotist's power something reminiscent of the father of the primitive horde, in front of whom one was compelled to behave in a passive and masochistic way. The important thing to keep in mind about this type of relationship is the fact that the hypnotized subject has only one interest in reality: the hypnotist-primitive father; the rest of the human race and the world seem to him devoid of interest. Another feature is worth noting: the hypnotized subject who places himself in a state of absolute dependence entirely abandons his own will. He accepts every decision from this primitive father and settles into a state in which he is without a will and capable of sacrificing himself totally. But this description, which is indeed in line with Freud by virtue of the prevalence given to the father, fails to take into account the reciprocity of the relationship, which is so obvious in analysis.

The other model, now current in the Anglo-Saxon literature and appearing increasingly in France, is that of the mother-child relationship.[1] Some have said that the figure of the good mother was indispensable to the patient in the role of the analyst; others have described how in the analysis the patient experienced the threat of the deadly and devouring mother.

In my opinion, these models, which are equivalent, have two drawbacks. First, they assume the distinction between two individuals, although the whole question is to determine whether separation has occurred and whether it is possible. Second, these models refer to the patient's history, that which really happened, although the time of the transference (if one may still speak here of time) is that of myth, which has an active role in history but which cannot be placed in the order of history. Some authors, especially among the Kleinians, have used the term "symbiosis," doubtless in order to suggest that only one life is in question here.[2] As if what the patient dreams of is to rediscover the blissful state of the cell before the first scission. It is true that in the neurotic or the psychotic this myth asserts that in the beginning there was one.[3] But this assertion is also an injunction: because there is only one, there will be only one, there should be only one. In other words, the myth implies violent opposition against both the unity of two and their separation.

One is reduced to considering this nonrelation in purely contradictory terms, one term canceling out the other. It is false to claim that there is no other in this state, because the other is indispensable. But this second proposition is equally false, because the other must be there in order to be assimilated, because the other cannot and must not be admitted. On the contrary, obviously, it is possible to support the truth of these propositions, since there must be another in order that he can be reduced; the other must exist before he can be reduced to nonexistence, but he is not really indispensable, since he must fade away. In the discourse of patients, one encounters this impossible combination of a "fear of being swallowed" and a "need for fusion," which is also a fear of fusion and a need to be swallowed.[4] Reciprocity is total here to the point that life becomes death. Life is fusion-union-love, and death is fusion-absorption-hate.

One could still doubtless speak of a relation, but only on the condition that one specifies that it contains its own negation: I can only be distinguished from the other as I am in the process of dying, because it is only through the other that I live. If this distinction does not take place, the danger remains the same, because we will both vanish into the absolute void. I bring you into being, says one (and the other), all the better to reduce you to nothingness. To which the other (and I) responds: I exist on the condition that only you exist; I will deprive you of neither water, air, nor light. I love you with a hate that creates me, so that you can hate me with a devouring love. Life and death are not separated here; *there is only room for one.* It is a commonplace to observe that one of the most notorious passions in analysis is that of annihilation, but one forgets to add that it is only the reverse of an unlimited power, for the aim of this passion is to lead the other to destruction and thus become the master.[5]

That such a nonrelation is something best shared should not surprise us, since the other's need always brings with it the impossibility of tolerating it. This initial myth is more or less at work in all relations between men and women, parents and children, those who govern and those who are governed, domestic or political tyrants being only the visible excrescence of an obscure multitude. What matters here is that this mode of nonrelation can eventually appear to be the privileged paradigm of the analytic relation. When the hostile and excessive transference emerges (these two adjectives are finally identical and convey the double demand of an impossible possibility),[6] the analyst should not have only the alternatives of falling from his position or being walled into it. He must be able to accept this relation by letting himself be absorbed to the limits of annihilation without rejecting the patient.

According to the principles of the nonrelation, the patient tries to provoke the analyst into a sadistic reaction that will console him in his nothingness, or into a depressive reflex that will give him the feeling of all-powerfulness. To interpret the end of the analysis, as Lacan does, either as the patient's unbeing (*désêtre*) or as the analyst's fall into the position of the *objet petit a* (Lacan's formula for the other, *autre*), corresponds perhaps to the observed facts, but it is also to recognize that the analysis comes to an end only on reaching the nonrelation we have just described, or more precisely, it comes to an end only upon the appearance of the motive force of the transference. The end of the analysis would be the realization of the transference in the psychical life of the patient, and not at all the dissolution of the transference; instead of delivering him from the initial myth, the end of the analysis would be the process of assimilating the patient into it. These formulations are in effect only a more developed way of defining the two reversible positions in which the patient is locked in his rage to create and to exterminate the other all at once. One would be mistaken to attribute unbeing only to the patient, and the fall to the *objet petit a* only to the analyst. The hesitation of the Lacanians in the attribution of these qualifications to one protagonist or another would suggest that these positions could be reversed. For to stay at that point is to admit that the path of the analysis can end in nothing other than the definitive fixations of the analyst and the patient in the paranoid and depressive positions defined by Melanie Klein as constitutive of the human being, but also as the most archaic and infantile.

After such a long detour, can analysis avoid this overwhelming regression which would signal at best the uselessness of the treatment, at worst its aberration, but which would perhaps explain the fascination that it exerts? As if each one sought not to understand more clearly the unconscious mechanisms that control him, not to rid himself of his symptoms, but to practice what one could call *the game of the other,* or the game of death, the most fascinating game because the stakes are at their highest and the game is always unresolved and because there is nothing more dangerous or more sterile. If this game is the motive force of the transference, if it is why one begins an analysis, without knowing it, if it is what keeps one going, it does not follow that the end should be marked by a transformation of the protagonists into the constitutive representatives of the game. For that would suppose that the analyst lets himself be carried away in the magic of the game and that his daily practice, also without him knowing it, maintains him in this rapture. This would be yet another way of explaining why "he whom psychoanalysis has once grasped, it never lets go."

Not only must the psychoanalyst recognize abstractly and in general that he is part of this game but he must let himself be effectively caught in it, though differently in each case. While being unconsciously subjected to the archaic nonrelation that constitutes the transference, he may of course try to defend himself against being seized in the alternate identity of life and death, of absorption and rejection, of assimilation and abandonment, by refusing to give up the impassibility and impenetrability that characterize analytic work according to the classical theory. But in this case, either the analysis will not work or dangerous processes will develop undetected. Neither is it a question of abandoning this type of behavior on behalf of the sadistic or depressive reactions, because then they would simply be replies to the assaults by the patient in the game of the other. The analyst has been touched; he does not refuse to be overtaken by the impossible and contradictory demands of the patient, that is, he actively takes part in the game, lets himself be at once all-powerful and less than nothing, at once exalted and suppressed. The difficulty is in maintaining two positions simultaneously: on the one hand, to be overcome by the meaningless reversibility without making the other submit to the same process, and on the other hand, to be outside the situation enough to be able to to assess what is going on and to express it. It is a question of keeping the right distance: to be close enough to be effective, without which the patient will not be able to enact the passion that possesses him and will not stop vainly clamouring about it and, to be far enough away not to become the patient's plaything, which would have the effect of plunging him into anxiety, for it would lock the analyst, along with the patient, in an infernal enclosure instead of getting him out of it. To tell the truth, the analyst will never find the right distance; he must produce it, in time, as the patient begins to put an end to his everlasting reiterations. Not only is it difficult for the analyst to recognize the terms of the demands that are put upon him but the effect upon him of these demands is produced well before he suspects it, for the patient, even in his blindness, has more than one detour through which to reach the analyst when the latter least expects it. Moreover, the analyst, like the patient, can only work from the unexpected. The game of the other can be as dull as its identity. Its form from moment to moment is equally unpredictable; were that not the case, the other would know how to fend off the blow.

It seems to me that the stagnation of certain analyses in this archaic nonrelation comes in part from the fact that the analyst cannot be placed by the patient, or cannot place himself, at the right distance or that he passes it by because he fails to perceive the respective positions of the players. There are at least four terms to consider here.

Such is the analyst's force that the patient's attempts to bring the other into his game resemble the struggles of a gnat against an elephant. The patient then falls into a more or less embryonic state and assumes the role of the son before the sadistic father of the primitive horde, or of the child before the all-powerful mother. He can never succeed in reversing the roles and thus in revealing the specificity of the game, and this leads to an endless process of unbeing in which the diminished patient enacts his part in the pleasure of annihilation.

At the opposite extreme, the patient thinks only of devouring the analyst. Absorption will indeed occur, but without any results, because the analyst will attempt the impossible task of finding any independence whatsoever, and he will remain paralyzed.

In another case, the analyst is an old hand at analysis and is always quite invulnerable. The patient cannot make the right moves in order to get the game started because the distance to the analyst is simply too great. Nothing happens, and this impasse can last for years.

On the other hand, the patient's obsessional and perverse defenses might be so effective that he never risks lowering his guard. His need of the other's nonexistence is conveyed only through repeated complaints, a form of demand in which one is so little engaged that one's true nature and reasoning never appear.

At one time or another, every patient and every analyst can adopt these different positions. The right distance is never something on which the analyst can count. At best, it is a point that one passes and repasses, each time using the occasion to make another differentiation.

The analyst's errors are not only inevitable—it is impossible for him to choose the right distance—they are indispensable to the progress of the analysis.[7] As we have seen, if it is not taken, nothing happens (because the patient can not unfold the absurdity of which he dreams), but if it does not slip away again, there is no possibility of analyzing this dream. Faced with a vain reiteration of the game, one must little by little separate the two identical terms that constitute it in order to create a succession of events. If the nonrelation is called archaic or prehistoric, it is only in a limited sense, since by definition it escapes time and cannot properly be made part of a history. One cannot even say on this subject what Freud said regarding a mother-daughter relation, that is, that it belonged to the obscurity of an "especially inexorable repression,"[8] comparable to the Minoan-Mycenean era in relation to classical Greece, for the mother-daughter relation belongs to history as much as Crete belongs to Minos, and Peloponesia to Mycenae. The game of the other finally gains nothing by being characterized as archaic, as if it were a beginning, or as prehistoric, as it it were from a time before history. It is preferable to define this myth as atemporal and ahistorical, as a phenomenon that escapes temporality. It is even difficult to speak of repetition in relation to it, above all in the sense of a past action as Freud uses it, since we are concerned here with an indefinite recommencement that brings nothing and produces nothing, with a simple reiteration that always begins again in the same state. The objective of the analysis is therefore to fall into the time of this ahistorical nonrelation, which is only possible if the analyst, while playing the game, dismantles its rules with the patient.

To tell the truth, the most controversial question about analysis, if one looks into what is currently being said, is not how to get out of the game of the other, but why to enter into it in the first place. There is no doubt that today, especially among British psychoanalysts, one no longer shares the opinion of Freud, who advised only to guard against the countertransference, that is, the feelings and thoughts brought on by the patient's influence. The problem here is not the eventual use of the effects of this influence in order to make better interpretations, but the conception of the analysis as partly situated within the discourse, in a relation of forces. Such a conception will not fail to appear absurd at first, since the discovery of analysis consisted precisely in avoiding the confrontation that is found at the beginning of hypnosis and since the long detour through discourse and the positioning of the analyst as one who listens to and undoes a closed discourse aimed precisely at avoiding the short circuit that provokes the symptom in the life of a relation. One has seen, I hope, that there are no major difficulties, that an analysis through language is enough, as long as the transference does not appear as such, as long as it remains a secret motive force capable of bringing to an end the discursive dysfunctions in which the subject is caught. But one has also seen that the transference can reappear as a decisive obstacle to the continuation of the treatment. Freud says that the patient exchanges one illness for another, a neurosis for a transference-neurosis, from which one cannot emerge. It is to confess that one has followed a long road only to come back to one's point of departure, only to run into this strange force that was the principle of the treatment. It is to recognize that the transferential relation is more powerful than all the work of analysis and that the latter, despite appearances, cannot make a dent in it.

It is a question, not of denying the importance of the word in psychoanalysis, but of wondering if the patient's eventual transformations in analysis are not due to something other than the effect of the word, that is, if the transference is curable through the play of words rather than through the play of the transference itself, which would have words as its medium: *in this hypothesis, it is not the word that liberates one from the direct confrontation between unconscious minds and bodies; rather, it is the word that makes it possible.* Can the illness of communication be effectively treated through the means of communcation? Does the fact that every human reality is impregnated with language mean that it all arose from language? Can man/woman be reduced to a being who speaks (*parlêtre*)? That is what one does when one makes language, under the rule of the signifier, the god who comprises all things. Rehabilitating language in analysis should not lead inevitably to a sort of assimilation of the other factors into language.

Let us grant that neurosis is a failure of symbolization. One can then ask what forces are capable of holding language at bay. What is so much stronger than language that it can inflict language[9] with distortions in which the individual's relation to himself and to others becomes impracticable or is even annulled, as in psychosis? Will someone answer by saying sexuality? Certainly not, since whatever is opposed to the functions of language is equally opposed to sexual functions. Sexuality, which establishes and supposes sexual difference, can easily be applied to the discontinuous and alternating structure of language. Let us hypothesize that the adversary of language and of sexuality would be located in the game of the other, which is also the passion of the one, for which the condition of mute and masturbatory autism would be the consummate image. From this perspective, the neurotic, that failed autist, would be someone who, luckily, would always insufficiently resist the necessity to speak and the need for sexual relations.

Before going further, this is a good occasion to get a better sense of this game of the other or this passion of the one. When Freud describes the unconscious (the system Ucs.) as having the features "exemption from contradiction, primary processes (mobility of investments), atemporality, and replacement of external by psychical reality,"[10] he gives us only negative definitions, which make the unconscious into a pure reversal of the conscious system,[11] that is, a system of reference opposite to the one in which we say we live: absence of negation, of determination, of time, of space, of relations to others, since external reality has disappeared, and, consequently, absence of relation to self. Regardless of what some people think, the Freudian unconscious comprises no positivity. It is not surprising that a few lines later Freud says that the unconscious processes "cannot in themselves be cognized and are even incapable of existing." They are supposed purely as a limit, in such a way that their alliance with preconscious and conscious processes can account for phenomena like the dream or neurosis, which are at once temporal and atemporal, in relation and in nonrelation, where yes and no are intermingled, and which rely on external reality even in the act of dismissing it. In the perspective of the argument of this chapter, this limit could be characterized as the initial myth of the identity of life and death. Freud expressed it elsewhere, by way of evolutionary theories, without being truly able to integrate it into the analytic experience, as the tendency of the living to return to an inanimate state.

To confuse, as analytic literature so quietly does, the dream processes or the fabrication of neurotic symptoms with unconscious processes is to fail to recognize the specificity of the hypothesis of the unconscious as a pure limit, unknowable and nonexistent; it also produces a number of false problems and provides solutions that resolve nothing. To assert, for example, according to the Lacanian adage that "the unconscious is structured like a language" is to confirm several untimely and imprecise propositions.[12] One begins by admitting that condensation and displacement are unconscious processes, although Freud was careful to call them signs (*Anzeichen*),[13] that is, indices or even symptoms of primary processes, because they are already a composite of the unconscious, the preconscious, and the conscious; then one identifies condensation and displacement with metaphor and metonymy; then all that remains is to generalize and take the figures of rhetoric as a whole as a model of the unconscious processes. One has thus given a status to the unconscious that it certainly never had in Freud (and for good reason), but one also gets entangled in excessive claims about the extent of the importance of language in analysis. However, if one stands by the strict hypothesis of the unconscious as a limit of the knowable and the existent, which is not structured and in fact marks the limit of language itself, then the distortions that are undergone by language and by sexuality in the neuroses and psychoses will be understood as unstable compromises, of varying degrees of intensity, between on the one hand, the force of language and sexuality and, on the other hand, the force of this limit, that is, the hypothetical or mythical site of the confusion of opposites, of the absence of negation, of unreality, of the lack of a separation between life and death.

We prefer to leave the metapsychology aside in order to consider some clinical problems. One of the forms of the game of the other, more frequent with men than with women, appears in what Anzieu has named the paradoxical transference.[14] The patient puts the analyst in the position of not being able to intervene, or more precisely, his intervention received an implacable reply that forces him to make another attempt that receives another implacable response. The analyst then succumbs to the same double impediment as the patient, because the latter is sent back by his interlocutor, in everything he attempts, to the equally impossible opposite of everything he has been able to say or do. He is caught between two terms that seem to be contradictory but are put in place in order to produce a radical inhibition in him. This has little to do with the difficulty of the obsessional neurotic to choose between two equally attractive possibilities neither of which he wants to lose. It does, however, resemble the state to which the psychotic is reduced, because his every word or action is disqualified in advance; he cannot escape from the identity of contraries.

The correlative of this position is the unendurable character of every loss. If the continuity of space is not perfect, if it is not without gaps, the whole of existence is threatened. The psychoanalyst's attention must be at once total and uninterrupted in order to ensure that the patient does not receive the impression of a definitive loss, of a fall into emptiness. It is not a question of the analyst's maintaining his wavering attention and inadvertently getting something through to the patient other than what is said or passed over in silence. It all happens as if two bodies were present and the surface of these bodies were unrolled on a single plane, so that there is a total adhesion between the two. Inadvertence is the moment when one turns away from the other and when his own surface is rolled up on him while detaching itself from the other. This turning away, this detachment, in the spatial sense of the word, this coming unglued, is inadmissable for those whom we encounter more and more often in analysis and whom one could call the "borderline cases," not only because they are at the borders of psychosis but because they are at the limits of existence or of its extinction.

There are other transpositions of this passion of the one alone. The hysteric, for example, will make both the demand and the response in relation to another. She desires at once for the other and for herself. She cannot endure the resistance of the other's desire; she imagines it, then produces it and carries it out, all the while complaining that the other cannot keep to himself and obviously has no consideration for her. She cannot imagine that her love is not the only law of the other, which reduces every other preoccupation to nothingness, but at the same time she demands the independence of the other, who obviously submits only to his own desire. She does not tolerate failure in love, which is why she has resolved the question of the other before it has been posed, thus signaling her failure, which remains totally incomprehensible and even strange to her.

The preceding remarks will surely elicit the objection that all the ostensible difficulties that you find in psychoanalysis are the result of your having reduced it to a dual relation, while it has been long established that it functions only when a third term is called in, the Other which is the signifying function (of language). This objection is doubtless pertinent if one has in mind the aim of the analysis or its culmination in the best of cases, but it is beside the point if the major obstacle to overcome is precisely the fact that there is no other. By getting overly excited about criticizing the dual relation, one fails to take account of the fundamental question, namely, that there are not really two individuals present, the analyst and the patient, that there is only room for one, that the sameness of the minds and the unity of the bodies is so pervasive that it is no longer even noticed. One must avert the uncanny process through which one fails to perceive the sameness. If only there were a dual relation, all the questions would be resolved, resolved in advance, and psychoanalysis would doubtless no longer be needed.

What becomes of language in the face of the assertive power of the one alone? It can only be reduced to a pure uninterrupted presence. In extreme cases where it appears in the pure state of the power of sameness, it is radically rejected as memory in order to become extrapolated as knowledge in the present. The patient says everything at once, he keeps all the words on an indefinite plane, or he writes incessantly in order to get it all down and to make sure that nothing is missing. If, in what would be the opposite case, he becomes silent—but in fact there is no link between one case and the other—it is in order to abolish space and the word so that the absence creates a pure emptiness between the other and himself. In benign cases, speech proceeds without direction and inconsistently; it slides without catching on to anything and without any effect on the sameness that is preserved and protected by chatter. The patient says anything whatsoever, and free association becomes an impregnable rampart against modification. The effective use of the word would suppose the establishment of a differentiation that is not of the order of language and that cannot be made to appear.

If it is true, as Lacan decisively emphasized, that psychoanalysis unfolds in the medium of language, this can only make us forget that its practice demands minimal conditions that are far from always being fulfilled, that it collides with forces that can hold it at bay, that it presents itself as a borrowed force. The certainty that language impregnates everything human, that man is a "being who speaks," that nothing in our world escapes the mark of language, should not be confused with the conviction that language is capable of making everything human submit to it, that it can hold back drives, impulses, the repetition-compulsion, perhaps even death as well, that is, that its force is limitless and that it is enough to bring it into play for every other force to be able to reenter its orbit. Because a great many psychoanalysts today do not distinguish the fact that man is subordinate to the signifier from the belief that everything in him is mastered by the signifier, they can blithely let it be understood that an analysis pushed far enough or lasting long enough will be able to overcome all obstacles that that the patient will finally be "confronted with the primary signifier" in order to attain "absolute difference."[15] If this were true, there would be no need to fear surreptitious slippages or protracted confusion.

But it is not at all clear that Lacanian theory does not end up in the same impasse that Freud encountered, as we saw in the preceding chapter: the play of free association does not succeed in undoing the force of the transference that was already the force of hypnosis, that is, the force arising from the connection between the ego ideal and the subjection or loss of subjectivity. If by chance the use of language in psychoanalysis ended in practically the same result, it would be the occasion to pose some radical questions on analytic method.

We would doubtless need a great deal of space in which to develop texts that are so difficult to grasp that a simplistic presentation would only make their refutation trivial. The last few pages of Lacan's seminar on *The Four Fundamental Concepts of Psychoanalysis* are exceptional in this sense, since they can be approached somewhat more directly.

At first Lacan has some fun with the *liquidation* of the transference (a term that Freud does not use, preferring the words *solution, dissolution,* and *destruction*). To liquidate the transference would be "to liquidate the unconscious."[16] Quite right: there will be a transference as long as there is an unconscious. But that is to play on words in order to create confusion, for here it concerns the transference to the analyst. Under the pretext that there will be a transference, he wants to make us believe that the transference to the analyst can be maintained, which is something quite different. Freud, in any case, was rather alarmed at the duration of the transference and, with untiring insistence, made its dissolution the obligatory endpoint of the treatment.

The argument on behalf of maintaining the transference is, to say the least, surprising: "It would be all the same if the subject who is supposed to know, supposed to know something about you, and who, in fact, knows nothing, should be regarded as liquidated, at the very moment when, at the end of the analysis, he begins at last, about you at least, to know something. It is therefore at the moment when he takes on most substance, that the subject who is supposed to know ought to be supposed to be vaporized." This passage reveals a troublesome slippage of the subject who is supposed to know, whom Lacan elsewhere calls the supposed subject, into someone who knows, and then into the analyst himself. Following Lacan's line of thought, one would think that at the end of the analysis the supposition takes a form such that, and in consequence of which, the analyst's knowledge appears null and without interest, in order that the patient can know something. This much can be deduced from Lacan's account of "the permanent liquidation of that deception by which the transference tends to be exercised in the direction of the closing up of the unconscious." But it is precisely this liquidation that must be repeatedly put into effect it is to be permanent, linked as it is to the hypothesis of the unconscious. In order to justify the preservation at the end of the analysis of the link to the analyst who knows, Lacan proposed a liquidation that cannot take place but that is of a different order. This link seals the definitive closure of the unconscious, since the subject who is supposed to know, quite to the contrary of what went on with the one who knows, is the condition of analytic work.

This is not a minor point, for it is through this link to the one who knows that the process of identification, which Lacan discusses next, will be put into operation and maintained. The effect of identification will be to establish the analyst and patient in a relationship of reciprocal destruction which Lacan expresses superbly: "The patient says to his partner, to the analyst, what amounts to this—*I love you, but, because inexplicably I love in you something more than you*—the object petit a—*I mutilate you.*" And at the other extreme: "*I give myself to you*, the patient says again, *but this gift of my person*—as they say—*Oh, mystery! is changed inexplicably into a gift of shit*—a term that is also essential to our experience." Through these formulations, Lacan presents the *objet petit a* "in a more syncopated way." Let us consider what is involved here, for there is nothing mysterious about it. If the patient says that he makes a present of shit for the analyst, in his role as analyst, it is in order to please or displease him. It is therefore not only the analyst who is put in the position of the *objet petit a* but the patient as well. Even though the statements are put in the patient's mouth, they should also be put in the analyst's mouth. Each one of them loves and mutilates, since if the analyst were not taking part in it, he would not let himself be mutilated. Likewise, each one gives and receives a gift of shit. One cannot fail to recognize in these lines the transposition of what Freud describes as the essence of hypnosis and the state of being in love which was earlier assimilated into the transference: the relation to the ego ideal, which is occupied by the hypnotist, produces the fascination, the paralysis, the subjection, and the loss of subjectivity. While Lacan insists on the reduction of the analyst to the position of the *objet petit a*, Freud sees only the effects of the relation upon the patient. In the same way, Lacan veils the coarseness of the words *paralysis* and *subjection* behind phrases such as "caused as a lack by *a*" and "to recognize himself at this point of lack";[17] such phrases change nothing, but only give the patient the certainty that his mutilation or his transformation into shit is a glorious event. In any case, what should be retained from all this is that Lacan's *objet petit a* is the obligatory correlative of Freud's ego Ideal.

A few lines later, Lacan explicitly rejects an expanded conception of the end of the analysis: "Any analysis that one teaches as having to be terminated by identification with the analyst reveals, by the same token, that its true motive force is elided. There is a beyond to this identification, and this beyond is defined by the relation and the distance of the *objet petit a* to the idealizing capital I of identification."[18] At first glance, one believes that this explains why the end of the analysis is the accentuation of the transference. On second glance, one sees that Lacan has only uncovered the hidden side of identification, which psychoanalysts silently pass over, that is, the effect upon the patient—and, reciprocally, upon the analyst—of the identification with "the idealizing capital I," which is the *objet petit a.* For one instantly sees that there is no distance between the capital *I* and the *objet a*; they are only two contrary and reversible aspects of the same reality. To mutilate the other or to be shit for him both of which occur in two directions, is to take successively or simultaneously the place of *I* and of *a.*

On the next page, Lacan tries to establish the difference between hypnosis and transference:

> To define hypnosis as the confusion, at one point, of the ideal signifier in which the subject is mapped with the *a,* is the most assured structural definition that has been advanced.
>
> Now, as everyone knows, it was by distinguishing itself from hypnosis that analysis became established. For the fundamental mainspring of the analytic operation is the maintenance of the distance between the I—identification—and the *a.*
>
> In order to give you formulae-reference points, I will say—if the transference is that which separates demand from the drive, the analyst's desire is what brings it back. And in this way, it isolates the *a,* places it at the greatest possible distance from the I that he, the analyst, is called upon by the subject to embody. It is from this idealization that the analyst has to fall in order to be the support of the separating *a,* in so far as his desire allows him, in an upside-down hypnosis, to embody the hypnotized patient.

This crossing of the plane of identification is possible. Anyone who has lived through the analytic experience with me to the end of the training knows that what I am saying is true.[19]

Hypnosis would be defined as the confusion between capital *I* and *petit a*, while the transference would separate one from the other. Nothing is less certain than whether or not I have succeeded in showing in the preceding remarks that the capital *I* and the *petit a* would engender one another reciprocally (as two figures in the game of the other) and that "the idealizing capital I" or the "ideal signifier" or the "ego ideal" (for these terms are interchangeable) brings along as its shadow the waste, the shit, the object that falls. Besides, this is just what Lacan himself explicitly says here, by asserting that the psychoanalyst, after having been the capital *I*, comes to embody the *a* and takes the place of the hypnotized subject. To let it be understood that the transference is "an upside-down hypnosis" resolves nothing, for then, since the analyst is a hypnotized subject, the patient would embody the capital *I*, which is precisely what must be avoided. But beyond that, already in hypnosis, for anyone who knows how to read it, the positions are reversed, and the hypnotist no less than the hypnotized subject is in a state of paralyzing fascination, since suggestion, as Freud demonstrated, goes in two directions. Lacan senses that his argument will not suffice, since at the end he is obliged to appeal to the testimony of his patients, who know that what he says is true, that the "crossing of the plane of identification is possible." This appeal to witnesses is not only a confession of the failure of the theoretical argument that precedes it; it carries no conviction, since by definition, no one is more deeply involved in the game of the capital *I* and the *petit a* than the patient who has become a pupil and disciple. Freud already observed that the production of the pupil and disciple signals the interminability of the treatment and represents a typical case of suggestion.[20]

The merit of Lacan is to have brought to light what otherwise would have gone unperceived. And as if it were not clear enough, he ends this seminar by recalling the "drama of Nazism," for which "no meaning given to history, based on Hegeliano-Marxist premises, is capable of accounting." Psychoanalysis is capable of accounting for it, because psychoanalysis knows that "there are certainly few [who] do not succumb to the fascination of the sacrifice in itself—the sacrifice signifies that, in the object of our desires, we try to find evidence for the presence of the desire of this Other that I here call *the dark God.*"[21] These final remarks come at just the right place to give their full weight to the reflections on the transference. If psychoanalysis can understand "the holocaust, the drama of Nazism," it is because it knows that in the transference there is no distance between the capital *I* and the *petit a*, between the desire of this Other and the subject, because one discovers there "desire in its pure state, that very desire that culminates in this sacrifice, strictly speaking, of everything that is the object of love in one's human tenderness." When Lacan, in order to conclude, affirms that "the analyst's desire is not a pure desire," one wonders why. For the "desire to attain absolute difference" through the subject's confrontation "with the primary signifier" can only be the desire of subjection, of annihilation, of the abolition of all difference, since difference is relative or else it does not exist, and "the love without limits" that then arises cannot be differentiated from death, which at best is known by mystics and at worst by psychotics and which would orient psychoanalysis either on the side of an initiatory process or on the side of brainwashing.

In any case it is sufficiently evident that the Lacanian theory of the transference, which should protect us against the errors of an idealizing identification—the principle of hypnosis—leads on the contrary toward every possible development of this form of identification, which at least reveals the errors in all their crudity and even cruelty. We find ourselves back before the same problem: the transference is not only the place where the most archaic sado-masochism emerges but also the occasion for its reproduction; there is an intimate structural connection between these two functions. The Lacanian theory has given language a privileged place in psychoanalysis: this theory may deliver us from the conceptual indigence so customary in this field; it may lead us to Baroque splendors. If one undoes some of its sophisticated constructions and if one ceases to be dazzled by its radiance, one again comes upon radically unresolved questions that will be very difficult to solve. It is at least preferable to perceive them as they are rather than to forget them by multiplying the detours; by constructing detours that lead back to the difficulty at the beginning, but without altering it, we are able, having once forgotten the difficulty, to confront it with a forcefulness renewed by our former misapprehension.

How can we get away from the *there is no other, there is only room for one*? How can we really make sure there are two? Not by appealing to a third, because the appeal to a third always supposes that two are already there, which is precisely what is in question. Doubtless the reference to a third is a clever procedure which enables the analyst to avoid the game of the other, to stay out of the relation and to remain invulnerable. But above all the appeal to a third realizes the illusion of the one; it hides the nonexistence of two by letting it be believed that these two are at once surpassed and preserved, while it is only the pretense of having established a relation. There certainly appear to be two separate and distinct individuals, but that is not true for the unconscious, for the utopia that is the limit and the force of psychical life. This could be expressed in the following way: *the principle of the life of the relation, its motive force and its source, is that there is no relation.* One finds oneself in the pre-linguistic, pre-Oedipal state (without temporal signification), or well within language and Oedipus (without spatial signification), in the sense that language has separated nothing and there were never two parents, only one, whose body is the only body or whose body has been abolished. Let us say it at once without a lengthy overture: there can be two only if following the one there have first been four.

One must give extended attention to the most archaic if one is to have a chance to get out of it; otherwise, the analyst develops on this misunderstood basis a construction that, while appearing to work upon it and reduce it, will do nothing but reproduce it. Some analysts, especially in the Anglo-Saxon tradition,[22] have grasped both the undeniable importance of this desire for fusion among certain patients, which places those patients at the limits of psychosis, and the necessity to account for it in the treatment by trying to find some solutions.

Some think that in order to respond to this primitive need, the psychoanalyst must play the role of the good mother. But this could only reinforce the need for fusion by beginning its realization. To tell the truth, since this need for fusion is ambivalence itself, the good mother is the one who sanctions the fusion by devouring her child; she is thus immediately transformed into the bad mother who thrusts the patient into a feeling of guilt. One then settles into an indefinite alternation between gratification and frustration. There are indeed four elements then—the good mother, the bad mother, gratification, and frustration—but that does not permit us to leave the field of atemporal symbiosis.

It is, however, from these four terms that temporalization, the first condition (or consequence) of every relation, is able to occur, at least in its most elementary mode. If symbiosis is indefinite, it is because each of its moments annuls the others. There is no succession because during the time of rejection everything concerning the act of being devoured is forgotten, and during the time of fusion there is no longer any trace of isolation. If psychoanalysis, through the intermediary of the analyst, could become the site of a first act of remembering, the four terms, that is, the two figures of the analyst and the two states of the patient, would no longer each be devoted to disappearing in order to bring about the appearance of the other; they could begin to exist together and to endure one another. The pure appearance-disappearance would become a genuine succession and alternation and would therefore be in time, or more precisely, would create time. Everything could then be multiplied by two: if one does not forget, the two figures and the two states appear as the opposite of one another in successive time or as the stable products of their opposites at any given moment. This crossing over is generalized. One can therefore say that the first distance is the simultaneity of the double reciprocal relation, or that the first temporalization is the extrapolation in space of the elements of the reciprocal relation.

But what are the conditions under which this first emergence out of symbiosis is possible? First, as we have said, one must let oneself become involved in it. A psychoanalyst who is locked into his role as analyst, who never lets himself move or be moved, who never deviates, either for the other or for himself, from his impassibility or from his insensitivity, which is what Freud recommended, will probably never see the appearance of this ahistorical nonrelation and will certainly never be able to make it appear. He will not be able to recognize that not only are the fascination of symbiosis and the need for annihilation experienced by his patient but he himself abundantly participates in them.

In the course of the analysis, one must be seized by the flux and reflux of symbiosis, but one must also be attentive to it and thus find one's position by keeping a part of oneself outside the atemporal and despatialized comings and goings. The right distance, at which the psychoanalyst does not yet know how to place himself, will be situated between the moments when he is seized by the flux and reflux and those during which he is released from it, either because he is registering them or because he is awkwardly resuming his role as analyst; these are moments during which he becomes a pure representative, a pure sign, of a world which no longer functions on a symbiotic mode, and which the patient perceives as inaccessible but as still having an existence and its own substantiality.

One is again in the presence of four terms: the analyst is seized or detached; the patient is here and elsewhere. This double duality is radically different from the duality that constitutes symbiosis, since the passage from the latter to the former has nothing to do with symbiosis. In order to prevent this passage, the patient may, for example, begin to complain repeatedly that he cannot attain fusion, but he is careful to leave the analyst outside this demand. He addresses the demand, not to the psychoanalyst, but to some other man or woman or even to a child. Psychoanalysis is then no longer the place where the desire for fusion is played out, and the words that are said there are no longer anything more than chatter, because since the analyst was never seized by the flux, his detachment is void of meaning and power. The necessary condition for something to happen (and of course at the same time the greatest risk) is that the psychoanalyst becomes the indispensable other.[23] If not, the essential things are played out on another scene cut off from all possibility of interrogation, because the partner who is then chosen (outside the analysis) practices the game of the other in an identical way, without any possibility of detachment. The transference is not strong enough to seize the patient's existence during the analysis, and not having been properly directed, the drama can neither be tied together nor unraveled.

It also can happen, on the contrary, that psychoanalysis becomes the site of such an unexpected regeneration of symbiosis that the patient's life becomes possible because of it. On the analyst's couch, he plunges into purifying waters and thus becomes able to endure normal life and external reality outside his sessions. Speech in analysis will be chatter that has only the appearance of analytic work but will subtly refrain from touching upon those elements that would risk threatening this blissful state. The transference responds so well to the demand for fusion that it is desirable to maintain it indefinitely. The analyst's intervention risks either never being understood or being understood so well that it will be deactivated in advance.

In such cases, the word is not automatically effective. Its force and its weight depend upon the way the transference is situated. If for any reason whatsoever the game of the other unfolds without involving the analyst, either in speech or in silence, on his own part or on the patient's, then the result will be exactly the same: it will be null and void. If the opposite were the case, the significance of speech would consist essentially in the fact that it defines the respective positions between doing and saying or of one's becoming the other. Masud Khan provides a remarkable illustration of these ideas.[24] Nothing is possible as long as the patient does not make the analyst enter into the battle of devouring energies and hate. Through his "bodily attention" the analyst resists absorption, and after a while his resistance enables the patient to speak his hate and to show the analyst its means and ends. The counter-transference is not, therefore, a mixture of feelings and attitudes. It is first the acceptance of confrontation and at the same time the refusal of the game of the other; afterwards, if the right remark comes from the patient, it becomes the verbal expression of the respective positions in which the patient has placed the analyst and in which the patient himself is placed. It is never a question of more or less emotional outpourings. *The moment of detachment is the putting into words of the moment of seizure.* Here, truly, saying is doing. The word puts into effect a distance in relation to symbiosis; it emerges from the seizure in proportion to its involvement. The word is released from the grasp of symbiosis because the word is the result of symbiosis, to the extent that the word expresses symbiosis in a singularly adequate way that departs from any well-known generalities. Language can thus effect a separation in the ahistorical if it takes it into account, obviously, but also if it derives its force from that ahistorical state. One could say that words are all the more effective when they struggle against the silence that attempts to suppress them. This silence in psychoanalysis is none other than "the unknowable and non-existent unconscious." It is perhaps in this context that one could interpret Freud's remarks on working-through, which are significant only if we understand them to mean that working-through is necessary in the treatment after the transference has been revealed as the carrier of the ultimate threat.[25]

We again find ourselves before four terms, but now they are indeed different. Each of the protagonists is at once the one who has been caught in the game of the other and the one who was unable (the patient) or did not want (the analyst) to catch the other. A qualitative change has occurred, because the act of getting caught, instead of remaining an indistinct process, unfolds in terms of particular spatial and temporal functions. And from that point, the figure of the analyst is multiplied into as many points of identification as the patient can discover with figures of his own life. This is the return to the plural transferences, which Freud spoke of and which have constituted the individual's personal history.[26] The patient's archaic unconscious statement was made in order to reach the other in such a way that there was no relation; language was there used as a contrary force in order to destroy space and time. It is this attempt to reach the other that must be worked-through, elaborated, particularized, differentiated, in order to produce distanciation and a return to temporality.

If one works at it, one may see language as the third element that permits the departure from symbiosis, on the condition that one keeps in mind that this third element can only take effect as a doubling of the respective positions already in place, that is, as the preliminary deployment of the four. If the analyst had not effected a separation in the midst of the immediate transference,[27] there would never have been a mediated transference and therefore there would never have been a way out of hypnosis. But one could just as well assert that sexuality is the third element, for symbiosis is as foreign to sexuality as to language. The assertion that putting the ahistorical nonrelation into words produces a temporal relation could be substituted with the formulation that when the body becomes sexualized, the other becomes possible. It appears as though psychically we have remained fundamentally at an evolutionary stage prior to the stage of sexual reproduction, or that the most secret thing in each of us carries the memory of this earlier stage and tries to return to it, thus blocking sexuality and language—most evidently in psychosis.

This is doubtless a new way to revive the Freudian myth of the return of all life to an inanimate condition. In any case, one encounters in many treatments—not all, obviously—either as an end or as a point of departure, the necessity of putting into operation an initial difference between life and death, of distinguishing one from the other so that they do not immediately join together, an initial detour.

When Freud calls upon the analyst, on the one hand, to make his unconscious into a pure receiver of the patient's unconscious and, on the other hand, to be as impenetrable and insensitive as a surgeon, he is moving in an innovative direction that may have unfortunate consequences, because this new demeanor is meant to make up a deficiency in the analyst's function. This operational receptivity forces Freud, in the logic of his proposition, to suppose an analyst without resistance, perfectly analyzed; he makes him into a being apart who would have a totally transparent unconscious, not marked by repression, which is plainly contradictory. Later Freud recognizes that a completely analyzed analyst does not exist, but for all that, he does not cancel his earlier suggestions. One must conclude that in order to function like that, the analyst must tend toward an unattainable ideal. To get closer to the ideal, the analyst will become more deeply involved in his analysis, but since that has no effect on the fact that the ideal remains inaccessible, he is forced, in his practice, to conduct himself before the patient as if there were no obstacles. The pursuit of his analysis, moreover, will then be simply the alibi that will permit him, while awaiting what never arrives, to play the role of the ideal, to put himself in this position in order to be able to work. Incapable of identifying with a pure function that, by definition, cannot be embodied, he is left only to imitate an ideal through his conduct, which is caricatured with the well-known answer for everything: I'm not really involved in it, so it's your problem. The telescoping of conduct and function, which is the logical consequence of the premises posed above, submits both of them to the category of the ideal: the demeanor gives the ideal an existence; the function is reduced to the condition of transcendental possibility that passes into practice under the form of a subject who is supposed to be analyzed.

In support of his argument, Freud used the comparison to the telephone: the voice transformed into electric waves goes from the transmitter to the receiver, which retranslates them back into sound. Communication from unconscious to unconscious, which occurs through gestures, intonations, glances, and words, is something we experience everyday; this is not the place to discuss it. Freud's error is in believing that the analyst's unconscious can be a pure receiver and that the message that he deciphers is exactly the one that the patient's unconscious transmitted. In reality, the patient's unconscious is not all there is to decipher: attention must also be given to the unconscious reactions of the analyst. The analyst's unconscious does not receive signals like a microphone or a magnetic tape. The analyst must listen, but from time to time he cannot avoid having to defend himself, because the patient wants to use the analyst as a consumable and expendable object. The analyst inevitably reacts to the patient's actions and statements; these reactions, which are within the scope of the analysis, must be taken into account. To acknowledge that they take place is extremely banal, but the question is to know what consequences are to be drawn from them.

In the expression "the patient's unconscious *and* the unconscious reactions of the analyst," we notice a difficulty in the *and*, the importance of which will be impossible to determine in advance. This coordinating conjunction has, however, the advantage of ridding us of the process of idealization, which is always catastrophic, since the analyst now can no longer boast that he is impenetrable and because if a patient considers him as such, it can only be by virtue of a particular transference (inscribed within the plural) that could be easily analyzed. The patient will very quickly notice if the analyst is taking his distance from this ideal figure and is no longer trying to imitate it. The analyst obviously loses his beautiful mastery (as well as a large part of his power) in this operation; a master, however, is never able to make the analysis move forward an inch: he can only make it regress toward magic and religion.

This *and* not only marks the end of the analyst's mastery, but permits the relation of the two, or more exactly, the four. The analyst learns from his reactions, but so does the patient who provoked them; likewise, what the patient transmits to the analyst to be deciphered is produced partly from the patient's own history and partly in reaction to this particular analyst. These entanglements must be unraveled and even eventually cut so that each one can find something which belongs to him and which he can appropriate or reappropriate for his own. This disentanglement, this unraveling, this cutting, is to be performed at the same time by the analyst and the patient; and it should no longer be supposed that the analyst must be perfectly analyzed, but that he agrees to place himself within the analysis and to yield to it. This is simply to reintroduce the analyst's analysis into the patient's analysis. This could end in total confusion, but the risk must be run in order to prevent the deadly process of idealization from occurring. The analyst, with or without his own analysis, is, in any case, present in the patient's analysis. If possible, it is better to draw the consequences from it.

The collusion between the analyst's demeanor and his function engendered the process of idealization. It is not, however, a question of totally renouncing the behavior imagined by Freud, that is, of putting in parentheses the analyst's subjectivity—impenetrability, unresponsiveness—because it does play a role. Such behavior imitates the unconscious as an unknowable and nonexistent limit in order to create the appearance of a figure of a pure alterity that hears, understands, and sustains everything. The analyst who becomes unknowable and nonexistent forces the patient to place himself in connection with the unconscious as a hypothetical limit and to speak from that position, which would never otherwise happen, since he is caught, like everyone, in the language game of social appearances and pseudo-communication. But this hypothesis of the unconscious has two faces, that of a pure alterity which brings out the improperly named unconscious subject and that of the negation of all alterity, the state of confusion in which there is no other because the subject vanishes into the unknowable and the nonexistent. If the analyst, in an impenetrable and insensitive state, is content to mime the first face of the unconscious and refuses to experience the second, which is its obligatory corollary, the division of these two faces will be made between analyst and patient; and the latter would then be definitively situated at the frontiers of the extenuation of language and sexuality. If, on the contrary, the analyst accepts the second face, he ceases representing the function in order to let himself be affected by the hypothesis of the unconscious. His task is to fill the interspace between them by learning what is happening to him in this precise situation in regard to the patient, so that the patient can also, as a result of this confrontation with the two sides of the unconscious (alterity and confusion), produce his own uniqueness.

The analyst's behavior is therefore a provisional enactment of his function. As soon as this happens, and on each occasion that it happens, demeanor gives way to the analyst's work as determined by the patient's work. One is then obliged to affirm that the analyst is present. Some will cavil at the analyst' "presence" under the pretext that the analyst should only be the representative of the function. But that is to go from Scylla to Charybdis. One then doubtless avoids the ridiculousness of an ineffable and salutary relation, but the analyst who insists on only wanting to be "no one" involves the analysis in a perverse process, where he could put nothing into play, where he would be a pure spectator, but in reality where he would protect himself from getting caught, while remaining content to see the other get caught.

It is certainly not a question of there being symmetry between the positions of analyst and patient, for there is no genuine reciprocity between them. The analyst does not have directly to share his personal history, his personality, or his anxiety, with which the patient has nothing to do; nevertheless, those things are precisely what enter into the analysis through the analyst's conscious or unconscious reactions to what the patient says. All this is necessary, for if the patient speaks to "no one," what support could there be for his plural transferences? He must have an interlocutor as a support for all his interlocutors past and present. On one side, the analyst is parceled out into traits for the patient's multiple identifications; on the other side, as the unique support for the patient, he is the site for the circulation of these identifications and transferences, which enables the patient to overcome his dissociations. For identity is nothing other than the possibility of the passage from one to another of these identifications that mark out the patient's life and that have been the anchoring points of his various drives and impulses. The analyst is not "no one"; he is, one could say, a résumé of the other, since he has not pushed confusion aside and has helped to effect the first separation.

six

the effects of analysis

The things that are in common last the longest. Take the following proposition, for example: psychoanalysis should have subversive effects not only on the individual—that goes without saying—but on society. This sort of statement is certainly aimed at sustaining the morale of psychoanalysts. Those who are in charge of the corporate development of psychoanalysis cannot be reproached for having tirelessly repeated such uplifting sentiments.

A journalist has precisely described how these kinds of statements circulate in the analytic milieu and how they are justified:

> If psychoanalysis has retained, in part, its scent of fire and brimstone and its subversive virtues, it is because through its actions it tends to undermine the structures that uphold the body of society. One must remember that most often psychoanalytic treatments end up, for those who really get into them, by radically putting into question their way of life. How many patients, during their treatment, have left their political party or gotten divorced or changed their profession? How many have abandoned the religious, political, or moral beliefs upon which they had until then built the fragile equilibrium of their lives? One could, of course, attribute these effects to the cunning influence of the psychoanalysts. But it is enough, in order to explain them, to think of the procedure Freud described; the golden rule of which is the absolute freedom of speech. This is the freedom that leads, in many cases, to the crumbling of beliefs and to a creative doubt.[1]

All of that is exactly right, but the question is to know what this alleged subversion consists in and in what instances it has taken effect. Those who, during treatment, abandon their religion, leave their politicaal party, get divorced, or change profession have come to psychoanalysis because they were already in considerable doubt about their values, because their lives, led according to these norms, which were inherited from one social group or another, had already become untenable, because the signposts upon which they relied had already ceased being of service, and because they felt lost. The work of undermining ideals which were chosen earlier because they were recognized by a particular group or environment has already been put into operation. If some ideals still hold fast, it is only by a thin thread of habit and convenience. The society itself or the ambient culture or the spirit of the age has already subverted all that religion, morality, and political parties had claimed to be the true bases of life. Psychoanalysis does not shake these values loose; it simply registers their dissolution or their derivative or borrowed force. Those who undertake treatment ask anxiously how and if it is possible to live among these ruins. Perhaps they do not yet know the answer, and cling to these worm-eaten walls as though to a fortress, but the damage is already done. The role of the treatment is certainly considerable if it succeeds in clearing away a building that has been reduced to ruins but that remains in the sense that any other construction in its place is prohibited.

If society believes that psychoanalysis emits an odor of fire and brimstone, it is doubtless because society cannot tolerate the fact that individuals who renounce its official values are not left in their misfortune and that other individuals, called psychoanalysts, enable these unfortunate disbelievers to find new foundations for their existence beyond the decaying basis of society. The society at large, or at least those who hold advantageous positions, may well think, since there must always be a scapegoat, that psychoanalysis has caused this loss of values; it would nevertheless be comical if psychoanalysts were to accept these accusations in order to regain their former glory, for they would then share the blindness of those in power. In effect, society or culture itself, no longer functioning according to the openly affirmed standards of work, family, homeland, or religion, emptied them of their force and efficacy; society itself spreads the plague. If the bearer of bad news must die anyway, he should at least not take himself for a martyr but only for the necessary victim of an error; otherwise he would display no more lucidity than do his detractors.

It is impossible to underestimate the wrongs and the misfortunes that befell psychoanalysts during fascist regimes. But can one deduce from that fact that psychoanalysis is subversive? A totalitarian government cannot endure anything short of total control; it will infiltrate all social organizations and all forms of public and private life. One always emphasizes the fact that psychoanalysis was tamed in Nazi Germany through the efforts of a certain Dr. Göring, the field-marshal's cousin, but psychoanalysis was not an exception; the same thing happened to every group, whether religious, political, or scientific. And on each occasion the intention was the same: to distort radically the aims of psychoanalysis in order to place them in the service of Nazi ideology. Every family was denounced by its children, who became informers in the widest possible sense. Psychoanalysts obstruct absolute powers, but no more or perhaps much less than do men of the church who cannot tolerate slavery, or a union devoted to justice, or a dedicated student group whose members do not fear death.

Without presuming what is happening in other countries, is it not somewhat rash to assert that in present-day France psychoanalysis is subversive? In an article that tries to demonstrate precisely the opposite position, Serge Viderman writes: "Doubtless one can try to coopt *the psychoanalysts*, but never psychoanalysis; it is fundamentally subversive; it overturns the scale of values and their transmutation."[2] In what way is psychoanalysis subversive if its best products, the psychoanalysts, are not subversive? Where does subversion come from if "since Freud, psychoanalysts have only repeated themselves"[3]? What good is it to separate the Freudian enterprise from its social manifestations or its practitioners— "the psychoanalytic enterprise can only evolve by entirely cutting off its dependence on the name of Freud"[4]— if this enterprise has only produced, as Viderman tells us, so many parrots? The same kind of break should be made in regard to Lacan: "One must radically distinguish the work Lacan produced from the institutions he founded. . . . On the level of institutions, one must consider Lacan as an accident in the evolution of the psychoanalytic movement."[5] The author, who does not want to place any limits on his inquiry (which is not to minimize the interest of his article), seems to be trying to avoid the most disturbing questions. Does not this willingness to distinguish radically the man from the work, and the institutions from the work, reveal that it is precisely the myth of being scientific which has led to the success of psychoanalysis—for the name of the man can be discarded only in genuine science—and that this scientific myth makes psychoanalysis a necessary part of a liberal society? What Viderman thinks is most subversive in psychoanalysis is precisely what is most readily coopted and what, as a consequence, accounts for the fact that the psychoanalysts themselves are coopted.

Psychoanalysis is concerned with what a technological and industrial society by definition relegates to the exterior: the world of the irrational, the world of dreams, madness, impulses, and fantasies. The seductive power of the Freudian myth rests not on the reinsertion of irrational elements into our civilization but on the project of a new rationality, of a new science of the irrational: psychoanalysis will produce a science of dreams; it will make deductions from fantasies and impulses; it will reintroduce slips of the tongue, omissions, and the unintended meanings of jokes into the field of determinism. The Lacanian myth is working in the same direction when it sets as its decisive task the constitution of mathemes, which means the end of pathos, of fantasy, and of the undetermined.

In other words, psychoanalysis produces a myth that does not introduce an alien force into the present system in the hope of overturning it, still less in order to explode it; on the contrary, it produces a myth that in principle domesticates what cannot be integrated into a scientific, technological, rational world and gives it the status of science and logic and thus makes it acceptable. By giving a scientific intelligibility to what was outside the field of science and technology, psychoanalysis at first creates the impression that it is subverting that field, but afterwards it becomes the means of extending science beyond its own limits. In other words, the technological society that rejected dreams, fantasies, and madness into the shadows of superstition, magic, or myth might feel threatened by their reintroduction into its midst. But, because these phenomena, which are constitutive of the human being, have been acclimated to the new formation of society, they can reenforce that society, because they place at its disposal what had, by definition, escaped it and what it therefore risked forgetting, although they were intrinsically necessary to its survival. In a period when science and the society it created risked being enclosed in scientism, psychoanalysis made it tolerable to integrate these foreign and neglected domains into science, but it risked making them dangerous enemies.

To sum up, I propose this formulation: the task of psychoanalysis in modern society is to administer the irrational as scientifically as possible. It is an indispensable task, for no society, not even the most technological, should disregard what is on its borders, what is at its limits, and what risks invading it at any moment. It is an administrative task which obviously comprises an economic aspect. Without the flow of money, the Freudian myth[6] could have no social impact in our society. One could say broadly that psychoanalysts as a whole are a marginal group, unable, whether because of their elevated or their lowly condition, to be integrated into the economic circuit of production; at the same time they are marginals who are reconverted to society through the lucrative detour of managing the irrational (in order to avoid speaking of the unconscious in this context). More particularly, they manage the irrational through the dysfunctions of the dominant class. The Freudian myth, marvelously refashioned by the Lacanian myth, has become at once so convincing and so necessary to the ruling class that the cash flow has been there to sustain this enterprise.

There are yet other developments that would have to be attributed to the connections between psychoanalysis and society at large. In particular, one would have to show how the art of the detour in psychoanalysis, the refusal of any confrontation by returning to another problem, the recognition of inevitable compromises and of their displacement into other more tolerable compromises, including uncensored speech, could well resemble the attempt by our democratic societies to repress all violence and to translate conflicts into a verbal context, in order to transform them into contracts, or to be exact, into compromises. One would probably see in them secret alliances and submission to identical models. In any case, whatever perspective one takes, it is not very likely that psychoanalysis in France is today an instrument of subversion. If it succeeds in permitting some people to live better or less poorly, is it not already valuable? What need is there for it to give itself an air of indigent revolutionary fervor!

We must return to the question posed at the beginning of this chapter, namely, What is the effect of psychoanalytic treatment? This is what happens to a segment of those who go to see an analyst (we will discuss another segment later): they begin an analysis when their religious, political, moral, or psychological convictions and certainties are no longer functional in their roles as signposts and defenses and give way to doubt and anxiety; beliefs, ideals, pretensions, and self-evident truths that formed a system which one could call ideological or symbolic and gave a certain coherence to the judgments that enable us to place ourselves in relation to self and other are exhausted and no longer do the work of organization, differentiation, and autonomization.

While the patient is trying to recover the force and consistency of these diverse referents, the analysis brings forth an underground world of impulses, love, hate, murderous and self-destructive desires, delusions of greatness and of collapse, unspeakable and unforgettable bliss, in such a way that the former ideological or symbolic system appears in the form it has already assumed, that of a useless and burdensome superstructure. I am no longer where I thought I was; I was not where I thought I had been. If one explains this as disillusionment, one will be able to speak of the subversive effect of psychoanalysis. None of the functions of a society or of a well-tempered psyche can present a serious resistance to the force of the unleashed impulses. An overturning of the individual's existence is then put into operation. He must stop preaching a faith he no longer practices, stop arguing on behalf of a project for liberation that has made him ill, stop living with a woman or a man whom he or she had chosen as part of an already too evident neurosis.

But is society threatened by all this? It seems to me that the individuals who have undergone analysis, even if they renounce the obvious and well-known beliefs, nonetheless adhere to a system of implicit values, which still permits a society to function effectively. The patients no longer have a message to transmit or to defend, and they find themselves spontaneously in agreement with their contemporaries, with the indifferent mass of whatever zealous or fanatical persuasion (except where their immediate interests are threatened), around a vague moral of mutual respect between individuals (leave me alone and I will leave you alone) and a search for an unstable equilibrium between a minimum of work and a maximum of leisure, between a minimum of conflict and a maximum of pleasure; the only gods that they cautiously venerate are sex and money.

Psychoanalysis, which undoes all the mechanisms of idealization, secretly rejoins the wishes of a materialist and democratic society, distrustful of everything that is not palpably profitable and supporting an aimless individualism. When one no longer believes in anything in analysis, one inevitably rejoins the petty bourgeoisie, with its small ambitions and its limited satisfactions. In the words of Theognis of Megara (a Greek poet of the sixth century B.C.), *Meden agan.* This was a refined expression for the Greeks, but it could also be the motto of a community where every excess is considered as the effect of an illusory belief: "Nothing superfluous." Psychoanalysis poses a difficult question to the patient: How can one live, how can one continue to exist, when everything—religion, politics, love—has been demystified? There is no other way but to see that everything is relative, to appreciate what happens from day to day, to impose only the most supple limits, but to impose the strictest limits on one's needs and desires,[7] because every excursion outside them would make one fall back on the illusion that one is able to reach the moon.

But it is difficult indeed to live without belief. The difficulty will have to be avoided. Psychoanalysis, which delivers us from every illusory belief, from every eloquent certainty, from every ego-centered pretension, and returns us to existence by letting forces speak that come from beneath consciousness, is certainly something good and beautiful. It is said that there is nothing better in our epoch than the work of demystification, of clearing away ruined ideals, of liberating authentic living forces, so that everyone can find his own path. Permitting others to discover the benefits of the treatment asserts itself as the only possible task. How could one not want to transmit what has been so beneficial for oneself? And this is why one takes up the cause of psychoanalysis, as Freud described it to Karl Abraham.

What happens then has been recounted many times already: all the abandoned beliefs are simply replaced by others that conform more closely to the present culture. But one never notices it oneself. One would not think that belief in the unconscious, in the fulfillment of desire in dreams, in paranoiac melancholy in the child, in the reign of the signifier or the mathemes, required any demystification. For these things do not involve belief or evidence; they are properly and repeatedly proven facts. These facts hold up all the better because the psychoanalysts who consider them as such protect themselves from hearing questions from other psychoanalysts, or better still, from other disciplines.

The remystification of the analytic field is so much more solid and unassailable than its constitution as a closed process of theorization had been. According to Lacan, an analyst is truly an analyst only in so far as he produces another analyst: didactic psychoanalysis would be the only pure psychoanalysis; psychoanalysis would only be intelligible by virtue of the "pass" (a procedure unique to the Ecole Freudienne), through which one becomes a psychoanalyst. Without any doubt, these are exciting ideas, because they push to the extreme certain processes that are unique to analysis but that can also surreptitiously justify a series of procedures which inevitably lead to obscurantism.

To begin with, if the explicit aim of analysis is to produce analysts, one no longer has to pose the question of the dissolution of the transference, for the patient who has become an analyst continues to experience the transference in relation to analytic theory or to the one who has created the theory. The transference is what holds his work and his relationship together. But there is something more: if becoming an analyst is the result and the key of analysis, then analysis has enclosed itself within itself; it becomes an inside without an outside and behaves like a delirious patient who can only speak about himself. Analysis can then no longer examine its relations to society at large; it becomes its own justification if the beliefs it holds no longer appear as such, because they have become only elements, necessities of its own functioning. This circularity of analysis founded on only its own discourse creates a mini-society that increasingly tends to magnify its own importance, since it is true that the values officially proposed by society no longer correspond to its present state and since analytic theory—and the myths it conveys—account for many contemporary phenomena, thus making it much easier to adhere to them. Lacan's genius has unquestionably been to drain diverse cultural currents for the benefit of analytic theory in such a way that there is now something for everyone. Thanks to this subtle game of negation, contradiction, and confusion, he has created the illusion that he had never formed a system of beliefs, which permits him finally to enclose this enormous machine within itself while producing, as an effect of the transference, the believers and the faithful, who are themselves subservient only to the task of creating other faithful believers, who need not admit it to themselves because, on the one hand, their beliefs are part of the available culture and, on the other hand, they claim that their objective is the demystification of this culture. This self-enclosure is an integral function, since it succeeds in creating the illusion that it is only using the procedures of disclosure.

Lacan, it seems to me, has drawn only the most extreme conclusions from certain premises of psychoanalysis. If the result is monstrous, in view of the increasing number of his disciples, at least it has the virtue of alerting us to the extremes to which we can be led, which can be eye-opening to those who care to look. Many terrified psychoanalysts exclaim against the scandal and make it clear that they are not on this path, although they only go halfway down every road and avoid going forward in order not to face an irreparable dilemma. But we are all in the same boat, and it is not a question of opposing one brand of psychoanalysis to another. We cannot even say that the Lacanian model is so pregnant with ideas that everyone can imitate it in his own way, creating more disciples and reutilizing the transference in order to effect and even create the tenuous link to society. One does not imitate; one is only seized, as he is, in the psychoanalytic whirlwind.

With these remarks on the effects of psychoanalysis on groups of psychoanalysts, we come back to the question raised in our preceding chapter, which revealed that the logic of the transference tended to produce both indistinctness and identity; far from accentuating individuation through verbal freeplay, the transference risked dissolving individuation, to the extent and degree that the treatment was followed through, into the sameness of hypnotic sleep, into an atemporal nonrelation, into the indefiniteness of pure reiteration.

Nevertheless, what was said earlier regarding the subversive pretensions of psychoanalysis does not appear to arise from this problematic. The question of the separation of individuals from one another was not posed, either because the analysis concerned patients who in a more or less obvious way remained suited to the culture and the life of society or, an inseparably related reason, because the treatment developed into the type of transference that Freud called "light and unexpressed." So, on the one hand, psychoanalysis has been able to appear entirely circumscribed by language and the word, in which case it was a question of loosening somewhat the connections that were tied too tightly by the present culture, and on the other hand, as a consequence, it has not been possible, because it was not necessary, to look into the very nature of the transference that had not surpassed the limits of sobriety and reason.

But beside those over-cultured people who demand that psychoanalysis lift the weight of the language of society, which they use in order to avoid hearing anything about their desires and impulses, there is a crowd of people who have not really had access to culture and social life. It is as if they were deprived of the common language, as if they were excluded from the human world; the reality of the body, of sex, and of so-called human relations is something that they have never experienced. In these cases, psychoanalysis unquestionably becomes, to use Freud's word, an "*after-education*" [Nacherziehung].[8] Its task is the restoration or even the founding of human relations that have never been experienced, for they are made by retreating from communication through an opening into misunderstanding (*méconnaissance*), through the combination of giving and refusing. In these limit-cases the body is not really closed, not really an outside with an inside, because the difference between the sexes, even if there has been a sexual experience, has not been established, because the word presents itself at the same time as a pure transparency and as total opacity; in these circumstances, the transferential relation, which cannot be repressed, veiled, or held back, appears in its raw state, tends to invade every aspect of the treatment, and becomes the privileged ground of this game of the other.

We find ourselves before a curious paradox: the treatment establishes that from which it is supposed to deliver us. Yet it is immediately obvious that this paradox can be turned around: the analysis proposes to the patient that the exclusionary relation to the human world which he is currently experiencing can become, thanks to the transference, the site of experimentation and work, and the starting point for a transformation. However, such a turnabout does not come on its own; it most often requires very long detours.

The psychoanalyst must first abandon the idea that the transference is the place where the patient remembers his past, in particular his infantile history. The patient's remembering is not even a reproduction of his infantile past; for it is really not a question of a life history in the case of someone who has only lived in those moments, always the same moments, when solitary allpowerfulness and abandonment to the other are indissociably combined. As long as his relation to the other is unarticulated, there cannot be structured space or temporal succession. Still less can language be taken as a stable field in which the misfires would indicate the subject's relation to his unconscious in order to modify it. For language is undone here to the point of becoming a support for anything whatsoever: the ahistorical relation, which is the only mode of existence, takes all the substantiality out of language.

The analyst should expect from the patient not only a temporal regression that takes him back to his earliest memories but a regression beneath the human. If the inhuman is defined negatively by the absence of codified and respected social relations and thus, for example, by savagery and monstrosity, then it is defined positively—the word *nonhuman* would be more appropriate—by the animal, vegetable, and mineral kingdoms. If the psychoanalyst is attentive to this, he will see this kind of regression, not only with psychotics or with those I called "borderline cases" but with neurotics during the particularly crucial moments of their analysis.

Such is the feeling of being devoured by the beast, and the psychoanalyst takes the role of this devourer from whom it is impossible to escape. What is then at stake, for example, is the system of relations between mother and daughter, which is not located at a specific moment in the patient's history, which is not inevitably linked to memories, but results in making the daughter into a child and a woman who is incapable of existing in any form whatsoever in the presence of her mother and who is later destined to disappear when she meets other people. What occurs in the absence of the other is an expansion of the limits of the universe; but in the other's presence what occurs is a disappearance. To the extent that a struggle can be begun between the daughter and the beast, between her, the little animal, and this devourer, her body can begin to acquire independence.

Another way for the patient not to separate from the other is to become a plant, to refuse movement and let himself be moved by the elements, with no concern but to remain fixed in that role. The paitent's coming to see the analyst does not constitute a break in this role; what is important for him is not manifesting any other life but this one during the session, not moving, having roots instead of legs. Through this form of existence, the patient is trying to avert his fear of being abandoned. If the ground proposed by the analyst appears sufficiently stable, the patient will take root in other places, at first very rarely, before a genuine passage from the one to the other can begin.

The patient, however, can also be a stone, the silence of which must be indefinitely endured. Proximity means only a relation between objects. The patient's speech is then reduced to the demand for the recognition of his pure being-there. If something else were expected, he would let it be done, as he gives his body to whoever wants it, thus excluding himself in a void of thought and senses. But the fact that he can be a rock for a long while, since there is a passion in this rock, a passion for water and light, will give him the leisure to animate himself in order to please himself and in his own way.

Why these regressions, regarding the many various meanings of which it would doubtless be necessary to be more specific? They should first be considered as places of refuge. These states provoke considerably enough distance from the human world to make those who choose them feel or consider themselves sheltered. However dependent they may be elsewhere, they find a true autonomy there, a domain, the most withdrawn domain there is, where they never risk being violated or disturbed. But if they come to see a psychoanalyst, it is because they hope to get out of that domain. These regressions then become the proof of it. Just like neurotics who in their first sessions check the lay of the land in order to see more clearly to what point they will be able to risk speaking there without having their words turn on them unexpectedly and murderously, those who present themselves as beasts, plants, or fossils want to know if, in their inhumanity, they will be able to make something heard to the supposed human whom they have approached. Then the path will be opened to their return or their introduction to the country of those who appear as men and women.

It will doubtless be said, however, that all this is madness and that one knows that appeals to the animal, vegetable, or mineral kingdoms often abound in delusions or hallucinations. But does not every analysis that takes speech apart create an experience approaching psychosis? Octave Mannoni has written that "we are all cured psychotics."[9] Would it be incautious to turn this formula around and assert that we are able to cure, owing to psychoanalysis, only if the treatment becomes an experience brought on by psychosis? The treatment involves both a loss of reality and a loss of subjectivity. "If you believe that I am someone," a woman said, "you are grossly mistaken"; or, "I must constantly make an effort in order to give substantiality to things and to people"—words which could express a former state of confusion or which described a perception that psychoanalysis had made possible. These losses are necessary to loosen the contraction of the defenses of repetition, but they entail these regressions in order to avoid (the previously indispensable defenses having been lifted) the possibility of running directly into death. This obliges one to take a long detour through all the past and present forms of this life so that later the body, then sexuality, then language can be reclaimed.

If there are so many suicides in psychoanalysis—I know that the question is very complex and can be approached on other fronts—it is perhaps because analysts do not permit this kind of regression, because they have decided once and for all that one would then have left the proper field of psychoanalysis, since according to the Lacanian adage, the unconscious would be structured like a language, although the unconscious is the undoing of language and the limit of the latter's extinction. To move away from language, not only the preverbal but outside the limit of the human, distinguished by language, to have access to realms where there are only signs or only excitations or simply even sensations that cannot be integrated seems ridiculous and insane. Ridiculous perhaps, but certainly insane. All the same, it is a madness that softens the violence of the un-word (*dé-parole*), of the rupture of syntax, of the appearance of the pure signifier stripped of meaning, a violence that could immediately thrust one into despair and self-destruction.

If there is a risk of death, it is because the patient, dispersed into his speech, finds himself before the "absolute master" without any defense against him, without the possibility of taking refuge someplace where the master would be ineffective. If there is only language, a language of which the subject no longer has any command, the subject is exposed to deliquescence, to the short circuit of the naked truth, which one identifies with nothingness. The individual undergoes decompostion in the abyss of a decomposed language, since he is prohibited from coming out of it. "What I have to say is an accumulation that deserves to be in the dust bin, the short ends of language, mutilated words and sentences." And again, "If I had my say, it would not be like this"; in other words, I am unable to intervene in the words that are spoken. "If this does not stop, there is nothing left but to blow my brains out. That is why I am a stone." If I am condemned to remain on the field of language, if I am unable to go somewhere else into the cries of animals, the sound of plants, or the silence of minerals, there is nothing left but to destroy myself.

I do not think that what appears in outline here is some surreptitious return to Jung—and after all, does it matter? Dogmatists bore me—for it is not a question of gaining access to the archetypes, to a redemptive savior, or to some *gnosis* that provides access to the secrets of nature. No knowledge whatsoever is required; it is rather an extreme retreat from all forms of wakefulness, a plunge into sleep, into the night of all consciousness, a way to find a mode of existence that avoids encountering the human even though that other mode is itself a human supposition.

All of this, in fact, is not so far from Freud's preoccupations, if one is careful to read him freely enough. Since he was always preoccupied with the connections between phylogenesis and ontogenesis, and emphasized that the unconscious could retain the traces of "the earliest and most obscure periods of the beginning of the human race,"[10] then why not also those which preceded the appearance of the human race proper and which were, from an evolutionary perspective, the preparation for it? Moreover, it is at the moment when Freud stops thinking about the transference that he launches into both the descriptions of "The Uncanny" and into the speculations of *Beyond the Pleasure Principle*. It appears as though it were intolerable for Freud to observe that the logic proper to the transference in analysis is at best the reproduction of the same—the mainspring of the uncanny—at worst the disappearance of the other, and that if the transference is to avoid death, it must take the long detour that leads back to the inanimate. One might conclude that at the time that he detached the uncanny from the experience of the transference in order to avoid seeing that the death drive was at work there, he was suggesting the regressions that are necessary to avert the mortal danger contained in the hypnotic and therefore transferential sleep.

A great many threads, perhaps always the same, reappear and are rewoven here. What presents itself again is the connection of analytic treatment to psychosis. At the end of his article "The Dynamics of Transference" (1912) Freud recognized that the development of the transference leads to uncontrollable situations that have all the characteristics of madness: "The unconscious impulses do not want to be remembered as the treatment desires them to be, but endeavor to reproduce themselves in accordance with the timelessness of the unconscious and its capacity for hallucination. The patient, just as in dreams, regards the products of the awakening of his unconscious impulses as contemporaneous and real."[11] From these limit-cases which he describes with precision, Freud is unable to proceed to a radical investigation of his practice of the transference and of his conceptions of analytic treatment. This is why his reflections on the uncanny, telepathy, or the death drive must be reconsidered from another perspective and developed on another level.

It is well known that Freudian psychoanalysis is concerned with neurosis, perversion, and paranoia, all disorders which can tolerate the existence of a society in which there are relations between distinct human beings, but that it has veered away from schizophrenia, where the inhuman is manifest through the nonexistence of all alterity. The reason for this has already been mentioned several times: analytic method must at any price be distinguished from hypnosis, for what is uncovered in hypnosis and in the phenomena of suggestibility is the unstable character of individuation, or, if you prefer, the appearance in each partner of what resembles the diagnosis for schizophrenia.

If one takes into consideration what I have called the immediate transference,[12] which is to be distinguished from the mediated transference, which arises in the linguistic dimension of analysis, one is led to the possibility of an experience that anyone who has dealt with schizophrenics would regard as very commonplace. If it can take place in analysis, not only with borderline cases but also with neurotics, it transpires through the immediacy of communication from one unconscious to another that dissolves the mediations of the word, in a way much like what, according to Freud, happens within the crowd or between mother and child.[13] But the inherent danger of this type of communication provokes defensive reactions, the search for the limits beyond which individuality will be constituted in the refusal of this nonhuman immediacy. Becoming a plant, an animal, or a mineral is to go into the midst of the nonhuman, not to say into an inhumanity where one is overwhelmed by fusion.

These regressions act, then, as an objective and soon as a starting point for the individual's reconstruction, and for the work of reappropriating the things from which individuality is formed but which do not really belong to it. These experiences to which I refer obviously do not take place for everyone, and they rarely occur in a definite order. I regroup them here artificially in order to clarify the argument. If one must make it clear that they have indeed taken place and that they effect lasting transformations, it indicates that they cannot be foreseen and they retain a large part of the mystery of their appearance.

How can we account for what can only be called a birth? Although the transference plays a decisive role, this birth does not occur through the analyst; that is, it was fantasized not as an escape from his body but as an escape from the patient's body. This amounts to a self-production that is concomitant to the impossibility of relying upon any paternal or maternal support: this act of self-creation takes place amidst a generalized deception and with the certainty that everything upon which existence has been based up to now has been an illusion. When the patient, regardless of gender, asks about the psychoanalyst's role, it is in a manner something like "You are not helping me; you are helping the thing create itself." The connection between analyst and patient is recognized then as "a link that separates." The psychoanalyst, who obviously shares the anxiety caused by the loss of habitual referents, discovers in the patient at this moment, before he has transmitted it, a capacity to live under his own forces and, at the same time, that which sustains another existence. This kind of experience is impossible to program and can only be the result of an attitude adapted to the circumstances. If the patient is overwhelmed by what happens, the analyst, in his turn, is gripped by a necessity to appeal to forces that are usually buried. If the link is to come apart in the immediate transference, the analyst—but it is not evident a priori, as one might think—must not be as dependent upon the patient as the patient must be upon the analyst, dependence being well able to accept indifference and cynicism.

I just used the term "force"; in describing the transference and what happens there, it is impossible not to use "force" in a range of intensities. Even if psychoanalysts hardly speak about it and carefully avoid problematizing the question, they cannot help referring to it. For example, they spontaneously refrain from recommending that a patient who has, as they say, a strong personality (even if it is difficult to be precise about it) go to see a spineless analyst (even if there is no scientific definition of *spineless*). The reason is simple: the transference will not take place. And if it cannot occur, it is because the patient will perceive too early that this analyst lacks substance, which is sometimes the case; that is, the patient's own force is too great, and the pressure he exerts or will exert on this analyst at certain very intense moments risks crushing the analyst entirely. This is why some analysts who have difficulties with a treatment send their patient to another analyst. It is always to someone who is stronger, someone who is not only shrewder or more experienced but will better withstand the blow or the shock.

The majority of analysts will shrug their shoulders if they happen to hear such remarks. Still they are necessary if we are to understand the experiences that I am describing. If they are possible, it is due to the immediacy of the transference. This immediacy is effective because it works on a level inaccessible to consciousness, where the processes at work during waking are short-circuited; it thus becomes, like sleep, restorative. Moreover, this immediacy permits the passage of forces from analyst to patient. The analyst must still be differentiated enough not to place the patient in a fusional state from which he cannot escape, but he must not hold himself back, he must not prevent his force from passing to the other, without which he would abandon the patient to his own force, without any relational potential. In both instances he runs the risk of abandoning the patient to an undifferentiation that will dissolve him.[14]

Another common experience in analysis is the progressive constitution of the body itself. As he moves toward differentiation, the patient learns or relearns the important role of the sense of smell.[15] One of the difficulties of the psychotic, and of anyone insofar as he participates in this breakdown, is to think of the body, at the same time and not alternately, as an outside and an inside; it is for him either a pure surface that does not roll up on itself or a pure interior that knows no other dimensions. An odor is something that both penetrates and envelops, that pervades the interior and, as it circles around, forms the exterior. The patient can go from a total absence of odors to a disgust for every bodily odor. It can so happen that this disgust is overcome through the perception of odors coming from the analyst or his immediate environment. A certain alterity is possible at this level. Then a process of relearning sounds, voices, and the sense of touch can be put into operation in order to establish distances and proximities. The body is then able to close upon itself, to acquire a genuine inside that can no longer be reshaped in any way by the others, that is no longer either transparent or empty, but possesses an outside that is also occasionally accessible.

What is striking about this stage is that memories can reemerge, as if the closure of the body enabled the patient's story to be constituted. These memories may be insignificant, but the analytic relation gives them substantiality. At first they are memories of what has happened during the treatment, and they sometimes give the impression of having been invented, as if the patient shaped his own myth little by little. The patient has never experienced this story; it is something that lives in the pure reiteration of all-powerful self-abandon. But due to the analytic relation that is his first story, the patient reconstitutes a past in his own way.[16]

When these conditions have been fulfilled, one encounters the various themes that are ordinarily discussed during the analysis. For example, the question of sex is then posed, often as a consequence of a question about the sex of the analyst. Even among people who have a sexual life, sexual differentiation is not to be assumed. This is well known. It is not rare for patients to affirm to men that they are really male and to women that they are really female, in words, that they are not of one sex only. It is not that they live in a continuously homosexual state, which would be a hasty conclusion, but that in sameness they can avoid posing the question of sex, that is, the question of sexual difference. Sexual differentiation, even if it is biologically assured, can only be psychically assured through social and cultural constructions that always render it uncertain, in spite of all that these cultural and social referents are lacking and will be lacking. They are always deficient in cases of psychosis, and of what there is of psychosis in everyone, which is the part that threatens to bring down the whole structure.

The preceding remarks cannot fail to produce some startled reactions, for what I am proposing is nothing other than a constitution or reconstitution of the ego, and of the body. The aims that are sometimes given to analysis, at least in France, are subtle and refined in quite a different manner. The psychoanalyst should no longer be preoccupied with the cure, under the pretext—and this is something on which everyone agrees—that the cure cannot be aimed for directly, because it is only possible to come to the end of symptoms through long detours. But the search for the cure, which Freud described with the words the "capacity of enjoyment and of efficiency,"[17] is rightly the aim of psychoanalysis, even if at the end of an analysis this capacity does not correspond to the representation that the patient has in mind when he begins his treatment. On several occasions Freud asserts that the "scientific results of psychoanalysis are at present only a by-product of its therapeutic aims, and for that reason it is often just in those cases where treatment fails that most discoveries are made."[18] Some would like to reverse the terms of this proposition and make the therapeutic efforts a by-product of scientific research. And so they do not have to pose the question of how the treatment works and of the decisive role of the immediate transference. When attention is only on the mediated transference, the effects of the immediate transference are ignored, and consequently, the way is open for the production of a fusional and indistinct condition under the pretext that the clearest distinctions have been calculated down to the point of the azimuth. Having done this because one has failed to ask oneself how individuation is established, since it occurs, by definition, in the mediated transference, one prohibits the patient from undergoing the regressions that he must experience in order to find a goal, the possibility of taking refuge in a "no" from everything that encloses and absorbs him in order to realize that he can be a distinct individual.

Moreover, if at the end of this process the ego or the body is reconstituted, it is not in order to produce monoliths. Here one meets what has been described many times. Confronted with sexual difference and the particularity of his own sexuality, the patient experiences the division in language which could be summed up in these words said in amazement: "None if this is being said to me!" The patient who fears separation, a synonym for abandonment, is henceforth able to sustain the certainty that no word, whether or not it has been formulated by the analyst, can comprise the totality of what the patient is or of what he believes he has become. There will always be something left over, and there is no revelation whatsoever to be expected from the other. It is up to each of us to believe our own thoughts and to decide for ourselves on the basis of our understanding, knowing that the other understands them only insofar as he misunderstands them. By learning little by little that he can no more communicate with himself than he can with any other interlocutor, the patient no longer expects any recognition that is not marked by misunderstanding (*méconnaissance*). At this point one can say that the transference has been resolved, because its absorbing mass, which had begun to break up during extreme regression, where nothing or no one could reach the patient where he had withdrawn, is repeatedly broken by the word, which can only find him by missing him.

The specificity of language is evident here with all the force that makes it decisive for psychoanalysis. If it can be functional from now on, it is because at first it was not considered as everything for mankind, even if it impregnates everything human. The difficulty is to make language relative, while as long as it is caught in the direct transference, it is unceasingly absolutized. And the psychoanalyst, when he attempts to theorize, when he claims to have discovered "the historical truth" or to have confronted the patient with "the primary signifier," is only clinging to delusions of infantile all-powerfulness in order to be able to produce, in those who believe him, only more or less latent stages of psychosis. There is no more "truth" than there is primary importance in psychoanalysis: all of that is only a fable for children. It is better for the patient to create his own myths or, if he becomes an analyst, to theorize, to remake his story on the level of a legend, to become singular through the plural characters in his own novel, a bit of the actor, a bit of the author in the theater of life.

seven

the patient: a novelist?

In an effort to discredit the scientific claims of psychoanalysis, Havelock Ellis explained that the technique of free association, the principal lever in the practice of analysis, was to be understood in the context of literary creation. Ellis had discovered that in 1857 a certain Dr. J. J. Garth Wilkinson proposed a new method that enabled him to write a volume of poetry: "'A theme is chosen or written down; as soon as this is done, the first impression upon the mind which succeeds the act of writing the title is the beginning of the evolution of the theme, no matter how strange or alien the word or phrase may seem.' . . . 'The first mental movement, the first word that comes' is 'the response to the mind's desire for the unfolding of the subject.'"[1] Wilkinson had already clearly perceived that "'reason and will . . . are left aside'" and that "you trust to 'an influx,' and the faculties of the mind are 'directed to ends they know not of.'"

If, in response to Havelock Ellis, Freud reasserts the scientific character of the analytic method, because analysis is founded on the principle of psychical determinism, he is still very far from denying filiation between methods of literary invention and free association as it is practiced in analytic treatment. Already in *The Interpretation of Dreams* he had cited Schiller's recommendation to Körner to be attentive to ideas that emerged in isolation and that seemed careless and bold:

> "The ground for your complaint seems to me to be in the constraint imposed by your reason upon your imagination. I will make my idea more concrete by a simile. It seems a bad thing and detrimental to the creative work if the mind of Reason makes too close an examination of the ideas as they came pouring in—at the very gateway, as it were. Looked at in isolation, a thought may seem very trivial or very fantastic; but it may be made important by another thought that comes after it, and, in conjunction with other thoughts that may seem equally absurd, it may turn out to form a most effective link. Reason cannot form any opinion upon all this unless it retains the thought long enough to look at it in connection with the others. On the other hand, when there is a creative mind,

135 / The Patient: A Novelist?

Reason, so it seems to me, relaxes its watch upon the gates, and the ideas rush in pell-mell, and only then does it look them through and examine them in a mass. You critics, or whatever else you may call yourselves, are ashamed or frightened of the momentary and transient extravagances which are to be found in all truly creative minds and whose longer or shorter duration distinguishes the thinking artist from the dreamer. You complain of your unfruitfulness because you reject too soon and discriminate too severely."[2]

This letter by Schiller had been brought to Freud's attention by Otto Rank, which led to its introduction into Freud's text in 1909. But in his polemic with Havelock Ellis in 1920 Freud goes further in his acknowledgment of sources:

Meanwhile it is safe to assume that neither Schiller nor Garth Wilkinson had in fact any influence on the choice of psychoanalytic technique. It is from another direction that there are indications of a personal influence at work.
A short time ago in Budapest, Dr. Hugo Dubowitz drew Dr. Ferenczi's attention to a short essay covering only four and a half pages, by Ludwig Börne. This was written in 1823 and was reprinted in the first volume of the 1862 edition of his collected works. It is entitled "The Art of Becoming an Original Writer in Three Days," and shows the familiar stylistic features of Jean Paul, of whom Börne was at that time a great admirer. He ends the essay with the following sentences: "And here follows the practical application that was promised. Take a few sheets of paper and for three days on end write down, without fabrication or hypocrisy, everything that comes into your head. Write down what you think of yourself, of your wife, of the Turkish War, of Goethe, of Fonk's trial, of the Last Judgment, of your superiors—and when three days have passed you will be quite out of your senses with astonishment at the new and unheard-of thoughts you have had. This is the art of becoming an original writer in three days."[3]

Freud says that he received the volume of Börne from which this text is taken as a present on his fourteenth birthday. Since he no longer has this particular passage memorized, he admits that this could be an example of cryptomnesia, because he has many other memories of the work of Börne, "the first author into whose writings [I] had penetrated deeply."[4]

Acknowledging his debt to Börne, Freud knows very well that there is a long tradition behind it. When he replies to Ellis that "Wilkinson's alleged new technique had already occurred to the minds of many others," he speaks as a connoisseur. However extensive Havelock Ellis's reading may have been, the expression *freier Einfall* ("a sudden free idea"), which is the most precise way to describe the method of free association, cannot resound in his ears as it does in Freud's. Freud cannot doubt for an instant that he is taking up a commonplace of German romanticism and that this same romanticism had indissociably linked, well before him, the *Einfall* ("the sudden discovery of idea, the lucky stroke"), *Witz* ("wit, joke"), and the dream.⁵ As for Börne's admiration for Jean-Paul's style — and nothing in literature presents his mixture of the rambling and the unbridled more exactly, and yet still with that secret unity, than the style that characterizes an analytic session when it stops groping about in chatter and rationalizations — Freud gives us several occasions to observe that he shares it.

More references could be found, but they would add nothing to the conclusion that presents itself, and in Freud's own words: the technique of free association is a technique of invention imported from the field of literature. It is therefore quite natural for the surrealists to find in psychoanalysis something to their advantage, since there is nothing more closely related to Freud's style of writing when he analyzed his dreams than the automatic writing of the surrealists, and if they were the first in France to show an interest in psychoanalysis, there is nothing surprising, for they found it helpful in holding the ambient rationalism at bay. Neither should we be surprised that Freud viewed their approval with circumspection.

For he must hold himself back from being an artist — such a title can only come from adversaries; he wants to be faultlessly on the side of science. He never intended to use Börne's method to become a writer, but to resolve problems posed by dreams or by pathology. His concern in the treatment is not to produce an "original writer" but to effect a cure. Nevertheless, these oppositions or conjunctions could not help being quite as obvious as they appeared at first sight.

Freud's case — and that of psychoanalysts — must be distinguished from those who undergo analysis. Even while using a method that came to him from literature, Freud has in some way overturned or misappropriated the foundations of literary creation. A writer uses his dreams in order to create his work, because he has established that sleep imparts to him materials of a richness, a complexity, a strangeness, to which the waking state has no access.⁶ Like Robert Louis Stevenson, for example, he knows that the *Brownies*⁷ who visit him recount something of his life, that they are, in their fantasy and their gratuitousness, more himself than he is, but he does not take long to recognize it; he goes on from there to weave a narrative, a story, a novel. Freud also continually uses his own dreams to construct his work, and he knows that his dreams are part of his individuality, but his aim is not to produce a literary text from them; it is to ravish their secret, to discover how they function, to take them apart and put them back together like machines. For him, free association is not an occasion to produce a more or less mastered work from the fantasy of the dream, it becomes the means to attack the dream's fantasy in order to explain it and therefore to make it disappear.

Freud places himself at a point diametrically opposite to literature, as close as possible to scientific effort to reduce every possible form of the irrational and the unreasonable in order to determine the exact reasons. These mechanisms that he has ravished from the obscure world of our sleep and our nights, and that he has suggested are similar to those of psychopathological aberrations, will in return enable him better to decipher those aberrations and, so he thinks, to deactivate them and put an end to their effects. From this perspective, Freud is convinced that the treatment is scientific and that it remains the aim of science; and therefore his interest in knowing where the method of free association comes from is only historical or anecdotal, since it has lost all of its literary significance by abandoning the role that literature accords to invention and creation.

But the way of finding a connection to literature can be rephrased as the question of finding out what the role of the treatment is. Is it the dismantling of the psychoneurotic mechanisms and the process of explaining and understanding them, or, on the contrary, is it itself the production of dreams and fantasies, pushed to the point of constituting a narrative or a legend? For Freud, there is no doubt, the aim of the treatment, through inference and interpretation and even constructions, is to bring something from the unconscious to consciousness, in order to make the unconscious intelligible, and to fill the holes in this discourse with articulations that will make what follows a logical necessity.

But there is no assurance that this will happen. It often happens that one observes a treatment in which understanding is not useful, in which knowing how one functions, what one repeats, or where one is riveted to an indestructible bliss produces no essential or lasting effect. To the contrary, if one succeeds in arousing a production of dreams or fantasies that brings forth a hitherto inaccessible state of regression, the alterations are working either without there being a need to interpret them or without there being the possibility for the analyst to produce a system of references that encompasses the patient's discourse. It is as if what the patient has attained, through his strange formulations, has become a new basis with new roots. It is a question not so much of bringing sleep into wakefulness as of unfolding sleep until its very substance is revealed.

Without actually inscribing his work as a text, the patient does something similar to the work of the writer, who understands from his anxieties and dreams enough to renew his writing and thus to give a status to that which haunts his sleep. Even if in appearance it is always through uncertain and unstable bits and pieces, "through temporary figures that are destined to be effaced sooner or later, once the real effect that the discourse aims at will have been obtained,"[8] like a writer, little by little, the patient "fixes" the features of his life into a narrative, but in this case they are fixed on and in the analyst, either by rediscovering the narrative or by having to invent it because it was never there.

Freud had perceived this type of relation at one time:

> I have not always been a psychotherapist. Like other neuropathologists, I was trained to employ local diagnoses and electro-prognosis, and it still strikes me myself as strange that the case histories I write should read like short stories and that, as one might say, they lack the serious stamp of science. I must console myself with the reflection that the nature of the subject is evidently responsible for this, rather than any preference of my own. The fact is that local diagnoses and electrical reactions lead nowhere in the study of hysteria, whereas a detailed description of mental processes such as we are accustomed to find in the works of imaginative writers enables me, with the use of a few psychological formulas, to obtain at least some kind of insight into the course of that affection. Case histories of this kind are intended to be judged like psychiatric ones; they have, however, one advantage over the latter, namely an intimate connection between the story of the patient's sufferings and the symptoms of his illness, a relation for which we still search in vain in the biographies of other psychoses.[9]

This passage does not associate the narrative with the cure. Moreover, it is the analyst, not the patient, who produces the narrative, and, to be precise, his concern is to gain an understanding of the illness. Nonetheless, it is the patient and his illness that force the analyst to become the page on which the narrative is to be inscribed. In transforming the patient into a poet, the narrative acquires a capacity to cure. It is decisive to the treatment that the patient reconstitutes or recasts the events and the characters in his own novel and thus provides himself with landmarks and roots. A genuine reconstitution of subjectivity is thus put into effect, which is in imitation of what the German romantics thought of the production of the novel in relation to the constitution of the subject.[10] It is worth noting that Freud here abandons his scientific pretensions; and one is right to read him as giving a cathartic value to the narrative itself.

There are two faces to psychoanalysis: the method of free association can lead either to the adoption of the connection that Freud maintained between dreams, jokes, and sudden ideas or to following the footsteps of those who regard dreams, jokes, and sudden ideas as sources from which to draw or as masters to be questioned.

In the first case, psychoanalysis wants to be scientific, since after having given free rein to the imagination, it must pull it back again in order finally to force it into a code, a logic, a formula. The fate of the individuals who undergo analysis is put in second place. If one is interested in their peculiarities, it is always in order to transform them into elements of a universal discourse, since the peculiarities have no importance in themselves. The patient's speech does not stop with himself, has not been made for him, and must be replaced in a chain of transformations destined to end in the institution of laws. When Freud confesses to Kardiner that he is interested less and less in therapeutic questions and more and more in his own theory,[11] he is not only perfectly aware of his present practice; he is defining the rule which has guided his work all along. The dreams of his patients have filled the same function as his own dreams, that of having to support a theoretical project on the dream itself; likewise, the diverse pathologies of his patients enabled him to extend all the limits of his theory in order to be able to develop from them a combination of psychoneuroses. Freud was then no longer a dreamer or a patient: he became, as a subject, the one who had pushed back the shadows of sleep or of madness. When psychoanalysis fails to be scientific, it is seeking not so much to heal as to understand; it makes individuals the preliminary material for its construction. And this accounts for the indispensable role of interpretation, which becomes the fertile moment of the analysis, not only of course for the patient but necessarily for the analyst as well. This also explains the inevitable production of disciples, who by adopting Freud's discourse on the dream, jokes, or sudden ideas, become the proofs for the theory. Analytic theory can be neither proven nor refuted;[12] its validity depends on those who believe it, and its universality on the greatest possible number who recognize its validity. Nothing would be altered in the case of the analyst who flees interpretation by taking refuge in silence, because what is at work is the analyst's effective aim in the transference. If he is too preoccupied with science, if he is trying to make scientific advances or verify hypotheses, he will inevitably transform his patient into a scientific object. The one who was supposed to be the patient is now only a personification of analytic theory; he is entirely an analytic interpretation.

(One may, in passing, consider the scientific nature of analysis. When the patient has lost all substantiality and resistance in order to be reduced to a pure effect of a coherent and rigorous discourse, since the rigor and coherence are always a function of the field in which the discourse is posed and depend on the tacit or explicit agreement of those who use such a discourse, what is taking place?[13] Everything can then swing toward fiction, a fiction sustained only by the fact that a number of subjects accept it as the truth. The theory can distinguish itself from fiction only through continuous criticism.)

The other face of psychoanalysis could be constituted through the patient's effort not only to speak of his dreams, his fantasies, and his sudden ideas but to work them out in order to recognize himself. This is nothing new to Freud, who, after he had recognized the failure of recollection in cases where the transference became explicit and overpowering, made *Durcharbeitung*, "working-through," the final stage in the analytic method. But Freud does not say much about working-through; by no means does he link it to free association in order to see it as a second stage of free association, as its resumption with a view toward its appropriation.

Working-through could be interpreted as resembling the transformations to which the writer submits the materials that his dream or sudden idea has given him: this raw input must be replaced by something readable, and as the change is occurring the patient stops being a receiver and becomes an author himself. This is the decisive step that must be made in every case. If the patient were content to let himself go with the flow of the words, he would be like an author who did not make use of inspiration, like a madman whose understanding no longer functioned well enough to understand what could be understood of his delusions. At the other extreme, an author without inspiration never leaves the closed field of repetitive chatter; he is like the neurotic who does not let himself be overtaken by the word, who does not lift prohibitions against speaking, so great is his need for mastery. Moreover, the need for mastery is recurrent and will transform the dreams into trifles and the sudden ideas into commonplaces. In this sense, the problem posed to the patient resembles the one that the writer encounters: to let things come without going mad, yet not to be content with letting things come, but to rework the material until it has substantiality and appears to have an organization.

For this, the analyst's interpretation is unnecessary: there is no need to know if such and such a dream or fantasy can be made meaningful through the categories of analytic theory or if it is attributable to an allegedly universal plan. "There is no need" means that it would be injurious, as we said earlier, because the peculiarity, the singularity, of the case would be reduced to a discourse that comes from somewhere else. In order for the patient to have a chance to be cured, to take his own bearings in existence and not to be expropriated by analytic theory, as he has been by others, he must not depart from the world of imagination, of dreams, fantasies, and myths; all that matters is that these dreams, fantasies, and myths that have come from sleep or from the treatment are assimilated into the waking state and are constituted as a text which will be a landmark and a reference for the individual. This text will play a role similar to that of the symbolic, with only this difference: that the symbolic claims to be universal or to be linked to a particular society, and that it has the effect of assimilating the patient.

We conclude from the preceding argument that the cure is an act of inspired creation. In other words, the analytic technique of free association necessarily comprises this working hypothesis (and the analyst's role is essentially to make it manifest): every patient is a genius.[14] The neurotic and even the psychotic are not suffering from too much imagination, but from too much reality. They are invaded by it because they dread it, and it freezes them in a repetitive process that prohibits the imagination from unfolding. Then come the permanent short circuits that doom the patient to sterility.

The hypothesis is not extravagant. It would not perhaps have surprised Freud, who knew, through Börne, that he was part of the German romantic movement. The dream of the Jena group was nothing other than the foundation of a community of artists which would gradually come about through the mediation of those "who have their center in themselves," something like an initiation to the genius of artistic inspiration.[15] They would thus be suggesting that genius is transmissible. Psychoanalysis can understand such an audacious idea, since in order to be effective, it must be supposed that the patient, and not the analyst, is a discoverer.

If one reverses the statement that every patient is a genius, one comes back to a traditional idea that no longer seems surprising: genius is part of mental illness. It is always associated with the risk of madness. Once invited by the muses into their kingdom, who knows if he will be able to come back again? There is no creation that does not bear within itself the threat of collapse in the most secret or the sharpest anguish. But genius, in its turn, shows the neurotic which way to go in order to break out of his imprisonment. Genius makes it possible for something else to speak, something useless, fantastic, and unexpected. Genius also provides the power to speak in this way and to give form to what is said, while madness remains elsewhere, incommunicable even to the one who is its victim. Artist and patient are thus confronted with the same problem: how, as Schiller expressed it, can one avoid being "ashamed or frightened of the momentary and transient extravagances which are to be found in all truly creative minds"? What distinguishes the artist from the dreamer, the incurable patient from the one who will be cured, is the degree to which they tolerate these seizures or "extravagances," the delay with which they overcome these experiences, and the precision of their ability to discriminate them.[16]

This difference deserves a close consideration, because no matter how mysterious it is, it is no less decisive in the unfolding of an analysis. At the end of his brief "Note on the Prehistory of the Analytic Technique," Freud cited Börne: "'It is not lack of intellect but lack of character that prevents most writers from being better than they are.... Sincerity is the source of all genius, and men would be cleverer if they were more moral.'" What follows is the passage in Börne from which Freud took his citation:

> The true scientific endeavor is not a voyage of discovery like Christopher Columbus's, but the voyage of Ulysses. Man is born in strangeness; to live is to seek his homeland, and to think is to live. But the land of one's thoughts is the heart; from this source one must draw what one wishes to drink fresh. The mind is only a stream into which thousands step, and disturb the water by washing in it, by bathing in it, by soaking their linen in it and performing other disgusting ac-

tivities. The mind is the arm, the heart is the will; one may cultivate force, increase it, develop it, but what good is it without the courage to use it? A shameful cowardice to think holds all of us back. More pressing than the censorship of governments is the censorship that public opinion exerts on our mental labors. It is not lack of intellect but lack of character that prevents most writers from being better than they are. The artist, the writer, want to dominate and surpass their colleagues, but in order to dominate them, one must be at their sides; in order to surpass them, one must take the same road. This is why good writers have so many things in common with the bad. In the good there is everything of the bad; it is only something more. The good completely follows the road of the bad, he only goes a little further. The one who listens to the voice of his heart, instead of the cries of the marketplace, the one who has the courage to propagate, while teaching, what the heart has taught him, this one is always original. Sincerity is the source of all genius, and men would be cleverer if they were more moral.[17]

More than one feature of this text was able to mark the fourteen-year-old Freud and to reappear much later in order to determine specifically the analytic method, but also to limit it. Is it not, for Freud, a voyage of Ulysses, a rediscovery of a past from which he was estranged, rather than the discovery of an America within, of nature's unseen and unheard secrets, or of Jungian archetypes? Börne's contest between heart and mind strongly resembles Freud's contest between the unconscious and consciousness, which is also determined precisely by the role censorship will play. As for sincerity, it is included in the "saying everything" without which psychoanalysis would not exist.

The conditions of literary creation are thus similar to those which rule over the progress of analytic treatment. More precisely, psychoanalysis makes a systematic use of certain procedures of literary creation. Psychoanalysis can therefore abandon the moralizing vocabulary that suits Börne so well: character, courage, sincerity, heart. But for all that, it is not really so far removed, since several questions remain in common, such as, Why is it that the technique of free association in certain cases either cannot really be applied or is ineffective?

To answer this question, one is forced to appeal to hypotheses that have not been thematized by analytic literature. What is the force that is able to overcome an internal opinion, what enables one to resist the tyranny of introjected values, if it is not the capacity to bear the isolation, or better, the possibility of being estranged, not only from others but from oneself? Which is to say that the patient must somehow have already touched the limits of madness. It is possible to come to the end of a mental illness only through the means that the illness itself uses, only through the breach that it has opened in the breakwater of worldliness.

The technique of free association can provide the occasion to listen to dreams, fantasies, and sudden ideas as long as two conditions are fulfilled.

The first is that the patient has reached the borderline of tolerance, that life is impossible for him at this level of suffering and powerlessness, that he no longer has anything to lose, that he has lost all faith in what he formerly thought or did. The proximity of death, which devastates the whole field of intersubjectivity, readies the ear for the unprecedented, not only because it is no longer surprised by anything but because the dreams, fantasies, or sudden ideas are viewed against the horizon of death. When an analysis is undertaken under the pressure of one's entourage or to be in style, or in order to take up employment, or simply because of the desire to know oneself better, it is a good bet that the treatment will never be more than a more or less sophisticated chatter. Stay awake at all costs, because sleep, the sleep of dreams, is too close to death and one might not be able to return. In other words, analysis is possible only in a state of extreme necessity; an approaching collapse demands that everything be risked. More particularly, the second condition is the capacity to risk everything: although everything is submerged in anxiety and confusion, where, at the other extreme, does the furious longing to get out of it come from? One must suppose something like the superego, something that has been torn away from the id and that is capable of understanding but that instead of tyrannizing the ego, serves as both its refuge and its capacity for criticism and renovation. In descriptive terms, this thing that resembles the superego would comprise the ultimate power to say no to subjective death, and it would remain until the final degradation,[18] the definitive loss of humanity. As a consequence, it would imply questioning the possibility of undoing all of one's self-images, all of one's illusory opinions, which would finally indicate that it is the origin of the first affirmation and the foundation of subjectivity, because it brings about the first separation.

It now appears that genius must find its way between two perils: opinion and death. If the writer, or any creative figure, produces a work in order that it will reach a great number of people, it will only reflect the mass, a kind of random patchwork without any specific character. If, on the contrary, he cannot prevent himself from being overwhelmed by the anxiety of death, upon which he should draw, he will no longer be anything. Hölderlin vanishing into the night. But these propositions cannot be understood without mediation. He who is an interlocutor with genius is an indiscernible mixture of culture and nothingness. Jean-Jacques Rousseau says that he writes his *Confessions* in order to justify himself before those who accuse him. But he is mistaken; the proof of it is that he is very poorly perceived. It is not for that reason nor for those readers that he writes, but for an interlocutor whom he will take years to find and to lose in the *Dialogues* and the *Rêveries*. Likewise, it is never only in the anxiety of death that genius finds its sources: every work of genius secretly or openly derives its support from a polemic, indeed a rivalry; and thus once again it involves opinion. Börne said that "good writers have so many things in common with the bad. In the good, there is everything of the bad; it is only something more. The good completely follows the road of the bad, he only goes a little further." The difference is that the bad cannot for an instant take his eyes off his interlocutor in order to model his reply on the other, while for the good, the polemic is only an occasion, necessary certainly, to look for answers elsewhere. For authors from Jean-Paul to Diderot (and many others), the constant concern is to mislead their reader so that they will not fall into the trap of his expectations; otherwise, writing becomes impossible. If genius responds so well, it is because the question no longer belongs to the other and because the confrontation no longer takes place with a too familiar stranger, but also because the interrogation threatens his own foundations and forces him to build them anew. Every polemicist who does not respond first and principally to the questions that concern him is contemptible, because they involve his existence, his life and his death.

What can the psychoanalyst do as interlocutor in order to bring forth the quality of genius? If, as we have seen, the analyst cannot maintain the role of theorist without endangering the patient, then the patient unquestionably needs to go through a first stage (not only chronologically, but logically first) in which someone thinks intelligibly about his suffering and on occasion shares these thoughts with him. But the reverse is also indispensable. The patient is able to plunge into the solitude that is necessary in order to renew his dreams and fantasies only if this solitude is repeatedly sustained and confirmed through the ignorance and solitude of the analyst. Then he becomes the privileged interlocutor of genius. In this sense, the analyst is there in order to understand that he understands nothing. The paradox is easily explained: if I have no one to talk to, I can neither speak nor write; then I must have an auditor or a reader. But if he understands me, if I cannot startle, mislead, or lose him, he will rob me of my speech and my writing.

I believe that it is in this position, at the limits of the absurd, that the analyst is placed by the patient at the most fertile moment of the analysis and most certainly at its end. I emphasize *is placed*, because the analyst would not know how to feign the role of ignorance on his own. When Socrates questions the slave in order to make him discover what he did not know, Socrates' ignorance is feigned, and the result is that the slave never says anything that Socrates had not already made known in his presence.[19] The maieutic technique is a method of pedagogic enslavement, a means of enclosing the other within the master's knowledge. Socrates is the enemy of any invention that he does not control. It is nothing like this for the analyst, because at certain moments the patient's speech places the analyst, who is genuinely stunned and isolated, into a state of anxiety where all landmarks have been removed. He believed he could precede the patient in the course of his development, and now, through the latter's problems, he finds himself somewhere else and without even the ability to tell where he is. Most often, the analyst's stupidity is tolerated no better by the patient than by the analyst himself, because the former appreciates neither his own solitude nor the strangeness of his speech. All that matters to him is that a certain intelligibility from the analyst return as soon as possible in order to comfort him with advice; he will force the analyst into further retrenchments and finally into responding. If that happened, it would all be to the analyst's benefit, for he would in some way see the horizons of his own theory, even if it were at the price of an upheaval, but this would turn against the patient, who is once again caught in the snares of an interlocutor who cannot resist recuperating and reintroducing into his own system the interpretation that the patient was forced to make of his experiences. From this point of view, I do not believe that any analysis can be terminated or that any transference can be lifted if the patient has not somehow experienced the underlying incomprehension of the analyst. If the analyst's intelligence, at first an indispensable aid, becomes an arbitrary trap because it functions without exception, either the analyst will drive the patient into a definitive infantilism or the patient, in order to put an end to the transference and to the hold the analyst has on him, will have to produce what I earlier called a monophemic discourse,[20] which perhaps is always at the same time a creative discourse.

This simple proposition describes the patient's position at the end of the analysis (an authentic artist could doubtless say as much): "I do not need to be understood or to be recognized." The force that pushes me toward "the capacity of enjoyment and of efficiency" (the two characteristics of the cure according to Freud) is not, at bottom, conditioned by the presence or absence of others; my gestures or my speech have enough importance that the approbation of others adds nothing of significance and has very little effect on my insights or my omissions. This position can express self-sufficiency, but it should not be confused with the paranoiac's position when he says, "No one understands me." This formulation conveys resentment and an exacerbated state of mind, even if it assumes the haughty form of a narcissistic wound: "I am understood by no one," which on occasion becomes "No one deserves to understand me," with the implication "But I never expected anything else." This is the source of the aggressivity of the paranoiac who, unable to be recognized directly for what he is or what he is not, will seek a negative recognition through conflict: "I am rejected only because of my value." He does not emerge from "mimetic rivalry";[21] he is nothing other than a neurotic to the second power. He turns his back on madness, and thus on every source of inspiration, in order to cling to a caricature of social conduct.

I do not refer to the paranoiac's position by chance. A psychoanalysis that clinically places paranoia among the psychoses and that, furthermore, wants to make it the model according to which every psychosis will have to be understood has already turned itself into an enterprise of enslavement. This thesis regarding paranoia is maintained for ideological reasons: it tries to prevent the question of the first person from being posed, a dangerous question in every civilization, but particularly our own, which survives only through the existence of the masses. There is an unquestionable complicity between the paranoiac and the mass. The paranoiac is able to subjugate the masses because he gives the impression of being independent and of speaking in his own name—a double illusion, shared by each member of the masses, which enables them to identify with him and therefore to allow themselves to be led by him without resistance. But from another perspective the paranoiac is the genuine, old-fashioned neurotic who will always exist and who is entirely dependent on the crowd, for, contrary to appearances, he has no existence on his own; only the crowd, despised or humiliated, can give him his demeanor and substantiality. He scorns and overwhelms the crowd through his rage at being unable to attain solitude and its correlative, ignorance. He must repeatedly be put in the state of being the one who is supposed to know; to know, obviously, for the other and in his place. When Lacan proposes the expression "the subject who is supposed to know" in order to define the analyst's position as the basis of the transference, he is giving a partial description of what is occuring; but because he wants to make it the expression of a law, he is no longer able to think of the abolition of the transference,[22] and therefore he inevitably leads the analytic relation back to that of the paranoiac and his crowd, which is in effect to enclose the analytic relation within the indefinite and the insoluble. The paranoiac and the crowd cannot exist without one another: he is always supposed to be a genius, and the crowd is always supposed to be mentally debilitated.

Paranoia never emerges from the problematic of neurosis and therefore of society; it is always the exasperation of a dual situation, that is, in the speech of the second person. When I say "I," I am speaking as "you." The Lacanian adage "Desire is the desire of the other" certainly applies to mankind as long as he lives in and through society; therefore it applies to the neurotic or the paranoiac, but it consequently prohibits any solitary access to desire if it claims to be universal. The question of speaking in the first-person singular can only be reopened through an effort bordering on schizophrenia, which is essentially a disorder of the first-person singular.²³ The schizophrenic speaks in the third-person "he"; at least this is the way he is understood in a descriptive sense. But his "he" is at first what the "I" has cast off, which is never anything other than "you." Because he resists the game of illusion and the mirror, the schizophrenic cannot speak like everyone else. He moves on the horizon of truth, because he knows that there is neither an other nor an Other; put more simply, he must repeatedly abolish the interlocutor who would send his own speech back to him and, at the same time, make a prisoner of it. His delusions, his diffusion, and his unspeech (*dé-parole*) present, beneath the features of a discourse that has lost all coherence and rigor, the only way to escape the other's tyranny. Delusion, diffusion, and unspeech are the manifest correlatives of a psychical function that I propose calling the "hyper-I" (*hyperje*). The "I" is usually only the expression of the ego and consciousness, and ipseity, or the self, is never more than its duplication; it must therefore be called a simple misunderstanding (*méconnaissance*) of the second person. If the neurotic (and the paranoiac, in spite of appearances) is entangled in the snare of opinion, the schizophrenic is caught on the side of radical absence, that is, by death. An untenable position, but it reveals to us a limit from which it is possible to emerge from a dual relation.

In "The Loss of Reality in Neurosis and Psychosis" (1924), Freud gives a remarkable definition of normal behavior:

> The initial difference is expressed in the final result: in neurosis a piece of reality is avoided by a sort of flight, whereas in psychosis, it is remodeled. Or we might say in psychosis, the initial flight is succeeded by an active phase of reconstruction; in neurosis, the initial obedience is succeeded by a deferred attempt at flight. Or again, expressed another way: neurosis does not disavow reality, it wants only to ignore it; psychosis disavows it and tries to replace it. We call behavior "normal" or "healthy" if it combines certain features of both reactions, that, like neurosis, it does not disavow neurosis, but strives afterwards, like psychosis, to change that reality. This normal behavior obviously leads to work being carried out on the external world, and it is not content, like psychosis, to produce internal changes. It is no longer *autoplastic* but *alloplastic*.²⁴

This combination of submission and alteration suggests a new approach to what occurs in artistic creation and in analysis. When the interlocutor, in his ignorance, stops being an individual who is only fixed on representing the possible, then reality in its turn ceases being insurmountable and becomes the play of possibilities, opened to multiple combinations. Only in this instant is the individual's singularity posed, for it becomes the place where the change occurs, which is posed in the first person, using forces that do not belong to it and that have never been codified by a "you" who would have been its support. One is then at the limits of madness, where ordinary space and the usual forms of language are destructured. What the schizophrenic experiences at the extreme point of dissociation is experienced by those who give in to "extravagances," always by necessity. The customary "I" is held at bay by the flux of questioning anxieties that have turned away from reality as it has been perceived up to now. This marks the appearance, in the first person, of the hyper-I, who, through this opened breach, comes to draw upon a new fiction that will make another reality readable and provide new landmarks to the individual who forms it. The difference between the psychotic and the creative artist is that the former, who remains imprisoned in the hyper-I, cannot cross the distance that separates it from the normal "I." The difference between the creator and the neurotic is that the latter does not want to understand any other discourse than the one that comes to him from a "you" that has been fabricated in advance, while the former feels constrained to produce what no interlocutor expects or at least what no interlocutor knows how to expect.

The explanations proposed here resemble many earlier solutions, most obviously those of German romanticism. Albert Béguin cites this passage from Herder on the magical power of *Märchen* ("fairy tales"): "As in dreams, we discover our double self in these tales: the one who dreams and the mind that contemplates the dream, the narrator and the auditor. . . . This involuntary and autonomous poetry of tales and dreams is a marvelous power accorded to man."[25] This is another, certainly discreet way of introducing a psychical category other than that of "the one who dreams" or "the narrator."[26] But Schelling, directly linked to the Schlegel brothers, allows us to understand the complexity of the necessary connection that the understanding and conscious reason maintain with madness. He distinguishes (after Kant and Hegel, although less decisively) the understanding and the reason, the former being active, the latter passive, gathering in the inspirations of the soul.[27] And finally Nietzsche, whom Freud said he never wanted to read because he felt himself too close to him, disdains the "I" of subjectivity, but to the Dionysian musician, who "is himself nothing other than the original suffering and the echo of this suffering," accords the right to say "I."[28]

These authors are not concerned with therapy, but would not their ideas apply to therapy? and why could we not situate therapy in relation to such ideas? While the psychotic oscillates between enclosure in the hyper-I, pure sterile affirmation without a determined object, and the collapse into confusion of death and life, the neurotic cannot emerge from the narrow circle of his ego and wishes to know nothing of what is on its borders. For the psychotic the cure consists in creating the relation that maintains the "I" together with the "you," in such a way that the alternation from enclosure to collapse becomes a succession and that afterwards a passage is possible across the hyper-I, from the borders toward the consciousness that will receive the echo of the hyper-I. For the neurotic the cure consists in the possibility of constituting a hyper-I that will enable him not to feel annihilated at the approach of anxiety and excess and that will filter the sudden burst of new connections. In other words, the cure consists in starting or restarting diverse processes and in putting into circulation between them elements of reality, tested through what "cannot be cognized and is even incapable of existing."

If Freud recognized that normal behavior involves a transformation of reality in a way similar to that of psychosis, he did not consider it necessary to conjecture a psychical function that could account for this phenomenon. Perhaps this is not by accident. The principle of determinism, to which he adhered, he tells us in his response to Havelock Ellis, with a "conviction amounting almost to a prejudice," leads him to reduce dreams, jokes, wit, parapraxes, and sudden ideas to the elements that consciousness is capable of embracing in their totality. Nothing must escape the understanding. And if, in his second model of psychical topography, he invents the superego, a function issuing from the id, in which the system of values is centered, he will hardly grant it any other function than that of tyrannizing over the ego—not a word about its transmission to the ego of the principles and the forces of an alteration coming from the id. The example of the poetic impulse could have risen to his imagination only if he had abandoned the shores of science and had embarked momentarily for the Cythera of the romantics.

notes

PREFACE TO ENGLISH-LANGUAGE EDITION

1. Gerald Holton, "On the Role of Themata in Scientific Thought," *Science,* April 1975.
2. See Serge Doubrovsky, *Parcours critique* (Paris: Galilée, 1979), p. 200.

CHAPTER 1

1. Walter Muschg, "Freud écrivain" (trans. J. Schotte), *La Psychanalyse* 5 (1959): 69-124. The original version is "Freud als Schriftsteller," *Die psychoanalytische Bewegung* 2 (1930): 467-509. There is no English translation.
2. Muschg, "Freud écrivain," p. 85.
3. Walter Schönau, *Sigmund Freuds Prosa: Literarische Elemente seines Stils* (Stuttgart: J. B. Metzlersche Verlagsbuchhandlung, 1968).
4. Ibid., p. 7.
5. The bibliography on Freud's style is very limited. There are some remarks in *Die Psychoanalytische Bewegung* 5 (1930): 510-11. Also see the following: Geraldine Pederson-Krag, "The Use of Metaphor in Analytic Thinking," *Psychoanalytic Quarterly* 25 (1956): 66-71; Martin Grotjahn, "Sigmund Freud and the Art of Letter Writing," *Journal of the American Medical Association* 200 (1967): 13-18; idem, "Sigmund Freud as Dreamer, Writer and Friend," *Voices* 5 (1969): 70-73; Conrad Stein, "Sur l'écriture de Freud," *Etudes freudiennes* 7 8 (1973): 71-119; Tzvetan Todorov devotes a chapter to Freud's rhetoric in *Théories du symbole* (Paris: Seuil, 1977); Jacques Derrida has done an important reading of *Beyond the Pleasure Principle* in *La Carte postale* (Paris: Aubier-Flammarion, 1980); Maurice Dayan, *L'Arbre des styles* (Paris: Aubier-Montaigne, 1980).
6. Ernst Bleuler, Karl Abraham, Georg Groddeck, Ludwig Binswanger.
7. For example, J. Lachelier, *Du fondement de l'induction,* where the reasoning is always deductive, i.e., it returns to what has been established by other means. We will see that Freud's reasoning is always inductive.
8. Sigmund Freud, *Die Traumdeutung,* in *Gesammelte Werke,* 18 vols. (Frankfurt: S. Fischer Verlag, 1940-68), 2/3:531-37. All future references will be to *G.W.* The passage appears in English in *The Interpretation of Dreams,* in *The Standard Edition of the Complete Psychological Works of Sigmund Freud,* ed. James Strachey et al., 24 vols. (London: Hogarth Press and the Institute of Psychoanalysis, 1953-74), 5:526-32. All subsequent references will be to *S.E.*.
9. On all these points the *Standard Edition* succumbs too often to easy solutions. It is therefore impossible to rely upon it.
10. *G.W.* 2/3:516-27; *S.E.* 5:512-22.
11. *G.W.* 2/3:527-30; *S.E.* 5:522-25.

12. The first two paragraphs are joined in *G.W.*, while *S.E.*, being more attentive to the manuscripts, separates them, and this conforms to our analysis of the text.
13. *G.W.* 2/3:593; *S.E.* 5:588.
14. For example, in this chapter: *G.W.* 2/3:541, 559; *S.E.* 5:536, 553.
15. *G.W.* 2/3:515; *S.E.* 5:510-11.
16. *G.W.* 2/3:515-16; *S.E.* 5:511.
17. On the metaphor of walking, see Schönau, *Sigmund Freuds Prosa*, p. 160.
18. *G.W.* 2./3:543; *S.E.* 5:538.
19. On parataxis, see Heidegger's commentary on the sentence by Parmenides, "It is necessary that being is saying and thinking." In order to get closer to the Greek original, Heidegger proposes a translation that cuts the sentence into four parts: "Needful: the saying also thinking too: being: to be." Here is Heidegger's commentary:

> We just now stressed the structure of the saying, only in order to get closer to the area of its problematic. The colons we inserted give a first, outward sign of the manner in which the words are put in order relative to one another. The Greek word for order and placement is τάξις. In our saying, the words follow upon each other without connection. they are lined up side by side; 'beside,' or more exactly 'by,' is παρά in Greek. The word order of our saying is paratactic and not, as the usual translation represents it: 'One should *both* say . . . *that*.' By this 'both' and 'that,' the words are put in a specific order. The connection coordinates them, puts them together in an order; in Greek, 'together' is σύν. We speak of 'synthesis.' The usual translation of the saying puts the words together in an order, by inserting connecting words. In regard to its word order the translation is syntactic.
>
> Syntax is the study of sentence structure in the widest sense. Our ideas of the structure of languages are formed in terms of syntax. Where we encounter languages that have no syntax, we normally understand their structure to be a deviation from, or a failure to attain, syntactic structure. Paratactic speech occurs also in syntactically structured languages, for instance among children. Then everything fits, since children, too, are considered primitive. A child might say about a passing dog: 'Bow-wow, bad, bite.' [Parmenides' phrase] sounds that way. (*What Is Called Thinking?*, trans. Fred D. Wieck and J. Glenn Gray [New York: Harper and Row, 1968], p. 183).

Jacqueline Sudaka has informed me that from a strictly grammatical point of view, Heidegger's translation is not justified. The infinitive clause, in Greek or in Latin, is never considered as paratactic. The only cases of parataxis in Greek are found in Homer, and they are found in such Latin writers as Ennius, Plautus, and Terence. I quote Heidegger because of his commentary on Parmenides.

20. *G.W.* 15:20; *S.E.* 22:20. Todorov cites this text and several others to show that Freud links together "madmen, savages, children." Todorov concludes that Freud does so in order to damn the *others*, who are outside this group.
21. *G.W.* 2/3:554; *S.E.* 5:549. Freud cites Nietzsche, for whom the dream is a way "to a knowledge of man's archaic heritage."
22. According to Littré: The joining together of words in a sentence and the sentences to one another. According to Dumarsais: "What, in each language, makes the words produce the meaning that one wants to produce in the minds of those who know the language" (*Oeuvres* [Paris, 1797], 5:2).
23. A deductive style, on the other hand, first provides the thesis that it wants to prove and then gives proofs.
24. *G.W.* 2/3:541; *S.E.* 5:536.
25. *G.W.* 2/3:604; *S.E.* 5:598.
26. *G.W.* 2/3:609; *S.E.* 5:603.
27. *L'Interpretation des rêves*, trans. Meyerson (Paris: P.U.F., 1950), p. 488; trans. Denise Berger (Paris: P.U.F., 1967), p. 508.

28. *S.E.* 5:598.

29. *G.W.* 2/3:516; *S.E.* 5:512.

30. See Octave Mannoni, *Fictions freudiennes* (Paris: Seuil, 1978); idem, *Un Commencement qui n'en finit pas* (Paris: Seuil, 1980); and Maud Mannoni, *La Théorie comme fiction* (Paris: Seuil, 1979).

31. *G.W.* 2/3:558; *S.E.* 5:552.

32. Freud is not unaware of the leap he is making, as he observes at the end of the paragraph: "I am aware that this assertion cannot be proved to hold universally; but it can be proved to hold frequently, even in unsuspected cases, and one cannot generally refute it." (*G.W.* 2/3:559; *S.E.* 5:554). The non-scientificity of analytic theory is clearly stated here. It is a discourse that can be neither proved nor refuted.

33. On the production of delirium by psychiatric knowledge, see Octave Mannoni's important article, "Président Schreber, professeur Flechsig," *Les Temps modernes* 341 (1974): 624-41. To be assured of the distinction between theory and delirium, the psychoanalyst would have to return to psychiatry.

34. *G.W.* 2/3:593; *S.E.* 5:588.

35. "R. Kuhn observes that, in reading Freud, one is often led in a direct way to the relation between the inspiration of his written text and the analytic situation, even and perhaps above all when this situation is not explicitly his theme." (J. Schotte, in *La Psychanalyse* 5 [1959]: 64). In his notes to Muschg's article, Schotte suggests that there is a link, through the style, between theory and practice. In particular, see his notes 21 and 25.

36. Letter 92, July 7, 1898. In Sigmund Freud, *The Origins of Psychoanalysis: Letters to Wilhelm Fliess*, ed. E. Kris, A. Freud, and M. Bonaparte, trans. E. Mosbacher and J. Strachey (New York: Basic Books, 1975), p. 258.

37. Hilbert, whom someone asked how a mathematician could become a novelist, answered: "It is easy. He did not have enough imagination for mathematics, but he had enough for novels" (*Critique*, April 1977). The citation in *Critique* is taken from Constance Reid, *Hilbert* (Berlin, Heidelberg, and New York: Springer, 1970), p. 175.

38. "Wen die Psychoanalyse einmal gepackt hat, den lässt sie nicht mehr los." Cited by Schonau in *Sigmund Freuds Prosa*, p. 87.

CHAPTER 2

1. *G.W.* 16:43-56; *S.E.* 23:257-69.
2. *G.W.* 7:426; *S.E.* 10:204.
3. *G.W.* 12:277; *S.E.* 18.:151. *G.W.* 13:16-17; *S.E.* 18:18-19.
4. *G.W.* 16:47; *S.E.* 23:261.
5. *G.W.* 16:45; *S.E.* 23:259.
6. *G.W.* 16:47-48; *S.E.* 23:261.
7. *G.W.* 12:277; *S.E.* 18:152.
8. Chap. 5, "The Wolfman Case-history" (1918), *G.W.* 12:81; *S.E.* 17:52.
9. Sigmund Freud, *L'Homme aux rats: Journal d'une analyse* (Paris: P.U.F., 1974), p. 267. Most of these notes by Freud are to be found in *S.E.* 10:259-318. There is no complete English translation of the French/German edition cited here. (N.L.)
10. *G.W.* 12:291; *S.E.* 18:163.
11. *G.W.* 16:47; *S.E.* 23:260.
12. *G.W.* 16:46-47; *S.E.* 23:260.
13. *G.W.* 16:48; *S.E.* 23:261.
14. *G.W.* 16:49; *S.E.* 23:262.
15. *G.W.* 16:50; *S.E.* 23:263.
16. *G.W.* 16:50; *S.E.* 23:263.
17. *G.W.* 16:52; *S.E.* 23:265.

18. See the following: "The Ratman Case-History" (1909), *G.W.* 7:704-5, n. 1; *S.E.* 10:181, n. 1. "Wolfman Case-History," *G.W.* 12:79-80; *S.E.* 17:50-51 (here the patient himself makes the construction). "The Psychogenesis of a Case of Homosexuality in a Woman" (1920), *G.W.* 12:277; *S.E.* 18:151. *Beyond the Pleasure Principle* (1920), *G.W.* 13:16-17; *S.E.* 18:18-19.

19. *G.W.* 7:405; *S.W.* 10:181, n. 1.
20. *G.W.* 16:52; *S.E.* 23:265.
21. *G.W.* 16:49; *S.E.* 23:262.
22. *G.W.* 16:48-49; *S.E.* 23:262.
23. *Beyond the Pleasure Principle*, chap. 3, *G.W.* 13:16; *S.E.* 18:18.
24. *G.W.* 16:52; *S.E.* 23:265.
25. "Ratman Case-History," chap. 1, *G.W.* 7:428 n. 1; *S.E.* 10:208, n. 1. "Lines of Advance in Psychoanalytic Therapy" (1919), *G.W.* 12:188; *S.E.* 17:163.
26. *G.W.* 16:53; *S.E.* 23:266.
27. *G.W.* 16:44; *S.E.* 23: 258.
28. *G.W.* 16:53-54; *S.E.* 23:266-67.
29. *G.W.* 16:54-55; *S.E.* 23:267-68.
30. *G.W.* 16:55-56; *S.E.* 23:268.
31. "Wolfman Case-History," chap. 5, *G.W.* 12:79-80; *S.E.* 17:50-51.
32. The term *Schwärmereien* refers to the realms of mystical effusion. (N.L.)
33. *G.W.* 16:56; *S.E.* 23:269.
34. *The Interpretation of Dreams* (1900), chap. 7, *G.W.* 2/3:541; *S.E.* 5:536.
35. Octave Mannoni, *L'Arc* 69 (1977): *D. W. Winnicott Issue*, p. 39.
36. Published after his death. Karin Obholzer, *Gespräche mit dem Wolfsman: Eine Psychoanalyse und die Folgen* (Reinbek: Rowolt, 1980). There is a French translation by Romain Dugas under the title *Entretiens avec l'homme aux loups* (Paris: Gallimard, 1981). (N.L.)
37. See Jürgen Habermas, *Knowledge and Human Interests*, trans. Jeremy Shapiro (Boston: Beacon Press, 1971), pp. 214-73.
38. Roustang refers to Lacan's attempt to derive a mathematical formula that would establish the scientificity of psychoanalysis. See Roustang's comments on the possibility of a psychoanalytic matheme in his *Dire Mastery: Discipleship from Freud to Lacan*, trans. Ned Lukacher (Baltimore: Johns Hopkins University Press, 1982), pp. 68-69. (N.L.)
39. See Vincent Descombes, "L'Equivoque du symbolique," *Confrontation* 3 (1980): 77-95.

CHAPTER 3

1. *G.W.* 15:51-58; *S.E.* 22:47-55.
2. Like *Vorsicht, foresight* signifies both foreseeing and precaution. Catherine Wieder has informed me that they both entail the same lexical and semantic field as *carefulness* and *caution.* She also pointed out that *Forsyth* derives from *farside* and signifies "he who comes from afar."
3. Ernest Jones, *The Life and Work of Sigmund Freud*, 3 vols. (New York: Basic Books, 1953-57), 3:375-107.
4. Charles Moreau, *Freud et l'occultisme* (Privat, 1976), which includes a complete bibliography on this question.
5. *G.W.* 17:23; *S.E.* 5:625.
6. *G.W.* 4:291; *S.E.* 6:262.
7. *G.W.* 17:27-44; *S.E.* 18:177-93.
8. *G.W.* 17:35; *S.E.* 18:184-85.
9. *G.W.* 13:165-91; *S.E.* 18:197-220.
10. *G.W.* 13:165; *S.E.* 18:197.
11. *G.W.* 13:176; *S.E.* 18:206.

12. *G.W.* 13:177, 190; *S.E.* 18:207, 219.
13. Jones, *The Life and Work of Sigmund Freud*, 3:395.
14. *G.W.* 1:569-73; *S.E.* 19:135-38.
15. *G.W.* 1:572; *S.E.* 19:138.
16. *G.W.* 15:45; *S.E.* 22:43.
17. *G.W.* 15:47; *S.E.* 22:44.
18. *G.W.* 15:49-50; *S.E.* 22:46-47.
19. *G.W.* 15:50; *S.E.* 22:47.
20. Ibid.
21. *G.W.* 17:31; *S.E.* 18:181.
22. *G.W.* 17:43; *S.E.* 18:193.
23. *G.W.* 15:38, 42; *S.E.* 22:36, 39.
24. "The Uncanny (1919)," *G.W.* 12:246; *S.E.* 17:234.
25. The question is posed with great acuity in René Major's *Rêver l'autre* (Paris: Aubier-Montaigne, 1977).
26. Paul Roazen, *Brother Animal: The Story of Freud and Tausk* (New York: Alfred A. Knopf, 1969), p. 78.
27. *The Freud Journal of Lou Andreas-Salomé*, trans. Stanley A. Leavey (New York: Basic Books, 1964), p. 114.
28. Ibid., p. 88.
29. *Studies on Hysteria* (1895), *G.W.* 1:310; *S.E.* 2:304.
30. *G.W.* 1:309; *S.E.* 2:303.
31. "Recommendations on Analytic Technique (1912)," *G.W.* 8:384; *S.E.* 12:118.
32. *G.W.* 8:381; *S.E.* 12:115-16.
33. *G.W.* 8:382; *S.E.* 12:116.
34. *G.W.* 5:295-96; *S.E.* 7:288. This date is wrongly given as 1905 in both *G.W.* 5 and *S.E.* 7. The error is corrected in *S.E.* 1:63. "Thought-reading" [*Gedankenerraten*] is a form of divination, decipherment.
35. *G.W.* 7:391; *S.E.* 10:166.
36. "Constructions in Analysis (1937)," *G.W.* 16:45; *S.E.* 23:258-59.
37. *G.W.* 1:572; *S.E.* 19:138.
38. *G.W.* 8:377; *S.E.* 12:112.
39. Helene Deutsch, "Okkulte Vorgänge während der Psychoanalyse," *Imago* 12 (1926): 420-21.
40. *G.W.* 15:59; *S.E.* 22:55.
41. *G.W.* 15:60; *S.W.* 22:56.
42. "The Dynamics of Transference (1912)," *G.W.* 8:371-72; *S.E.* 12:104-5.
43. *G.W.* 8:366; *S.E.* 12:100.
44. *G.W.* 12:248; *S.E.* 17:236.
45. *G.W.* 12:251; *S.E.* 17:238.
46. *G.W.* 12:257, 259; *S.E.* 17:243, 245.
47. *G.W.* 12:257; *S.E.* 17:243.
48. *G.W.* 15:59-60; *S.E.* 22:55-56.
49. *G.W.* 5:289; *S.E.* 7:283.
50. See *Interpretation*, no. 21 (Spring 1978), the "Son psychanalyste" issue, in particular the article by J. Bigras, "Le Vénération," pp. 17-32.
51. Wladimir Granoff, *Filiations: L'Avenir du complexe d'Oedipe* (Paris: Editions de Minuit, 1976), p. 108.
52. I remember a psychoanalyst who, in the course of his "pass"—he was, of course named an "Analyste de l'Ecole freudienne de Paris"—was amazed to discover, little by little, how his own story seemed to him more and more like that of Lacan himself.

CHAPTER 4

1. *G.W.* 5:280; *S.E.* 116-17.
2. Jean Laplanche and Jean-Bertrand Pontalis, *The Language of Psychoanalysis*, trans. Donald Nicholson-Smith (New York: Norton, 1974), pp. 456-57.
3. Ibid., p. 457.
4. *G.W.* 5:279; *S.E.* 7:116.
5. *G.W.* 5:281; *S.E.* 7:117.
6. *G.W.* 5:282; *S.E.* 7:118.
7. See above, chap. 3, n. 34.
8. *G.W.* 5:281; *S.E.* 7:117.
9. This will be explicitly recognized later in *Introductory Lectures on Psychoanalysis* (1916): "All the libido, as well as everything opposing it, is concentrated on the relation to the doctor . . . in place of the various unreal objects of the libido there appears a single, imaginary object in the person of the doctor" (*G.W.* 11:473; *S.E.* 16:454).
10. "Freud's Psychoanalytic Procedure," *G.W.* 5:5; *S.E.* 7:251.
11. *G.W.* 5:14-15; *S.E.* 7:258.
12. *G.W.* 5:15; *S.E.* 7:259.
13. *S.E.* 7:258; *S.E.* 1:63. See Léon Chertok, "La Découverte du transfert," *Revue française de psychanalyse* 32 (1968): 503-29.
14. *G.W.* 5:299-300; *S.E.* 7:290-91. This prefigures Freud's development of these ideas in *Group Psychology and the Analysis of the Ego* (1921).
15. *G.W.* 5:301; *S.E.* 7:292.
16. *G.W.* 5:17-18; *S.E.* 7:260-61.
17. See above, chap. 3.
18. *G.W.* 5:313; *S.E.* 7:301.
19. *G.W.* 7:336; *S.E.* 10:101-2.
20. *G.W.* 7:339; *S.E.* 10:104. Italics added.
21. *G.W.* 8:105; *S.E.* 11:141-42.
22. *G.W.* 8:364-66; *S.E.* 12:99-100. Italics added.
23. *G.W.* 8:369; *S.E.* 12:103.
24. *G.W.* 8:370; *S.E.* 12:104.
25. Ibid.
26. *G.W.* 8:371; *S.E.* 12:105.
27. *G.W.* 8:373; *S.E.* 12:107.
28. *G.W.* 8:374; *S.E.* 12:108.
29. *G.W.* 8:373; *S.E.* 12:107.
30. *G.W.* 8:366; *S.E.* 12:100.
31. *G.W.* 8:373; *S.E.* 12:107.
32. *G.W.* 8:274; *S.E.* 12:108.
33. *G.W.* 8:381-82; *S.E.* 12:115-16.
34. *G.W.* 8:382; *S.E.* 12:116. In "On Beginning the Treatment" (1913) the tone will not be the same: "No one who is familiar with the nature of neurosis will be astonished to hear that even a man who is very well able to carry out an analysis on other people can behave like any other mortal and be capable of producing the most intense resistances as soon as he himself becomes the object of psychoanalysis" (*G.W.* 8:458; *S.E.* 12:126).
35. *G.W.* 8:371; *S.E.* 12:105.
36. *G.W.* 8:366; *S.E.* 12:100.
37. *G.W.* 8:371; *S.E.* 12:105.
38. *G.W.* 8:384; *S.E.* 12:118.
39. *G.W.* 8:366-67; *S.E.* 12:101.

40. *G.W.* 8:373; *S.E.* 12:107.
41. Ibid.
42. *G.W.* 8:374; *S.E.* 12:108.
43. According to the bibliographic note on *S.E.* 12:146, this article would be the first appearance of the concept of the repetition-compulsion. We will see later that Freud might also have drawn his concept of the death drive from his reflections on the transference.
44. *G.W.* 10:127; *S.E.* 12:148.
45. *G.W.* 10:129; *S.E.* 12:149-50.
46. *G.W.* 10:130-31; *S.E.* 12:151. Here Freud distinguishes the mild and unexpressed transference (*mild und unaugesprochen*) from the hostile and overpowering one (*feindselig und überstark*); in his *An Autobiographical Study* (1925), he will oppose the tender and measured transference (*zärtlich und gemässigt*) to the impassioned or hostile one (*leidenschaftlich, feindselig*).
47. *G.W.* 10:130; *S.E.* 12:150.
48. *G.W.* 10:129; *S.E.* 12:149.
49. *G.W.* 8:473; *S.E.* 12:139.
50. See *G.W.* 10:131; *S.E.* 12:151, *G.W.* 10:133; *S.E.* 12:153, and *G.W.* 8:368, 374; *S.E.* 12:102, 108.
51. "In the early years of my psychoanalytic practice I used to have the greatest difficulty in prevailing on my patients to continue their analysis; this difficulty has long since disappeared, and I now have to take the greatest pains to induce them to give it up." "On Beginning the Treatment," *G.W.* 8:462; *S.E.* 12:130.
52. *G.W.* 10:132; *S.E.* 12:152.
53. *G.W.* 10:133; *S.E.* 12:153.
54. *G.W.* 8:374; *S.E.* 12:108, *G.W.* 10:134; *S.E.* 12:153-54, 146.
55. Freud will acknowledge it in his autobiography: "Without difficulty we can recognize it [the transference] as the same dynamic factor that the hypnotists have named suggestibility, which is the support of the hypnotic *rapport.*" *G.W.* 14:68; *S.E.* 20:42.
56. *G.W.* 10:136; *S.E.* 12:155-56.
57. Cited by Léon Chertok, "Hystérie, hypnose, psychopathologie, histoire et prospective," *Annales médico-psychologiques* 2 (1974): 699.
58. *G.W.* 10:317; *S.E.* 12:168.
59. *G.W.* 10:317-18; *S.E.* 12:168-69.
60. "When Freud asserts that, in hypnosis, the hypnotist has taken, for the subject, the place of the ego ideal, he is describing a type of relation that is also that of the psychoanalyst with his patient." Léon Chertok, "Freud et les théories de l'hypnose: Histoire et interrogation," *Revue de médecine psychosomatique* 18 (1976): 156.
61. These connections had been established in "Psychical Treatment" (1890): "The hypnotist says, 'You see a snake, you smell a rose, you hear the loveliest music,' and the hypnotic subject sees, smells, and hears what is required of him by the idea that he has been given. How do we know that the subject really has these perceptions? It might be thought that he is only pretending to have them; but after all, we have no reason to doubt them, for he behaves exactly as though he had these perceptions: he expresses all the appropriate emotions, and in some circumstances he can even describe his imaginary perceptions and experiences after the hypnosis is at an end. We then understand that he has seen and heard just as we see and hear in dreams, that is, he has *hallucinated.* He was evidently credulous in relation to the hypnotist that he is *convinced* that there must be a snake to be seen when the hypnotist told him so, and this conviction had such a strong effect on his body that he really saw the snake, which is something that can sometimes happen even to people who have not been hypnotized. It may be remarked in passing that credulity such as the subject has in relation to his hypnotist is to be found outside hypnosis in real life only by *a child toward his*

beloved parents, and that such an attitude of similar subjection on the part of one person toward another has only one correspondence, though a complete one, namely, in certain *love-relationships* where there is extreme devotion" (*G.W.* 5:307; *S.E.* 7:296).

62. *G.W.* 13:126; *S.E.* 18:114-15.

63. In chapter 10 of *Group Psychology and the Analysis of the Ego,* the relation to the hypnotist is called a transference (*G.W.* 13:141; *S.E.* 18:126). Herman Nunberg made this connection in his article "Transference and Reality," *International Journal of Psychoanalysis* 32 (1951): 1-9.

64. In *An Autobiographical Study* (*G.W.* 14:68; *S.E.* 20:42), Freud says that the impassioned or hostile transference paralyzes (*lahm legt*) the patient's work of association.

65. *G.W.* 5:50, n. 1; *S.E.* 7:150, n. 1.

66. In this sense, the transference of neurotics can no longer be distinguished from the transference of psychotics. Freud thought that psychotics were incapable of transference. This proposition can now be reversed: the psychotic reveals the true nature of the transference.

67. *G.W.* 10:131, 133; *S.E.* 12:151, 153.

68. *G.W.* 5:5; *S.E.* 7:251.

69. *G.W.* 12:308-12; *S.E.* 18:263-65.

70. *G.W.* 11:472; *S.E.* 16:454.

71. *G.W.* 11:470; *S.E.* 16:452.

72. *G.W.* 11:464; *S.E.* 16:446.

73. *G.W.* 11:470-71; *S.E.* 16:452-53.

74. *G.W.* 11:464-65; *S.E.* 16:446-47.

75. *G.W.* 14:207-96; *S.E.* 20:177-258.

76. *G.W.* 16:57-99; *S.E.* 23:209-53.

77. *G.W.* 13:279, n. 1; *S.E.* 19:50, n. 1.

78. *G.W.* 13:278-79; *S.E.* 19:49.

79. *G.W.* 21:280; *S.E.* 19:50.

80. The sense of guilt seems to me to proceed directly from the fact of the myth of the first separation, of the initial individuation. I cannot forgive myself for having separated myself, for having differentiated myself from this first love-object, who absorbed me in order to survive and who without me, according to this logic, is condemned to death. It does not matter whether I abandoned the other, who was not really other, or I was abandoned by the other; the result is the same: I am guilty of having caused the other to be threatened by death, even though he certainly threatened me with death, because the other was everything to me. Identification (in the configuration of this myth) is logically only a secondary stage, a duplicate, a palliative, an attempt to restore the lost unity. There can be identification (and identification can then appear as the individual's first necessary gesture), because there had formerly been nonseparation, identity. If this first identification has the effect of subjection to the point of self-sacrifice, it is because death is finally the only way to efface individuation. And so Freud writes that "the sense of guilt is dumb" (*G.W.* 13:279; *S.E.* 19:50); it works silently, like the death drive, speaking only in order to create illness.

These remarks are also addressed to the analysis of depression post partum. The woman who identifies with her newborn child cannot forgive herself for having separated herself from her own mother. But this clinical fact is only the second apperance among others of a generalizable and perhaps universal structural reality.

CHAPTER 5

1. See, for example, Julien Bigras, *Le Psychanalyste nu* (Paris: Robert Laffont, 1979), where the preoccupations are very near to those developed in this chapter. See also the journal *L'Ordinaire du psychanalyste* 11, which includes several articles on this question.

Monique Schneider's "L'Ordre symbolique, la dévoration et l'infanticide," in *Etudes freudiennes* 15-16 (1979): 203-18, decisively reveals the identity between absorption into the mother's womb and being devoured by the symbolic father. The question raised in this chapter has already been explicitly posed by Solange Nobécourt, "Chapalu reste," *Documents confrontation*, May 1978, pp. 5-19. It is significant that the conference in May 1978, from which Nobécourt's essay originates, has had so little response.

2. See, for example, Jose Bleger, *Simbiosis y ambiguidad* (Buenos Aires: Paidos, (1967).

3. Serge Leclaire has raised this question in two articles: "Heimlichkeiten," *Interpretation*, no. 21 (Spring, 1978); and "L'Angoisse de l'assujetti devant le pas d'un," *Lettres de l'Ecole freudienne*, no. 26 (March 1979).

4. "For dissociation is the other side of fusion, and destructive anxiety the opposite of the desire for fusion" (Nicole Fabre, *Avant l'Oedipe* [Paris: Masson, 1979], p. 92).

5. All that is said here about the transference strangely resembles Etienne de La Boétie's sixteenth-century treatise *Le Discours de la servitude volontaire* (Paris: Payot, 1978); see particularly Claude Lefort's essay in this volume, "Le Non d'un." Through the perspective of a relation like this, one could think about the connections between psychoanalysis and politics.

6. The proximity of the excessive to the hostile transference has already been emphasized by M. Neyraut in *Le Transfert* (Paris: P.U.F., 1974), p. 95.

7. These themes have already been developed in Joyce McDougall, *Pleas for a Certain Degree of Abnormality* (New York: International Universities Press, 1980); Harold Searles, *Collected Papers on Schizophrenia and Related Subjects* (London: Hogarth Press, 1965); and idem, *Countertransference and Related Subjects* (New York: International Universities Press, 1979).

8. *G.W.* 14:519; *S.E.* 21:226.

9. One will reply that language supposes dysfunction but that is a play on words. Why are there degrees of dysfunction that range from usability to a complete breakdown?

10. *G.W.* 10:285-86; *S.E.* 14:187.

11. "The unconscious must be the precise contrary of the conscious" (*G.W.* 7:403; *S.E.* 10: 180).

12. Regnier Picard, "Si l'inconscient est structuré comme un langage," *Revue philosophique de Louvain*, November 1979, pp. 528-68, is a discussion of this adage from a linguistic and psychoanalytic perspective.

13. *G.W.* 10:286; *S.E.* 14:187.

14. Didier Anzieu, "Le Transfert paradoxal," *Nouvelle revue de psychanalyse* 12 (1972): 49-72.

15. Jacques Lacan, *The Four Fundamental Concepts of Psychoanalysis*, ed. Jacques-Alain Miller, trans. Alan Sheridan (New York: Norton, 1978), p. 276.

16. Ibid., p. 267.

17. Ibid., p. 270.

18. Ibid., p. 271.

19. Ibid., p. 273. The phrase "an upside-down hypothesis" must have inspired Jacques Nassif's discussion of "the beginnings of psychoanalysis" in his *Freud, l'inconscient* (Paris: Galilée, 1977).

20. *G.W.* 11:470; *S.E.* 16:452.

21. Lacan, *The Four Fundamental Concepts of Psychoanalysis*, p. 275.

22. I am thinking particularly of Searles's work (see n. 7 above).

23. Does not the fact that a psychotic in an institution is usually treated by several physicians confuse the problem of plural transferences?

24. Musad Khan, *Le Soi caché* (Paris: Gallimard, 1976), pp. 180-210.

25. *G.W.* 10:133-35; *S.E.* 12:153-56.

26. See above, chap. 4.

27. See above, chap. 3.

CHAPTER 6

1. Catherine David in *Le Nouvel observateur*, no. 807 (April 28-May 4, 1980): 94.
2. Serge Viderman, "La Machine dé-formatrice," *Cahiers confrontation* 3 (1980): 32.
3. Ibid., p. 29.
4. Ibid., p. 32.
5. Ibid., p. 34.
6. *Myth* is here to be understood in the strongest sense of the word: as a collection of representations in which a society finds itself and which help to locate it.
7. The religion of desire, which Lacan has helped to found, can be accurately enough described as the possibility of walking a little on the feet of others without being or feeling guilty about it.
8. *G.W.* 11:469; *S.E.* 16:451.
9. Octave Mannoni, in *L'Arc* 69 (1977): *D. W. Winnicot issue*, p. 39.
10. *G.W.* 2/3:554; *S.E.* 5:549.
11. *G.W.* 8:374; *S.E.* 12:108.
12. See above, chap. three.
13. *G.W.* 15:59-60; *S.E.* 22:55-56.
14. It is enough to reread the last chapter of the *Introductory Lectures on Psychoanalysis* to realize the importance accorded to suggestion in analysis. The word is used as a synonym of transference. Psychoanalysis is distinguished from hypnotic method because the latter uses direct suggestion, while the former "makes use of suggestion to modify the outcome of conflicts." Far from misunderstanding or ignoring, in analysis, the importance of suggestion, the nerve center of hypnosis, Freud is concerned to recognize and use it in order finally to decompose it. To speak of forces in regard to the transference and to suggest that the cure takes place through the passage of forces going from analyst to patient is, obviously, to return to ancient definitions of magic (see Hegel's *Encyclopedia*, no. 405 — reference provided by Jean-Luc Nancy in an unpublished work) or to some recent remarks on witchcraft (see Jeanne Favret-Saada, *Les Mots, la mort, les sorts* [Paris: Gallimard, 1977], chap. 12). If psychoanalysts condescend to open this question, it would be possible both to see that, through the direct transference, psychoanalysis enters the realm of magic and tries to understand something about it, even though the immediacy of this kind of relation makes theoretical development very difficult.
15. Françoise Dolto has done important work regarding odors in her therapy with children and even the newborn infant, using, for example, a scarf that the mother has worn in order to wrap the child who must be hospitalized.
16. This is nothing new, as one can see in a note to the Wolfman case: "If we do not wish to go astray in our judgment of the reality, we must above all bear in mind that people's 'childhood memories' are consolidated at a later period, usually at the age of puberty, and that this involves a complicated process of remodeling, analogous in every way to the process by which a nation constructs legends about its early history." (*G.W.* 7:427n; *S.E.* 10:206n).
17. *G.W.* 11:472; *S.E.* 16:453.
18. "Ratman Case-History," *G.W.* 7:428n; *S.E.* 10:208n.

CHAPTER 7

1. "A Note to the Prehistory of Analysis" (1920), *G.W. 12:310; S.E.* 18:263.
2. *G.W.* 2/3:107-8; *S.E.* 4:103.
3. *G.W.* 12:311-12; *S.E.* 18:264-65.
4. *G.W.* 12:312; *S.E.* 18:265.

5. Philippe Lacoue-Labarthe and Jean-Luc Nancy, *L'Absolu littéraire: Théorie de la littérature du romantisme allemand* (Paris: Seuil, 1978), reveals the connection between *Einfall,* "the sudden idea," and *Witz,* "wit, humour" (esp. pp. 74-75). Thomas Mann emphasizes Freud's affinities with German romanticism, particularly Novalis: "his theory of the libido . . . is romanticism become scientific" (*Die Stellung Freuds in der modernen Geistesgeschichte,* bilingual ed. [Paris: Aubier-Flammarion, 1970], p. 145).

6. "The true poet is, as he writes, only the auditor, and not the master of his characters; that is, he does not compose in dialogue by serving his replies one after the other, according to a stylistic of the soul that he would have learned with difficulty; but, as in dreams, he watches them come alive and he listens to them. . . . It is natural that the accomplices in our dreams surprise us with answers that we, nevertheless, have inspired in them — in the waking state as well, each idea shoots up like a flash, and we still attribute it to our own effort. But, in dreams, we are without consciousness of the effort; we must refer the idea to the person who appears to us and to whom we attribute this effort" (Jean-Paul, cited in *Romantiques allemands,* ed. Albert Béguin [Paris: Gaillimard, La Pléiade, 1973], p. xviii).

7. In "A Chapter on Dreams" (in *Across the Plains, with Other Memories and Essays* [New York: Scribners, 1892]), Robert Louis Stevenson describes his "Brownies": "That part [of my work] which is done while I am sleeping is the Brownies' part beyond contention; but that which is done when I am up and about is by no means necessarily mine, since all goes to show the Brownies have a hand in it even then" (p. 248).

8. Bernard Pingaud, "L'Ecriture et la cure," *Nouvelle revue française,* no. 214 (1970): 159. Also see his "L'Oeuvre et l'analyste," *Les Temps modernes,* no. 233 (October 1965): 638-46. In rereading these texts, it strikes me that I have neglected to speak about the specificity of writing; this is probably because I use the comparison with literary creation really only in order to perceive one of the possible forms of the analytic cure.

9. *Studies on Hysteria, G.W.* 1:227; *S.E.* 2:160-61.

10. Lacoue-Labarthe and Nancy, *L'Absolu littéraire,* pp. 192-93, 204-5, and passim.

11. A. Kardiner, *Mon Analyse avec Freud* (Paris: Belfond, 1978), pp. 103-4.

12. *G.W.* 2/3:559; *S.E.* 5:553. See also above, chap. 1, n. 32.

13. The same question can be posed in regard to every science, even mathematics. In this sense, A. Warusfel writes of Euclid: "Let us not be too quick to criticize. First, we do not know what the centuries to come hold in store for us; the notion of 'rigor' is evolving continuously and although we have made decisive progress (certain demonstrations can be proven by machines), 'personal conviction' often remains the true touchstone. On the other hand, no mathematical demonstration, at whatever level, is complete, even if it satisfies the present requirements of rigor. . . . The concern not to miss the forest for the trees and, at the other extreme, to put in the limelight only the important points of a proof, makes sure that, contrary to widespread opinion, *one continuously cheats in mathematics!*" (*Les Mathématiques modernes* [Paris: Seuil, 1969], pp. 9-10).

14. "It is necessary to call for genius from everyone, but without counting on it. A Kantian would call that the categorical imperative of genius" (Friedrich Schlegel, cited in Lacoue-Labarthe and Nancy, *L'Absolu littéraire,* p. 82).

15. Ibid., pp. 191-92. On the notion of genius and its relation to literary creation, see P. Grappin, *La Théorie du génie dans le préclassicisme allemand* (Paris: P.U.F., 1952).

16. Harold F. Searles, who does not take himself for a genius, writes: "I have realized that the anxiety, the confusion, and the despair that I have always felt in the course of preparing a text, had a special relation with the panic that chronically seizes the schizophrenic who is totally disoriented in relation to the steady principles of organization that could render the chaotic perceptions that assail him intelligible and manageable" (*Counter-Transference and Related Subjects* [New York: International Universities Press, 1979], p. 5).

17. Ludwig Börne, *Gesammelte Schriften* (Hamburg: Hoffmann and Campe, 1835), vol. 3, pp. 233-34.

18. Bruno Bettelheim, *The Informed Heart: Autonomy in a Mass Age* (Glencoe, Ill.: Free Press, 1960).

19. One understands Nietzsche's anger against Socratism for having deflected Euripides from the Dionysian sources of the tragic (*The Birth of Tragedy*, trans. Walter Kaufmann [New York: Random House, 1967], p. 86).

20. See the conclusion of chap. 2, above.

21. This is René Girard's expression for "the cultural mechanism by which the human community is founded" (see Josué Harari's introduction to *Textual Strategies: Perspectives in Post-Structuralist Criticism*, ed. J. Harari [Ithaca: Cornell University Press, 1979], p. 57). If artistic creation arises, in part, from this mechanism, one might think that it loses its specificity and acquires another meaning, precisely because its origins are outside the social field.

22. See above, chap. 5.

23. I am indebted for these ideas to J. Schotte, professor at the University of Louvain-la-Neuve, who also brought to my attention the text of Freud cited below.

24. *G.W.* 13:365-66; *S.E.* 19:185.

25. Cited in *Romantiques allemands*, p. 1561.

26. Michel Foucault has shown that it is necessary to distinguish the author from the writer in order to understand the role of a work in the social field (in "What Is An Author?" in Harari, *Textual Strategies*, pp. 141-60). This opposition has already been presented, from within, by an individual who produces texts. Robert Louis Stevenson, a writer in financial difficulties, turns his thoughts toward his dreams: "What I call I, my conscious ego . . . is no storyteller at all . . . so that, by that account, the whole of my published fiction should be the single-handed product of some Brownie, some Familiar, some unseen collaborator, whom I keep locked in a back garret" ("A Chapter on Dreams," in *Across the Plains*, pp. 248-49).

27. "The basis of the understanding itself is therefore madness. Madness is thus a necessary element, but it must not come to the foreground, and must not be actualized. What we call understanding, if it is effective, living, active understanding, is properly speaking nothing other than *regulated madness*. . . . Men who have no madness in them are men of an empty and sterile understanding. From which the reverse proverb: no genius without a grain of madness; from which also the divine delirium mentioned by Plato and the poets. . . . Understanding and reason are the same thing, but considered in a different way. . . . In the understanding, there is, by all evidence, something more *active*, and in reason, something more *passive*, something that abandons itself. . . . What reason does not accept, what it resists, what it does not allow to be written in itself, is not inspired by the soul, but comes from the personality" (Friedrich W. J. Schelling, *Oeuvres métaphysiques*, trans. Emmanuel Martineau and Jean-François Courtine [Paris: Gallimard, 1980], pp. 246-48).

28. Nietzsche, *The Birth of Tragedy*, p. 50.

This book was composed in Baskerville text and display type by David Lorton, from a design by Lisa S. Mirski. It was printed on 50-lb. Glatfelter paper and bound in Kivar 5 by Thomson-Shore, Inc.